*Samuel Johnson
on Shakespeare*

Samuel Johnson
on Shakespeare

THE DISCIPLINE
OF CRITICISM

Edward Tomarken

THE UNIVERSITY OF GEORGIA PRESS

ATHENS AND LONDON

© 1991 by the University of Georgia Press
Athens, Georgia 30602
All rights reserved
Designed by Betty Palmer McDaniel
Set in Linotron 202 Ehrhardt
The paper in this book meets the guidelines for
permanence and durability of the Committee on
Production Guidelines for Book Longevity of the
Council on Library Resources.

Printed in the United States of America
95 94 93 92 91   C   5 4 3 2 1
Library of Congress Cataloging in Publication Data

Tomarken, Edward, 1938–
Samuel Johnson on Shakespeare: the discipline of criticism /
Edward Tomarken.
p.   cm.
Includes bibliographical references and index.
ISBN 0-8203-1358-0 (alk. paper)
1. Shakespeare, William, 1564–1616—Criticism and
interpretation—History—18th century.   2. Johnson, Samuel,
1709–1784—Knowledge—Literature.   3. Criticism—Great
Britain—History—18th century.   I. Title.
PR2968.T66   1991
828'.609—dc20   90-23164
CIP

British Library Cataloging in Publication Data available

TO
Annette Porter Tomarken

CONTENTS

Acknowledgments

ix

Abbreviations

xi

Introduction

1

CHAPTER ONE

Morality in *Henry IV*

14

CHAPTER TWO

Critical Editing of *Troilus and Cressida*

35

CHAPTER THREE

History of Criticism in *Twelfth Night*

51

CHAPTER FOUR

Feminist Satire and Bibliographic Idcology in *The Taming of the Shrew*

71

CHAPTER FIVE

Mimetic Theory in *King Lear*

89

CHAPTER SIX

Imagination in *The Tempest*

112

CHAPTER SEVEN
Evaluation of Closure in *Hamlet*
130

CHAPTER EIGHT
Aesthetic Empathy in *Macbeth*
152

CONCLUSION
Toward a New Humanism
175

Notes
181

Index
197

ACKNOWLEDGMENTS

At an early stage Ralph Cohen, Robert Dent, and J. Paul Hunter read the entire manuscript. I wish to thank them for their constructive criticism and valuable suggestions. At later stages a number of my colleagues at Miami University read various single chapters. I am grateful to Dale Bauer, William Campbell, James Clark, Richard Erlich, Patricia Harkin, Britton Harwood, Thomas Idinopulos, Robert Johnson, Frank Jordan, Susan Kammeraad-Campbell, Andrew Lakritz, David Mann, Armand Michaux, John Parks, Christiane Phillips-Heim, Constance Pierce, William Pratt, Susan Kay Sloan, James Sosnoski, Marilyn Throne, and Randolph Wadsworth for their helpful advice concerning scholarship and style. My research for this book was aided by a sabbatical provided by the English Department of Miami University and by two grants, a summer research grant awarded by Miami University Research Committee and an American Society for Eighteenth-Century Studies grant to study at the William Andrews Clark Memorial Library in Los Angeles. I received valuable assistance from the librarians at both the U.C.L.A. and the Clark libraries, as well as at the British Library, the University of Kent at Canterbury Library, and particularly from William Wortman at the Miami University Library. At the University of Georgia Press, I was fortunate in having two prompt and discerning readers, Paul Korshin and John Burke, Jr., in addition to the courteous and able editorial assistance of Karen Orchard and Nancy Grayson Holmes. Brenda W. Kolb copyedited the manuscript with great care and tact.

The editors of the following publications have given me permission to re-print portions of chapters 6, 7, and 8: *English Studies 2: Essays in Honour of Marie-Thérèse Schroeder-Hartmann, Eighteenth Century Life,* and *The CEA Critic.*

Personal acknowledgments are the most deeply felt and therefore the most difficult to articulate. Stephanie and Michael Shea have continued to provide friendship and support, and Bernard and Monique Labbé provided a welcome refuge in France, Le Moana, for writing large portions of the book. My family on both sides of the Atlantic provided the quotidian pleasures that make life worthwhile. Pamela Porter offered hospitality and good humor for our stays in England, and Martin and Elizabeth Porter presented wonderful Sunday lunches that included the convivial laughter of Anthony, James, and Christopher. Peter and Dana Tomarken welcomed me to their home while I was working at the Clark Library; Jason, Alexis, and Candace provided much-needed relief from the rigors of scholarship and tolerated my bad jokes. James Tomarken never let me forget the relationship between good humor and morality. Emma Tomarken listened patiently and sagely to the manuscript and contributed to the last sentence. As the dedication indicates, my greatest debt is to my wife, who never stinted of her time for me while working under difficult circumstances as a teacher, administrator, and researcher.

ABBREVIATIONS

Dictionary   Samuel Johnson. *A Dictionary of the English Language.* 4th ed. 2 vols. London, 1773.

Dryden   John Dryden. *The Works of John Dryden.* Ed. Maximilian E. Novak. Vol. 13. Berkeley: Univ. of California Press, 1984.

Garrick   David Garrick. *The Plays of David Garrick.* Ed. Harry William Pedicord and Frederick Louis Bergmann. 4 vols. Carbondale: Southern Illinois Univ. Press, 1980.

Hill and Powell   George Birkbeck Hill and L. F. Powell, eds. *Boswell's "Life of Johnson,"* by James Boswell. 6 vols. Oxford: Clarendon Press, 1934–64.

Lives   Samuel Johnson. *The Lives of the Poets.* Ed. George Birkbeck Hill. 3 vols. Oxford: Clarendon Press, 1905.

Notes   All references to Samuel Johnson, *Notes to Shakespeare,* provide first the volume and page number in the original edition (London, 1765) and then the volume and page number in the edition by Arthur Sherbo (New Haven: Yale Univ. Press, 1968).

NV   Horace Howard Furness, ed. *A New Variorum Edition of Shakespeare's "Twelfth Night."* 1901. Reprint. New York: Dover, 1964.

Preface   Samuel Johnson. *Preface to Notes to Shakespeare.* Ed. Arthur Sherbo. New Haven: Yale Univ. Press, 1968.

SCH   Brian Vickers, ed. *Shakespeare: The Critical Heritage.* London: Routledge and Kegan Paul, 1974–81. Because they

represent the most readily available versions, these vol-
umes are cited in the text. Whenever possible, notes provide information on the original sources.

Shakespeare   In any given discussion, the text of Shakespeare's play referred to is, unless otherwise indicated, that used by the
editor or critic being discussed.

W   William Warburton, ed. *The Works of Shakespear.* 1747.
Reprint. New York: AMS Press, 1968.

*Samuel Johnson
on Shakespeare*

Introduction

As if miraculously transported from the bygone era of his studies, a doctoral candidate enters the room and faces his examiners. After handshakes, some cordial and others frosty, the thesis defense begins. Congratulating the student on restoring much of the original text in his thesis, a new edition of Shakespeare, the bibliographer, having mentioned that some quartos were not consulted that should have been, poses his question: "While your textual procedure seems competent and sensible, with a few unfortunate lapses, I found no outline of a concept of copy text in your *Preface.* Why not?" The candidate replies that precedent was his principle: he generally based his text on the oldest authoritative copies. When there was a discrepancy or another viable alternative, the decision was usually made on critical, not bibliographical, grounds, for he found that the distinction between these two aspects of the discipline was exaggerated and seldom defensible.

While the bibliographer becomes uneasy, the eighteenth-century specialist brightens at the mention of criticism, announcing his pleasure that the edition includes previous notes by commentators in his field. He is puzzled, however, by the fact that competent scholars, like Theobald and Warburton, are treated less favorably than amateurs at this endeavor, like Dryden and Pope. To his supervisor's surprise, the candidate seems eager to reply: "Surely," he begins, with an awkward movement of his arm, "the critical acumen of the father of criticism and the satirical insight of our greatest ironist are more important than the cold pertinacity of Theobald and the pedantry of Warburton." "Shakespeare," he continues, now feeling the enthusiastic fit, "is our greatest humorist and we can only do justice to the text of his plays by attending to that aspect of his talent with critical intelligence. Take Falstaff—."

His supervisor interrupts, gesturing to the Renaissance expert, who has a question. Indicating his approval of the historical research on his period— particularly on Elizabethan witchcraft—the latter is, nonetheless, disturbed to find the personal judgments of the present day foisted on a text from the past. "How else," the candidate begins, catching his supervisor's eye and quickly lowering his voice, "how else, sir, are we to make Shakespeare alive for us today? If we editors do not make clear how the past pertains to the present, how can we expect the reader to see our texts as anything but quaint curiosities from the past?" "Then," the professor rejoins, "have you your own idea of how the past and present are to be related?" "No," comes the unhesitating reply. "Many such theories are already available. Literary criticism as a discipline must be capable of absorbing a number of them, for the means by which we bring dead texts to life must be based on larger and more fundamental principles than any single theory."

The theorist intervenes: "But you told us that you have your own conception of the task of a bibliographer and, just now, that you have an equally singular one concerning literary criticism, yet you make no claim to a new theory. How would you suggest that we judge your work that you claim is innovative in all aspects of our discipline, from bibliography to literary theory, but contains no new theory?" "Ah," replies the candidate, deliberately avoiding the fixed gaze of his supervisor, "that is precisely where literary criticism joins with morality. You need only decide whether or not my edition shows how Shakespeare makes us better able to understand and endure the human dilemma." Cacophonous laughter ensues. The candidate withdraws into himself, assuming various postures, finally resembling the shape of a book.

This book is about the ethical commitment at the basis of literary criticism as a discipline. Including the full range of our endeavor—from bibliography to literary theory—Samuel Johnson believed that his critical edition of *The Plays of William Shakespeare* was dedicated to improving the human condition. Modern critics and theoreticians avoid morality because they associate it with didacticism, with pietistic sententiae that are not pertinent to authorial intent or artistic structure. In distinguishing morality from didacticism, my first task is to show that, for Johnson, criticism requires, not intrusive sententiae, but evaluative interpretations, decisions about how literature applies to the human dilemma. The humanistic element in Johnson's morality leads to a new approach to criticism, a new humanism.[1]

Perhaps modern critics' neglect of this moral dimension explains why my book is the first devoted to this topic and the first to focus on Johnson's *Notes to Shakespeare*. Another reason for the neglect of Johnson's longest critical work except for the *Lives of the Poets* is that the portions of the *Preface*, often published separately, and the sections from the *Notes*, occasionally included, are extracted from their context in order to exemplify "neoclassical" dicta that are generally regarded as quaint and dated. Scholars who have studied the *Notes* carefully have integrated them into studies of larger issues, such as Johnson's literary criticism, morality, or rhetoric. While referring to central concerns from these kinds of works, I am interested in the *Notes* first and foremost as "naked criticism." This intrinsic interest in the material means that no attempt is made to move from the *Notes* to new generalizations about Johnson's literary criticism, morality, or rhetoric. My contention is that Johnson's interpretation of some of Shakespeare's dramas speaks directly to us, raising new questions and presenting new resolutions for modern Shakespeareans, theoreticians, and literary critics in general.

No attempt is made to refute the position that the *Preface* is a largely derivative work. I do claim, however, that some insights in the *Notes* are original and that pertinent sections of the *Preface* have new theoretical significance. Seeing Johnson as an eclectic critic whose practical and general remarks often extend well beyond the larger system or systems that form their basis, I do not pursue an alternative, totalizing framework. Rather, I am interested in demonstrating how Johnson's kinds of textual insights form the foundation of literary criticism as a discipline and in characterizing the nature of that endeavor.

Although lacking an overall, coherent theory, Johnson developed and abided by certain critical principles. Modern systematic inquiry into Samuel Johnson's literary criticism began with Jean Hagstrum's *Samuel Johnson's Literary Criticism*, first published in 1952. Recognizing that Johnson was neither a theorist nor an adherent of any single critical system, Hagstrum nevertheless demonstrated that implicit in Johnson's commentary about literature is a set of consistent principles. At the heart of Johnson's criticism, Hagstrum concluded, is a concept of wit as a union of the familiar and the unfamiliar. This principle was regarded as distinctly empirical: "Reading is itself an experience within the larger experience of all of life, and art is therefore to be judged, as all experience must finally be judged, by the canons of morality, truth, and empirical validity."[2] In the same year, William R. Keast wrote "The Theoretical Foundations of Johnson's Criticism." Furthering Hagstrum's position, Keast argued that, for Johnson, the audience of literature is the common reader: "The common voice of the multitude" enables Johnson to find "a stable basis in nature on which to rest critical inquiry and judgment." By means of this principle, Keast concluded, Johnson shifts "the emphasis in criticism from art to nature."[3]

While Hagstrum and Keast proposed a view of Johnson's criticism based upon consistent empirical principles, William K. Wimsatt, Jr., and Cleanth Brooks, in 1957, pointed to what they saw as Neoplatonic aspects that resulted in inconsistency: "In Johnson the literary theorist we confront a system of ideas (in part rigidly consistent, in part rather manifestly inconsistent, in part at least paradoxical) which constitutes a massive summary of the neo-Platonic drive in literary theory and of its difficulties." The problem, according to Wimsatt and Brooks, is that the "principle of the neo-classic universal," which is present throughout Johnson's writings, is inconsistent with that "deeper strain of particularism tied in closely with one of his most basic inclinations, that toward introspection and personal morality." Johnson's *Preface to Shakespeare* featured prominently in this debate. In response to Wimsatt and Brooks's assertion of the predominance of the general in Johnson, one critic cited portions of the *Preface* that favored the concrete in Shakespeare. But Wimsatt replied that the theory of the neoclassical universal was by its very nature subject to inconsistencies.[4]

This disagreement persisted during the next decade and was described in the following terms by Jean Hagstrum in a new preface to his book: "Before accepting the essentially empirical approach of my study, which invokes for Johnson psychological, educational, and rhetorical norms and which denies neo-Platonic content to his notion of generality, the student will wish to read Professor Wimsatt's brief but stimulating analysis of Johnson's thought as a 'massive summary of the neo-Platonic drive in literary theory and of its difficulties' and to study the ninefold definition of what neoclassical theorists meant by universality."[5] Since Johnson made no definitive statement on this philosophical issue and since Hagstrum accepted that other critics of the period, namely, Dryden and Reynolds, did evidence Neoplatonic elements in their theories, critics recognized the need to study the criticism of Johnson in relation to that of other critics of his age. But with this matter remaining unresolved, scholars were left without any guidance as to whether to focus on the particular or the general in a study of the criticism of the era.

In the 1960s, the empirical position was reinforced by two studies of Johnson's morality: Robert Voitle and Paul Alkon both demonstrated the centrality of ethics in Johnson's thought and critical procedure.[6] In the 1970s, however, the earlier dichotomy once again became manifest. Leopold Damrosch, Jr., examined the particular in Johnson: emphasizing the *Lives of the Poets,* not the Shakespeare criticism, Damrosch argued for the modern utility of Johnson's criticism.[7] William Edinger, on the other hand, made considerable use of the *Preface* to delineate a general "neo-classical" rhetorical position.[8] R. D. Stock, studying the intellectual context of the *Preface,* also located Johnson's position within the larger framework of "neoclassical dramatic theory."[9] Since the *Notes* to Shakespeare remained unexamined, it was assumed by the 1980s that Johnson's Shakespeare criticism could safely be relegated to the orthodox neoclassical realm, that which is of merely historical interest, as opposed to the aspect of his criticism that remains pertinent for us. In the 1980s, two studies attempted to remedy this situation. In 1982, John Needham placed Johnson's Shakespeare criticism in the tradition of Coleridge, Eliot, and Leavis.[10] In 1989, G. F. Parker defended Johnson on Shakespeare by presenting the commentary in terms of a consistent mimetic theory based on the concept of general nature in the *Preface.*[11]

My own approach appropriates from my predecessors in the following ways. Believing, as do Hagstrum and Keast, that Johnson proceeds by way of critical principles, not merely by way of the vagaries of taste, I accept, as Wimsatt and Brooks assert, that these principles do not cohere into a consistent theory. Viewing Johnson as in the last analysis an eclectic critic, I make no attempt to resolve the debate concerning the empirical particulars versus the Neoplatonic universals. In the tradition of Voitle and Alkon, the centrality of Johnson's morality is a focal point: Johnson's comments, which in isolation seem didactic and therefore dated, will be seen in context to raise ethical issues that remain important to us. Profiting from the research of Edinger and Stock, my study attempts to understand Johnson in relation to other critics of his age, particularly other eighteenth-century editors of Shakespeare. But, like Damrosch, I feel we must make a case for the usefulness of Johnson's criticism to the modern reader. Johnson, as Needham urges, deserves his place along with Coleridge, Eliot, and Leavis, but we must also recognize, as Parker argues, that he derives from a very different kind of critical tradition than that of nineteenth- and twentieth-century critics.

I differ from my predecessors in one key respect, and that has a number of ramifications. My study stems from a suggestion provided by the scholar responsible for making the full body of Johnson's Shakespeare criticism available to the modern reader. In 1956, after publishing the first complete twentieth-century version of Johnson's *Notes to Shakespeare,* Arthur Sherbo stated that Johnson's greatest contribution to Shakespeare criticism resided, not in the *Preface*, but in the *Notes*. Sherbo goes on to point out that "the method of sampling Johnson's notes by culling a remark here and another there to prove a particular point of view . . . is almost as dangerous as a total neglect of them." [12] The past thirty years, however, have produced little work that does not either ignore the *Notes* or subordinate selected remarks from them to the *Preface*.[13]

I begin with the *Notes* to a specific play, explaining how they constitute an interpretation, and then refer to an appropriate generalization in the *Preface*. In itself, this approach constitutes an innovation, since the *Preface* is so often printed on its own and treated as a separate document that few modern readers know that it was originally conceived as an introduction to the *Notes*. No attempt, however, will be made to provide another holistic framework for understanding the *Preface* or the *Notes;* rather, I shall suggest how Johnson's views point beyond the limitations of the literary theory of his day and pertain to present-day theoretical inquiries. Nor will an attempt be made to place Johnson in any particular tradition comprised of great critics; rather, he will be viewed in terms of his predecessors, contemporaries, and successors in the belief that the history of criticism reveals that innovation results from variation and recombination of earlier critical views.

My method operates simultaneously on two levels. The critical principles that are shown to provide the basis for Johnson's *Notes* are analogous to the metacritical foundation of my own procedure. Johnson's questioning of the end of *Henry IV* is transformed into the concept of critical teleology; the difference between Johnson and Dryden on *Troilus and Cressida* becomes a bibliographic principle; the distinction between the Victorians and Johnson on *Twelfth Night* leads to a tenet for the history of literary criticism; Johnson's defense of Pope's text of *The Taming of the Shrew* leads to a notion about the modification of ideology; Johnson's objection to the death of Cordelia points to a new approach to the history of literary theory; his view of Caliban bears upon the history of ideas; his reading of the graveyard scene in *Hamlet* suggests a new concept of closure; and his interpretation of *Macbeth* provides the basis for a reconsideration of aesthetic empathy. I do not wish to claim that any of these "new-fangled" ideas are Johnson's; they result from my attempt to adapt Johnson's critical procedures to the problems of our day. As Johnson's great "imitation," *The Vanity of Human Wishes*, makes Juvenal pertinent to eighteenth-century England, this study is an "imitation" of Johnson's Shakespeare commentary.

Although not previously the subject of a full-length analysis, Johnson's

Notes have for many generations been treated with respect by Shakespeare-ans. One need only consult an annotated modern edition, an Arden or vari-orum text, of almost any drama in the canon to find Johnson's "common-sense" readings invoked as important touchstones.[14] The difficulty is that this commentary is treated in a miscellaneous manner, giving rise to the mislead-ing impression that Johnson's edition is a conglomeration of notes which do not constitute coherent analyses of Shakespeare's dramas.

My decision to dispel this illusion by beginning with the *Notes* as practical criticism, then proceeding to the *Preface* or the level of theory, and then mov-ing to a formulation integrating them, is fundamental to this study. Practical criticism came first for Johnson. In the 1750s and 1760s, he prepared himself for his final great critical work, the *Lives of the Poets* (1779–81), by immersing himself in literary textuality. During the period of the *Notes to Shakespeare* (1745–65), he assembled the *Dictionary* (1755), a compendium of citations from English literature, and produced the periodical essays (1750–60), which were expanded notes on mainly literary issues.[15]

Literary criticism as a discipline, as a kind of inquiry with its own method and subject matter, must begin by focusing upon the art of interpreting texts, or practical criticism. Although literary criticism is heavily dependent upon bibliographic scholarship and literary theory, the one for establishing the subject matter and the other for articulating methods of approach to the subject matter, each of these aspects of our discipline is common to other fields in the humanities, if not the sciences. All researchers, from archaeolo-gists to historians of science, are likely to be concerned with bibliographic questions about the authoritative text, while theory, formerly the province of philosophers, is now the concern of almost every kind of intellectual pursuit. The singularity of literary criticism must reside in the ways literary critics interpret literary texts.

Such a seemingly uncontroversial position is by no means generally ac-cepted in our profession. In a recent address which he delivered as president of the Modern Language Association (MLA), J. Hillis Miller proclaimed the "triumph of theory" because the most important problems for literary criti-cism are related to ideology. Yet the issue of *PMLA* that begins with this presidential address also contains essays arguing against the utility of ideo-logical theories, ranging from a critique of "new historicism" for its ideo-logical preoccupation to a feminist argument that the available ideological theories are male-oriented.[16]

Although Hillis Miller believes that this resistance to theory does not sig-nal a "crisis in the humanities," some of the members of the MLA manifest a deeper anxiety. Many of my colleagues feel uneasy about beginning with a philosophic system or theory, particularly one concerned with a problem as far removed from their routine concerns as ideology. Although ideology is a topic of concern in this study, I believe that we need to formulate our own theories, ones that appropriate useful concepts from other disciplines but that develop from our craft and serve our purposes as literary critics. Such a procedure, long and arduous, cannot be accomplished in a single book, by a single critic, perhaps not even in a single generation. But instead of deciding a priori that the initial issue is ideology or advocating any particular theory, we can, in my view, more fruitfully begin this project by examining the sorts of concepts, theoretical and practical, that enable critics, particularly great ones like Samuel Johnson, to accomplish their task.

An initial outline of criticism as a discipline, this book is not an attempt to arrive at a totalizing framework. On the contrary, as a discipline, criticism must be able to contain a number of competing, if not contradictory, systems. Although I believe no single theory can hope to encompass literary criticism, we should be able to delineate characteristics essential for a proper training in the field, traits shared by our greatest practitioners, such as Dryden, Johnson, Coleridge, and Arnold.

Why choose Johnson's *Notes* for such an undertaking? If Dryden is, as Johnson called him, the father of criticism, Johnson is the father of criticism as a discipline. Where before Johnson's Shakespeare edition (or even after it) do we have an instance of a great critic attending to the canon of the greatest writer in English literature in a manner that covers the range of criticism— from bibliographic and textual notes to critical comments and theoretical generalizations? This work of 1765, the first to cover the full gamut of our discipline, represents the classic document of criticism as a discipline. It is perhaps for this reason that Johnson's Shakespeare resists containment in any single theory. The project is larger than any system. In analyzing it, we are in the presence of the first achievement of the greatest of professional critics. Its most distinctive characteristic, in my view, is the combination of theory and practice, notes and preface, and my purpose is to raise to the level of principle the foundation of this achievement.

Each of the eight chapters proceeds from specific textual matters, or practice, to general concerns, or theory, and the book as a whole moves from the predominantly practical to the more theoretical issues. Devoted to a different Shakespearean play, every chapter considers Johnson's position in relation to critics of his own day, to some after his time, and to appropriate passages of the *Preface* that pertain to modern theory.

Instead of attempting to survey all of Johnson's Shakespeare commentary, which could reinforce the misperception that his remarks were miscellaneous, I have decided to focus on eight plays that are characteristic of Johnson and manifest his relevance to modern criticism. Tracing the development of his remarks on individual plays and relating them to the final summary statements enables me to demonstrate that the *Notes* constitute interpretations, critical positions that raise serious issues for present-day theorists.

The eight dramas selected represent the various types of Shakespearean plays: a history play, an early and a middle comedy, a romance, or late comedy, as well as a problem play, or tragicomedy. Of the tragedies, *Macbeth* was included because Johnson first introduced his edition by way of samples from his research on Elizabethan witchcraft and because it was comparable to *Richard III. Lear* and *Hamlet* were obvious choices, since they involve textual and critical issues important both in Johnson's day and in our own. *Henry IV, Parts 1 and 2* was selected not only because of the important insights concerning Falstaff but also because of the references to *Richard II* and *Henry V,* thus providing a broad range of Johnson's opinions on the histories. Because of its continual references to Dryden, *Troilus and Cressida* suggested a comparison between Johnson and the great Restoration critic that would highlight the differences and similarities between the art of editing and that of adapting. *Twelfth Night* permitted me to compare Johnson with a Victorian editor, particularly interesting since the difference between Johnson and Furness over Malvolio is still pertinent in our time. *The Taming of the Shrew* offered the opportunity of relating Johnson to Pope and to modern feminists. *The Tempest* was chosen because Coleridge makes reference to Johnson in his remarks, leading me to compare an eighteenth-century and romantic view of Shakespeare's last play. In addition to the textual problems of the three tragedies selected, each presented an important problem for literary theory. *King Lear* enabled me to demonstrate how a mimetic question can apply to modern readings of the tragedy. *Hamlet* was included because it highlighted Johnson's much neglected but crucial concepts of humor and closure. And *Macbeth* became the final topic because of the equally important notion of aesthetic empathy. Since this study does not cover all of the plays in detail, I have included in the text and notes references to the other plays in an attempt to demonstrate how these eight focal points are central to Johnson's *Notes to Shakespeare.*

The goal of every chapter is to arrive at a principle that seems to me essential to literary criticism as a discipline. Focusing on Johnson's morality and its function in textual commentary, chapter 1 demonstrates that interpretation for Johnson involves evaluation, a decision about how the literature relates to the human dilemma. Here we confront the recent critical interest in ideology, a term postformalists use to refer to how literature pertains to concerns beyond the bounds of the literary. Global systems of thought, ideologies are generally seen as far removed from literary criticism. Johnson's morality, on the other hand, relates the discipline of criticism to ideology. Specifically, Johnson's disapproval of the end of *Henry IV* indicates how ethical literary judgments contribute to the modification and questioning of ideology. My conclusion is that literary criticism can contribute to what some philosophers have called the "democratic hegemony" of orthodox political theories, that is, the development and alteration of ideologies. This conception is derived from the research of Ernesto Laclau and Chantal Mouffe, especially as it bears upon morality.[17]

Because the ethical dimension of criticism is somewhat subjective, Johnson believes that the critical editor should make his position explicit. Chapter 2 examines what Johnson characterizes as his innovation as an editor, strictures, or brief summaries of his notes. Here I suggest that criticism needs to follow Johnson's example, making overt the interpretive principles that form the grounds for editorial decisions. At this point in the study two terms become prominent—interpretation and closure. They are loosely defined in relation to one another. Closure is not merely or necessarily the end of a drama but a significant conclusion, and interpretation involves a judgment about what constitutes a significant conclusion. My reason for avoiding a rigid definition is that since these terms concern the point at which literary analysis refers beyond the literary, they can only be clarified when seen in context. Johnson's strictures show us that criticism is a teleological activity and that his innovation is to make plain the nature of his critical goal. The result is that we understand how Johnson relates a specific Shakespearean drama to the extraliterary domain. The importance of making explicit the ethical and ideological issues involved in this critical procedure are further discussed in the Conclusion.

Since interpretation inevitably leads to individual differences, chapter 3 considers how Johnson's new editorial policy relates to his assessment of his predecessors. My contention is that, in place of Johnson's explicit view, the implicit one of the editor of the "new variorum" produces a distortion of the history of criticism: the anomaly is ignored or misunderstood because of an overriding interest in a critical consensus. The result is that important critical innovations pointing to new directions for the history of criticism are passed over in a concern to find *the* tradition. The belief in a single tradition is called into question; different histories derive from different critical approaches to the literature. Interpretation not only forms the basis of explication of texts but also is fundamental to the history of literary criticism.

But the nature of critical differences, Johnson suggests, goes beyond criticism. A consideration of satirical technique, chapter 4 demonstrates how the assessment of humor provides a point of mediation between bibliography and ideology. Here the connection between practical criticism and literary theory becomes an issue: a textual decision about whether or not the drama is to be presented as a play-within-a-play bears upon the concerns of feminist criticism. Here I demonstrate that the separation of bibliography from literary theory has hampered both endeavors. Decisions about what constitutes the text cannot be divorced from interpretation of the text. In this way the book moves to the higher register of theory while maintaining contact with practical criticism.

Since ideologies are few in number and kind and often result in or from ultimate political differences separating the right from the left, the problem is how these extremes relate to one another within the confines of criticism. Can literary theory accommodate or mediate between ultimate differences? In the context of the debate over poetic justice, chapter 5 shows how mimeticism, the theory of Johnson's day, bears upon modern criticism and theory. Johnson's question about the death of Cordelia points to the limitations of formalism and postformalism; the answer to his question goes beyond the bounds of mimeticism. My point here is that we cannot ignore the questions that derive from outmoded theories or ideologies, because new theories and ideologies for the most part develop from modifications and recombinations of old ones.

At this juncture it becomes clear that the problems arising in criticism cannot be restricted to literary criticism or literary theory. Critics need help not only from their predecessors in the field but also from experts in other fields. Turning next to Johnson on the creative imagination, chapter 6 considers the relationship of criticism to other disciplines—in this case, the history of ideas. Appropriation, or acceptance and modification, is the key to this relationship. For instance, the concept of the imagination is accepted from the history of ideas, but the assumption that the transition from Johnson to Coleridge involves a radical "dissociation of sensibility" is modified to one of continuity in discontinuity. Demonstrating that literary methodology employs not merely literary concepts but also concepts from other disciplines, I contend that literary criticism can only come into its own as a separate discipline if it is seen as a part of the larger humanistic endeavor to understand man's place in the cosmos.

This concern with the extraliterary clarifies the way in which literary criticism is referential, pointing beyond the realm of language to that of action, conduct, historical events. The last two chapters analyze the structural means by which literature refers beyond itself and the role of the reader in defining the nature of that referent. The formal aspect, the assessment of a significant conclusion or closure, and the reader-response aspect, the explanation of aesthetic empathy, are both functions of the critic's view of the human predicament. In order to begin formulating a criticism that is not a new mimeticism, that insists on referentiality only on the symbolic level, I suggest how interpretation involves both a formalist/structuralist and a hermeneutic/reader-response element. Focusing on Johnson's belief in the appropriateness of humor in tragedy, chapter 7 examines value judgments as they pertain to the decision about closure. Here we see that humor in a tragic situation, what might be called serious comedy, leads the critic to values that may not necessarily be consistent with his ideological position. Johnson sees in the graveyard scene of *Hamlet* a gallows humor that, if pursued, could call into question the social hierarchy accepted in his society. Thus, a critic's sense of humor, like the moral judgments discussed in chapter 1, can contribute to the modification of ideology.

Finally, in analyzing Johnson's notion of dramatic action, the last chapter demonstrates how the art of interpretation calls for an innovative concept of aesthetic empathy, one that involves the interaction of interpretation and empathy. Johnson does not see *Macbeth* as being centrally about Macbeth or ambition because neither the character nor the idea of ambition is sufficiently developed to evoke our empathy. We return to ethical judgments, which, in chapter 1, were seen as elemental; for Johnson, the critic's most fundamental task is to decide where literature touches upon the human dilemma. The means by which contact between them is achieved involves aesthetic empathy. Johnson argues that we are moved by the situation, not the character of Macbeth; the tragedy is therefore seen less as personal and more as contextual. By way of literary criticism, I conclude that literature can refer beyond itself, not, as was believed in the past, by imitating life, but by way of the art of interpretation, a circle that hermeneuticists tell us is a literary planet orbiting in the extraliterary solar system.

The Conclusion provides a vantage point for reconsidering Johnson's place in the history of Shakespeare scholarship. This reassessment is made possible by a new methodology that relates the literary to the extraliterary. Humor is a key to this method. Undermining ideas held sacred in our discipline as well as in others, from conceptions of the self to theories and ideologies, the stage lights of comedy with a serious purpose expose the vulnerabilities of human thought. This process of revealing the fissures in the seemingly impervious provides the basis for building new conceptions. Understanding the value and significance of this procedure and how to appropriate from it is the special task of literary criticism.

CHAPTER ONE

Morality in *Henry IV*

Samuel Johnson is surely the most revered moralist of English literature, yet his ethical pronouncements on Shakespeare alienate modern critics. One of the most regularly cited passages in this regard is the section of the *Preface* where Johnson accuses Shakespeare of sacrificing virtue to convenience, that is, of neglecting opportunities for promoting piety and decency. Most modern commentators, on the other hand, admire Shakespeare for refraining from such obtrusive lectures. At his best, however, Johnson the moralist is not didactic, not in favor of tedious declamations on virtue and vice, but concerned with an ethical dimension that is inherent in the structure of the work of art. *Henry IV* is particularly exemplary in this regard because it is approached by Johnson in moral and by moderns in political terms. Understanding the basis of Johnson's moral position throws new light on a section of the *Preface* that is traditionally seen as manifestly didactic and reveals how an ethical interpretation of *Henry IV* relates to modern commentary. Specifically, Johnson's moral view bears upon Shakespeare's political position, suggesting how the critic's ethical decision can contribute to the modification and undermining of ideology, to what Laclau and Mouffe have called the "democratic hegemony" of orthodox political theory. My conclusion is that we need to recognize the ethical dimension basic to literary criticism because literary analysis relates to ideology by way of morality.

The innovative elements of Johnson's Shakespeare criticism become apparent when the *Preface* is treated as a preface to the *Notes*. Studies of the *Preface* in isolation have made clear that most of its ideas are derivative.[1] But Johnson's traditional generalizations also serve to summarize and bolster innovative readings of the plays found in the *Notes*. Such eclectic moments in literary criticism are not mere aberrations of interest only to those concerned about the specific text, but are of general significance for literary criticism and theory. One of the reasons for the emergence of new literary methodologies and the modification of ideologies is the inadequacy of old terminology for communicating an innovative interpretation. Johnson's reading of *Henry IV* moves beyond the limitations of didactic criticism and raises a new kind of question for modern Shakespeareans.

Prominent in terms of the discipline of criticism is the need to study literary theory in relation to textual analysis. For Johnson, the *Preface* represents his attempt to theorize about his practical findings in the *Notes*. Like most critics, he had to formulate his innovative interpretations in traditional terms that were becoming inadequate because of new insights such as his own. For the history of literary criticism such practical breakthroughs are crucial, since they are often the points of transition between different theories and ideologies.

FALSTAFF IN CONTEXT

The following passage from the *Preface* is immediately recognized as exemplary of the critic often called the great moralist: "His [Shakespeare's] first defect is that to which may be imputed most of the evil in books and in men. He sacrifices virtue to convenience, and is so much more careful to please than to instruct, that he seems to write without any moral purpose" (7:71). The *Notes* to *Henry IV* conclude with a summary statement, the last paragraph of which uses similarly didactic terms: "The moral to be drawn from this representation is, that no man is more dangerous than he that with a will to corrupt, hath the power to please; and that neither wit nor honesty ought to think themselves safe with such a companion when they see *Henry* seduced by *Falstaff*" (4:356; 7:523–24). Johnson believes that Shakespeare's purpose is to disclose the dangers of being seduced by the kind of person Falstaff represents. By implication, if Henry is vulnerable, who, however honest or intelligent, is safe from the wiles of a Sir John? In this sentence, Johnson begins to distinguish himself from his contemporaries. Since the Restoration, critics had discussed Falstaff apart from the other characters and the action of *Henry IV*. Johnson, it should be noticed at the outset, is interested, not merely in Falstaff, but in his relation to Prince Hal and, by extension, to the audience.

Johnson's contemporaries discussed Falstaff as if he were a drama in himself. In 1698, Jeremy Collier could not disguise his delight that "the admired Falstaff" goes off in disappointment: "He is thrown out of Favour as being a *Rake*, and dies like a Rat behind the Hangings. The Pleasure he had given would not excuse him. The *Poet* was not so partial as to let his Humour compound for his Lewdness" (*SCH* 2:88).[2] Collier's didactic position enables him to avoid deciding why we feel attached to a rake who deserves to be punished for his lewdness. But Johnson does not see the matter in these simplistic terms and therefore feels obliged to explain the positive as well as the negative side of this great comic character. His explanation needs to be cited in its entirety, because, in my view, it has not been surpassed:

> But *Falstaff* unimitated, unimitable *Falstaff,* how shall I describe thee? Thou compound of sense and vice; of sense which may be admired but not esteemed, of vice which may be despised, but hardly detested. *Falstaff* is a character loaded with faults, and with those faults which naturally produce contempt. He is a thief, and a glutton, a coward and a boaster, always ready to cheat the weak, and prey upon the poor; to terrify the timorous and insult the defenceless. . . . Yet the man thus corrupt, thus despicable, makes himself necessary to the prince that despises him, by the most pleasing of all qualities, perpetual gaiety, by an unfailing power of exciting laughter, which is more freely indulged, as his wit is not of the splendid or ambitious kind, but consists in easy escapes and sallies of levity, which make sport but raise no envy. It must be observed that he is stained with no enormous or sanguinary crimes, so that his licentiousness is not so offensive but that it may be borne for his mirth. (4:356; 7:523)

This statement stands apart in its own day, accounting in very penetrating terms for the attractive qualities of Falstaff without in the least diminishing his faults. Other eighteenth-century critics chose to defend or attack Falstaff, emphasizing either his rejection by Henry V or his ability to captivate the audience. The latter position reached its culmination in Maurice Morgann's defense of Falstaff's "cowardice" on the battlefield. Although Morgann's essay appeared after Johnson's edition of *Henry IV,* the debate about Sir John began much earlier (*SCH* 6:164–80).[3] In 1709, Nicholas Rowe admitted that the great Shakespearean comic figure was a "Thief, Lying, Cowardly, Vainglorious, and in short every way Vicious." Nonetheless, he found the rejection of Sir John difficult to accept, for the playwright has given his character "so much Wit as to make him almost too agreeable; and I don't know whether some People have not, in remembrance of the Diversion he had formerly afforded 'em, been sorry to see his Friend *Hal* use him so scurvily when he comes to the Crown in the End of the Second Part of *Henry IV*" (*SCH* 2:195).[4] Similarly, Charles Gildon, in 1710, found the Falstaff of the second part less diverting than that of the first part: "Tho the Humour of *Falstaff* be what is most valuable in both these Parts yet [it] is more excellent in the first, for *Sir John* is not so Diverting in the second Part" (*SCH* 2:248).[5] In 1733, William Warburton, on the other hand, focused upon Hal, not Falstaff, and applauded Henry's final judgment of his drinking friend: "The *King*, having shaken off his Vanities, in this Scene reproves his old Companion Sir *John* for his Follies with great Severity. He assumes the Air of a Preacher . . . bids him seek after Grace . . . and leave gourmandizing" (*SCH* 2:534).[6] Warburton believes that this final judgment of Falstaff has been prepared for since the first act, when the prince, in soliloquy, establishes a clear distinction between himself and the knight. For Warburton, Falstaff is a minor character in a drama about the development of a prince into a king. In this respect, however, Warburton is in the minority. Most eighteenth-century commentators considered Falstaff to be the main character. In 1744, for instance, Corbyn Morris wrote a "Character of Sir John Falstaff," which, he admitted, was "chiefly extracted from the *first Part of Henry the IVth*": "Sir *John Falstaff* possesses Generosity, Cheerfulness, Alacrity, Invention, Frolic and Fancy superior to all other Men. The *Figure* of his *Person* is the Picture of Jollity, Mirth, and Good-nature, and banishes at once all other Ideas from your Breast; he is happy himself, and makes you happy. . . . If you put all these qualities together, it is impossible to *hate* honest *Jack Falstaff;* If you observe them again, it is impossible to avoid *loving* him" (*SCH* 3:125–26).[7] In 1756, John Upton asserted that the two parts of the play must be seen as separate, a position that permitted avoidance of the problem of the rejection of Falstaff in the second part of *Henry IV.*[8]

When Johnson set about editing *Henry IV,* two related issues had been contested for some time: whether Falstaff finally deserves our praise or blame, and whether the two parts of the play should be seen as separate entities.[9] Indeed, Johnson refers in his notes to Rowe, Gildon, and Upton as well as to Warburton, indicating his awareness of both sides of the debate. His reply to Upton is most pointed: "Mr. Upton thinks these two plays improperly called *the First* and *second parts of Henry the Fourth.* . . . These two plays will appear to every reader, who shall peruse them without ambition of critical discoveries, to be so connected that the second is merely a sequel to the first; to be two only because they are too long to be one" (4:235; 7:490). Johnson refuses to avoid the thorny problem of Falstaff's place in the body politic by separating

the first part from the second part in which Hal turns upon Sir John. Instead of resorting to character criticism, Johnson faces this issue by locating
Falstaff in context. At the same time he is not content, as is Warburton, to
see Hal's "imitate the sun" soliloquy (1:2, 190–212) as satisfactory preparation for Henry V's turn upon the companion of his princely days. In order to
understand this matter in its full complexity we must first consider Warburton's position. In a part of Theobald's *Preface* now attributed to Warburton,
the following attitude toward Hal's soliloquy is set forth.

> And our Poet has so well and artfully guarded his Character from the Suspicions
> of habitual and unreformable Profligateness that even from the first shewing
> him upon the Stage, in the first Part of Henry IV, when he made him consent
> to join with *Falstaff* in a Robbery on the Highway, he has taken care not to carry
> him off the Scene without an Intimation that he knows them all, and their un-
> yok'd Humour; and that, like the Sun, he will permit them only for a while to
> obscure and cloud his Brightness, then break thru' the Mist when he pleases to
> be himself again, that his Lustre, when wanted, may be the more wonder'd at.
> (*SCH*, 2:479)[10]

Johnson would probably not have known that this portion of Theobald's *Preface* was by Warburton, but he did respond to a more cryptic manifestation of
this attitude in his comment on Warburton's note to a line in Prince Hal's
soliloquy in act 1.

> PRINCE HENRY. So, when this loose behaviour I throw off,
>   And pay the debt I never promised;
>   By how much better than my word I am,
>   By so much shall I falsifie men's hopes;
>   Just the contrary. We should read FEARS. WARBURTON.

Johnson comments on Warburton's note as follows: "To *falsify hope* is to *exceed hope* to give much where men *hoped* for little. This speech is very artfully
introduced to keep the Prince from appearing vile in the opinion of the audience; it prepares them for his future reformation, and, what is yet more valuable, exhibits a natural picture of a great mind offering excuses to itself, and
palliating those follies which it can neither justify nor forsake" (4:123; 7:458).
Warburton implies that only those who have a negative view of the prince,
those who have "fears" rather than "hopes" for him, misguidedly believe that
he will not be able to disassociate himself from Falstaff. Johnson sees the
matter in more complex terms. The audience is prepared for the prince's reformation while at the same time shown that he willingly participated in and
enjoyed the follies of Falstaff and his other drinking companions.

Johnson has thus radically altered the kind of question raised by *Henry IV*. Realizing that Hal is attracted to the world of Falstaff while knowing from the outset that such a companion cannot be acceptable to a king, we understand that Shakespeare is interested not in the characters as individuals but in the context of their friendship. Thus, those of Johnson's predecessors who, like Gildon or Morris, focused upon Falstaff or who followed Warburton in centering upon Hal are equally far from the mark. Johnson stands alone in his own century in refusing to separate the character of Falstaff from the play of which he is a part and in resisting the notion that *Henry IV* is a play about Henry V.

Although a number of his contemporaries claimed that we cannot but love Falstaff, Johnson asserts that in both parts of the play Sir John uses his inimitable wit and humor to evade responsibility for his folly. And while others of his contemporaries argued that Prince Hal never becomes seriously involved in the episodes at the tavern and at Gadshill, Johnson attends to Hal's actions as well as his words and sees that Henry V is right to repent of the activities of his youth. But if in these respects Johnson was alone in his own time, he has much company in the present day. Few now discuss Falstaff separately or assert that Prince Hal only appears to be partaking in the pranks of the subplot. Johnson speaks to our age, placing Falstaff firmly in the context of *Henry IV*.

Indeed, it is probably for this reason that the only comic scene in *1 Henry IV* that Johnson does not like—where Hal seems to imply that he will later reward Francis for serving out his indenture time (2.4)—involves an attempt to prepare for Hal's taking the throne (4:152–53, 7:468). Johnson is the first to consider how the drama shapes our attitude toward Falstaff and leads us to a conclusion about the development of Prince Hal. Who would deny that these are the central questions? While using the didactic terminology that led his contemporaries to defend or attack Falstaff, Johnson steers a middle course, facing issues that still concern us two centuries later.

THE POLITICAL QUESTION

Even if modern commentators address the same issues as Johnson, they arrive at different conclusions: Johnson's position, properly understood in its own terms, raises a serious problem for modern critics. Present-day commentary on *Henry IV* is for the most part divided between two schools of thought that date back to the middle of this century. Some, like John Dover Wilson and E. M. W. Tillyard, believe that Hal's final rejection of Falstaff shows that Henry is ready to assume his responsibilities as sovereign of the realm. Others, such as John Danby and A. P. Rossiter, accept that it is politically expedient to reject Falstaff but find it difficult to accept in human terms: if Henry V has finally become a perfect Machiavellian monarch, he has done so at the cost of turning upon the manly sympathy of his princely days. Tillyard defends his view in the following terms: "The structure of the two parts [of *Henry IV*] is indeed very similar. In the first part the Prince is tested in the military or chivalric virtues. . . . In the second part, the prince prove[s] his worth in civil life" by accepting the rule of the Lord Chief Justice and rejecting his old companions.[11] For Tillyard, the rejection of Falstaff is the key moment in the play, an act that unifies the two parts of *Henry IV* because it represents the "Elizabethan standards" of political and social life. But Clifford Leech finds problems with this position: "When one is interpreting a Shakespearian play, one is always in danger of being reminded that Shakespeare was an Elizabethan, that the assumptions and standards of judgment were therefore different from ours. . . . But he was also a human being with a remarkable degree of sensitivity. . . . We do him, I think, scant justice if we assume that he could write complacently of Prince John of Lancaster, and could have no doubts about Prince Hal."[12]

This difference of opinion remains unresolved. In 1983, Harold Toliver wrote in defense of Tillyard's position, and Harry Levin reformulated the opposing view.[13] The twentieth-century debate concerns the political significance of the rejection of Falstaff: should the historically informed audience regard Henry V's commands at the end of the play as right and proper under the circumstances or as expedient but heartless?

Although employing moral terminology, Johnson makes plain that the ethical issue is closely related to the historical and political purport of the drama. At the outset, internal evidence is cited for the assertion that Shakespeare "designed a regular connection of these dramatic histories from *Richard the Second* to *Henry the Fifth*" (4:109; 7:453), and Johnson reproduces Theobald's notes at the beginning of both of these plays and for all the other histories, explaining that the action of the drama refers to actual historical events. These notes are not included in the Yale edition of Johnson's *Notes to Shakespeare* because Johnson left Theobald's comments unchanged. But, as is made clear in the *Preface,* Johnson left without comment only those notes of his predecessors that he regarded as important and with which he agreed. Further evidence that Johnson is aware of the play's political message appears in his comments on Hotspur and the other rebels. The note to Hotspur's famous boast to "pluck bright honour from the pale fac'd Moon" begins with

Warburton's attack on Gildon and Theobald, who characterized this speech as madness. Rather, Warburton asserts, it is "sublime" and comparable to the words of Eteocles. Characteristically, Johnson remains independent of both these positions, equally wary of seeing Hotspur either as a madman or as a tragic hero: "Though I am far from condemning this speech with *Gildon* and *Theobald* as *absolute madness*, yet I cannot find in it that profundity of reflection and beauty of allegory which the learned commentator [Warburton] has endeavoured to display. . . . The passage from *Euripides* is surely not allegorical, yet it is produced, and properly, as parallel" (4:133–34; 7:462).

Although not accepted without reservation, Warburton's comparison of Eteocles and Hotspur does demonstrate that Hotspur should not be dismissed as a madman. Few modern critics would contest this assessment, for Hotspur overreaches himself in refusing to accept his place in the body politic. Johnson evidences a similar sensitivity to the political implications of personality in his comment on the other leaders of the rebellion. In act 1, when Worcester first mentions the conspiracy against the king, Johnson explains: "This is a natural description of the state of mind between those that have conferred, and those that have received, obligations too great to be satisfied" (4:137; 7:463). This personality conflict is seen as a result of the political dilemma of the play: having been helped by nobles like Worcester to a crown that he could not acquire without their aid, Henry IV must expect that they will object to his absolute rule over them.

THE COMIC SPIRIT OF FALSTAFF

The Falstaff–Prince Hal relationship functions as part of a play about the development of a Tudor monarch. Johnson's first note suggests how personal and historical/political matters are intertwined. Concerning King Henry IV's complaint about the wildness of his son, Johnson points out that this element of Hal's personality had been anticipated in *Richard II*, an indication that Shakespeare "designed a regular connection of these dramatick histories" (4:109; 7:453). Another note on this same scene goes one step further, placing a moral as well as a personal issue firmly in the political context. Henry IV asserts that he wishes to pursue the "holy wars," occasioning Johnson's discussion of whether the Crusades were a right and proper pursuit for a Christian, a passage that concludes with the observation that since the Muhammadans had set out to destroy them, the Christians were obliged to defend themselves. Here Johnson considers the Crusades, an event that appears to be only tangentially related to the play, because he wishes to prevent the king's remark being taken as merely a political ploy, a pious platitude useful for impressing his subjects. Rather, he suggests that the playwright wanted the audience to intermingle religious and moral considerations with political problems, to feel some sympathy for a monarch who comes to regret the means by which he came to power. King Henry IV's sincere and truly Christian remarks help prepare us for the remorse he is to feel later on. Throughout his notes on the history plays, Johnson points out the necessity of understanding how the characters relate to the historical context. Near the beginning of *Henry V,* he remarks: "At this scene begins the connection of this play with the latter part of *King Henry IV.* The characters would be indistinct, and the incidents unintelligible, without the knowledge of what passed in the two foregoing plays" (4:383; 8:536).

But with the entrance of Falstaff a different sort of editorial comment appears, one of several notes that dwell on Sir John's language. Johnson goes to great lengths to explain Falstaff's humor; indeed, nearly half of the notes for the play, approximately sixteen of the thirty-six pages in the Yale edition, are devoted to explaining the jokes and quips between the knight and his companions, a fact that is even more remarkable when one recalls Johnson's remark on Shakespeare's puns in the *Preface:* "A quibble was to him the fatal Cleopatra for which he lost the world, and was content to lose it" (7:74).[14] This sentence is often cited as an example of Johnson's limited understanding of Shakespeare's language, but it is usually misleading to separate Johnson's theory from its application. In the editing of *Henry IV,* he labored continually with quibbles. For instance:

> PRINCE HENRY. Thou judgest false already: I mean, thou
>   shalt have the hanging of the thieves, and so become
>   a rare hangman.
> FALSTAFF. Well, *Hal,* well; and in some sort it jumps
>   with my humour, as well as waiting in the Court, I
>   can tell you.
> PRINCE HENRY. For obtaining of suits?
>
> *Suit,* spoken of one that attends at court, means a *petition;* used with respect
> to the hangman, means the *cloaths* of the offender. (4:118; 7:456)

In this instance, Johnson's explanation helps us understand the precise way in which the prince is deflating his drinking companion. Hal implies that his friend is as unlikely to be involved in any ceremony at court as in one on the gallows. The suggestion that Falstaff belongs in neither place, both being too extreme, is to be kept in mind when we come to the conclusion.

But Johnson's sensitivity to Shakespeare's language is not restricted to the conversation of Falstaff or to the use of the pun. At the first entrance of Hotspur, Johnson explains the connotation of the image of the "Severn's flood," which was so "affrighted" that it "ran fearfully among the trembling reeds" (1.3.104–5). Previous commentators had censured this passage as nonsense, for it represents a "stream of water as capable of fear." But Johnson explains that "*Severn* is here not the *flood*, but the tutelary power of the flood, who was frightened, and hid his head in *the hollow bank*" (4:129; 7:461). Characteristically, Johnson's aversion to puns does not prevent his careful analysis of language in order to clarify the important ideas of the play. Johnson is anxious to make sense of Hotspur's words so that the reader can distinguish the rebels' from the king's party in subtler terms than those of sanity and insanity. Johnson's analysis of the language of these characters leads to an important, if subtle, distinction between Hotspur and Hal. Percy is seen as one able to do much but who would do more than he is able. The prince, by virtue of his relationship with Falstaff, is implicated in the folly of humorous role-playing and merry quips, indicative of the flexibility and capacity for change of a "great mind." [15]

The self-defeating nature of Hotspur's ability is an early focal point. In the third scene of act 1, when the conspiracy is first mentioned, our attention is directed to Hotspur's response to what he most wants to hear: "*Worcester* gives a dark hint of a conspiracy. *Hot-spur smells it*, that is, *guesses it. Northumberland* reproves him for not suffering *Worcester* to tell his design. *Hot-spur*, according to the vehemence of his temper, still follows his own conjecture" (4:136; 7:463). Hotspur's vehemence does not permit him to pause even as the conversation turns to his own obsession. The limitations of this rugged soldier are seen in the conversation of the conspirators, who must wait for Hotspur's enthusiasm to subside before they can get down to the details of the uprising.

Although different from his fiery counterpart, Hal is not seen in wholly flattering terms. For example, the prince at the tavern (2.4.12) characterizes himself as "no proud Jack, like Falstaff, but a Corinthian." A modern editor glosses the last word of this line in the following complimentary terms: "a boon companion. . . . Corinth was noted for gay dissipation." Johnson is much less flattering: "a wencher" (4:151; 7:467). In *Richard II*, Johnson characterizes King Henry V by referring to "his greatness in his manhood" and to the "debaucheries in his youth" (4:92; 7:450). Further reference to the distinction between these two characters is provided by the immediately preceding note in *1 Henry IV*, which concerns Hotspur's conversation with

Lady Percy. While the prince revels in low comedy, Hotspur sets his military duty above the love of his wife.

Refusing to gloss over Hal's failings, Johnson nonetheless fosters our sympathy with and understanding of the personable qualities that distinguish him from Hotspur. Hal's reflections on Hotspur are paraphrased by Johnson for purposes of clarity: "That is, *I am willing to indulge myself in gaiety and frolick, and try all the varieties of human life. I am not yet of* Percy's *mind,* who thinks all the time lost that is not spent in bloodshed, forgets decency and civility, and has nothing but the barren talk of a brutal soldier" (4:155; 7:469). In fact, near the end of *Henry V,* Johnson chastises Shakespeare for contradicting the nature of this distinction, which has been established in preceding dramas: "I know not why *Shakespeare* now gives the king nearly such a character as he made him formerly ridicule in *Percy.* This military grossness and unskilfulness in all the softer arts, does not suit very well with the gaieties of his youth, with the general knowledge ascribed to him at his accession, or with the contemptuous message sent him by the *Dauphin,* who represents him as fitter for the ball-room than the field, and tells him that he is not to *revel into dutchies,* or win provinces *with a nimble galliard*" (4:479; 8:565). We gradually come to realize that Hal is a fuller human being than Percy: as Hotspur ignores his own domestic duties in his military obsession, the prince can be expected to respond to the full range of womankind, from wench to lady.

Hal is most notably to be distinguished from Hotspur in his association with Falstaff. Johnson gives his highest praise to the scene (2.4) where Falstaff takes the part of the king and admonishes the prince for his errant ways:

> FALSTAFF. *Harry,* I do not only marvel, where thou spendest thy time, but also how thou art accompanied; for though the camomile, the more it is trodden on, the faster it grows, yet youth, the more it is wasted, the sooner it wears.

> This whole speech is supremely comick. The simile of camomile used to illustrate a contrary effect, brings to my remembrance an observation of a later writer of some merit, whom the desire of being witty has betrayed into a like thought. Meaning to enforce with great vehemence the mad temerity of young soldiers, he remarks, that *though* Bedlam *be in the road to* Hogsden, *it is out of the way to promotion.*" (4:166; 7:472–73)

This digression, a rarity in Johnson's edition, serves to illustrate a linguistic abuse, a form of bathos, a trope that at once advances and subverts the speaker's purpose. Of course, Falstaff deliberately turns the trope upon himself, and that is why the scene is supremely comic. In fact, we are invited by our editor to pause over this particular comic moment, because it epitomizes what Johnson means by Falstaff's humor as consisting "in easy escapes and sallies of levity, which make sport but raise no envy" (4:365; 7:523). As the player-king, the knight scolds the prince in "high-flown" style—modern editors trace the camomile image to Lyly's *Euphues: Anatomy of Wit*[16]—which, in calling attention to itself, distracts our attention from the main purpose of the speech, saving the prince from some embarrassment about the question of "how thou art accompanied."

Falstaff's humorous skill here is of the sort that will not excite envy because he turns it upon himself and thereby allows Hal an easy escape. The authority of the player-king is, to some extent, undermined by his misuse of euphuistic rhetoric. Not simply a humorous character, Falstaff demonstrates that his inimitable comic spirit derives from his ability to see how others view him. He knows that the king finds him an unsuitable companion for his son, that the son accepts the justice and the humorlessness of his father's attitude, and that the audience enjoys the skill with which he plays upon these perspectives.[17]

This portrait of Sir John reveals not only the complexity of his sense of humor but also a side of his disposition that is often neglected. In the third scene of the third act, Bardolph abuses his drinking companion in obvious physical terms, telling Falstaff that he is so fat as to "needs be out of all compass." The knight's reply—"thou art the knight of the burning lamp"—elicits the following comment from Johnson: "This is a natural picture. Every man who feels in himself the pain of deformity, however, like this merry knight, he may affect to make sport with it among those whom it is his interest to please, is ready to revenge any hint of contempt upon one whom he can use with freedom" (4:188; 7:478). Johnson wants us to see genuine anger on the part of the knight; for a moment, the vulnerable man is revealed behind the clown's mask. The full picture of Falstaff, including his vulnerability to insult, is important to Johnson for two reasons. It will be a factor in Hal's final rejection of him and will also serve as a reminder that Falstaff in anger, as in enjoyment, is aware of how he appears to others. The point to be emphasized at this stage is that it is precisely this comprehensiveness of response, this broad range of human awareness, that accounts for the prince's and our attraction to Falstaff.

Yet Johnson provides no excuses for Falstaff on the battlefield. On the contrary, he is seen in contrast to the courageous prince. Explaining the famous image in which Vernon describes the prince and his comrades riding off to battle as "all furnish, all in arms, all plum'd like estridges, that with the wind, baited like eagles, having lately bath'd" (4.1.97–99), Johnson remarks that "a more lively representation of young men ardent for enterprize perhaps no writer has ever given" (4:199; 7:482). Falstaff, on the other hand, is described, not in the sublime terms of lively enterprise, but in terms of sheer cowardice, which he inadequately disguises as a joke. On the battlefield, when Sir John hands Hal a bottle of sack in place of a pistol, Johnson, unlike Maurice Morgann, does not attempt to excuse the knight's behavior.[18] Instead, he points to the comic way Falstaff tries to cover up or pass over his own cowardice.

> FALSTAFF. If Percy be alive, I'll pierce him.

> *Falstaff* takes up his bottle which the Prince had tossed at his head, and being about to animate himself with a draught, cries, if *Percy be alive I'll pierce him*, and so draws the cork. I do not propose this with much confidence. (4:222; 7:487–88)

Johnson speculates tentatively about this pun to make clear that Falstaff quibbles about the name of the enemy and pierces no more than a bottle of sack, while, in battle with Percy, Hal risks his life. In this way, we notice that the prince is beginning to pursue a way of life different from that of Falstaff.

THE ATMOSPHERE OF *2 HENRY IV*

Johnson records the change in the atmosphere in the second part of the play in a comment on Northumberland's acknowledgment of the death of his son Percy and his decision to join the rebellion.

> NORTHUMBERLAND. But let one spirit of the first-born Cain
>   Reign in all bosoms, that each heart being set
>   On bloody courses, the rude scene may end,
>   And darkness be the burier of the Dead!

> The conclusion of this noble speech is extremely striking. There is no need to suppose it exactly philosophical; *darkness* in poetry may be absence of eyes as well as privation of light. Yet we may remark, that by an ancient opinion it has been held, that if the human race, for whom the world was made, were extirpated, the whole system of sublunary nature would cease. (4:242; 7:493)

Remarking on the ancient belief in the possible return of chaos and old night, Johnson stresses the poetic expression of Northumberland's personal grief and desire for revenge. It is a commonplace among modern critics that, unlike *1 Henry IV,* the second part is marked by an increasing sense of decay, corruption, and the questioning of authority. Johnson apparently agrees.

Similarly, important historical and political information is contained in a note on Lord Bardolph's speech (1.3.36–62). Here Johnson refuses to accept Pope's emendation, which was adopted by Theobald, Hanmer, and Warburton. The problem is that in Pope's version Lord Bardolph recommends no delay, while, in the original, he cautions against haste. Siding with Johnson against Pope and the others, most modern editors offer a paraphrase (without acknowledgment of their debt to Johnson) of his explanation of this passage, which A. R. Humphreys labeled "the chief crux of the play." [19] Johnson is the first to realize that the uprising must be seen to be hurried, for the substantial political charge against the rebels is not that their claims were unjustified but that they acted before exhausting all alternatives to war.

Most of Johnson's notes, however, are devoted to explaining the puns and jokes of Falstaff, Hal, and their retinue at Mistress Quickly's inn, for the humor of these characters represents for Johnson significant entertainment. In the last act of *Henry V,* Johnson remarks: "The comick scenes of the history of *Henry* the fourth and fifth are now at an end, and the comick personages are dismissed. . . . I believe every reader regrets their departure" (4:474; 8:563). But in *2 Henry IV,* the reader is made aware of a change in tone. When Falstaff addresses Hal as "a bastard son' of the King's," Johnson remarks that "the improbability of this scene is scarcely ballanced by the humour" (4:283; 7:503). Unlike the scene in part 1 (3.3.85ff.) where Falstaff also abuses the prince, which Johnson characterized as a "merry dialogue" (4:193; 7:480), this scene lacks the deft sense of humor we expect of Falstaff. Particularly improbable here is Falstaff's insulting of the king, something he carefully avoids in the previous scene. It seems to me that Johnson is assuming that an eighteenth-century audience, like an Elizabethan one, would tolerate the knight's abuse of the prince, his drinking companion, but not of the king. Aside from the breach of decorum, this remark manifests Falstaff's insensitivity to his public spectacle, his blindness to the negative impression he is making upon others. Yet, as we have seen, his great comic genius resides in precisely such an awareness. Johnson suggests that in preparing the way for the rejection of Falstaff, Shakespeare sacrifices the most important element of one of his greatest creations, Falstaff's ability to turn his sense of humor against himself.

JOHNSON AND MODERN CRITICS

However, there are major differences between Johnson and present-day critics concerning Falstaff. Although they may disagree about the proper attitude to the end of the play, contemporary commentators agree that Falstaff changes in the second part and becomes less likable, his humor being darker and more corrupt. The knight's treatment of Shallow and Silence (3.2) is now generally regarded as shabby. Clifford Leech goes so far as to suggest that "we have come to wonder whether there is ultimately much to choose between Falstaff and Prince John."[20] For Johnson, on the other hand, the difference between these two characters must never be obscured. With regard to the gulling of Justice Shallow, Johnson explains that Shallow's description is equivalent to admitting that he "is King *Arthur's* fool" (4:301; 7:506–7). We are reminded that Shallow, as his name suggests, is a low character and a fool; the implication is that if Falstaff had not taken advantage of him, someone else would have. Indeed, Falstaff himself says as much.

> FALSTAFF. If the young Dace be a bait for the old Pike, I see no reason in the law of nature but I may snap at him.
>
> That is, *If the pike may prey upon the dace, if it be the law of nature that the stronger may seize upon the weaker,* Falstaff *may with great propriety devour* Shallow. (4:302–3; 7:507)

For Johnson, the devouring of Shallow is natural to Falstaff, who, we recall, was characterized as one who preys upon the weak; this behavior represents no change in Falstaff. Far from condoning the knight's actions on the battlefield or toward Shallow, Johnson sees each as cowardly and worthy of punishment; they are both, however, to be distinguished from major crimes. Prince John's action at Gaultree is described in unmistakably Johnsonian terms: "It cannot but raise some indignation to find this horrible violation of faith passed over thus slightly by the poet, without any note of censure or detestation" (4:317; 7:512). Moral outrage is expressed here because this breach of trust, while it may have been necessary for political purposes, represents a cold and calculated act of deception and inhumanity.

We may be tempted here to apply the passage from the *Preface* cited at the beginning of this chapter and conclude that Johnson required a didactic interjection. But the condemnation of Prince John should be understood in the larger context of Johnson's overall view of the drama. In neglecting to condemn the action of Prince John at Gaultree, Shakespeare obscures the difference between Falstaff and Prince John, namely, that the former's humanity makes him appealing to us in spite of his folly and vice. Prince John, on the other hand, remains unmoved by the humor of the fat knight. And both Falstaff and Johnson are mindful of this fact.

FALSTAFF. Good faith, this same young sober blooded Boy doth not love me; nor a man cannot make him laugh.

Falstaff speaks here like a veteran in life. The young prince did not love him, and he despaired to gain his affection, for he could not make him laugh. Men only become friends by community of pleasures. He who cannot be softened into gaiety cannot easily be melted into kindness. (4:320; 7:513).

Able to deceive others without a pang of conscience, this young prince is incapable of responding to Falstaff. Indeed, his crime seems to be defined by this inability. For Johnson, a man capable of gaiety would be too gentle, too kind to treat his fellow human beings as did Prince John at Gaultree. And in spite of his continual sloth and cowardice, few believe Falstaff capable of such an act. For this reason Johnson asserts that Falstaff "is stained with no enormous or sanguinary crimes." Crime involves the active betrayal of one's humanity; folly and vice, the result of passivity and self-indulgence, involve serious errors but not what Johnson calls "malignancy."

Prince Hal, on the other hand, comes finally to take his place somewhere between the warm but self-indulgent Sir John and the cold and, at times, unscrupulous Prince John. For Johnson, the play should conclude in a manner that does justice to the distinction between these three characters. To say that he is dissatisfied or even deeply disappointed is an understatement. The resolution occasions a most uncharacteristic exclamation from a critic who is widely praised for his judiciousness and common sense: "I fancy every reader, when he ends this play, cries out with *Desdemona, O most lame and impotent conclusion*" (4:355; 7:522). The reference is to Desdemona's protest at Iago's indiscriminately negative characterization of women. What disturbs Johnson about the end of this play is not Hal's change in attitude toward Falstaff but his sending him to the Fleet. Indeed, so far as I can ascertain, Johnson is the first to attend to the fact that the judgment of Falstaff involves two separate and different punishments. With regard to the first decision, the banishment of Falstaff from court, Johnson has no difficulty: "Mr. *Rowe* observes, that many readers lament to see *Falstaff* so hardly used by his old friend. But if it be considered that the fat knight has never uttered one sentiment of generosity, and with all his power of exciting mirth, has nothing in him that can be esteemed, no great pain will be suffered from the reflection that he is compelled to live honestly and be maintained by the king, with a promise of advancement when he shall deserve it" (4:353; 7:521).

Rowe and those who adopted his position are being warned not to be sentimental about Falstaff. Unlike many eighteenth-century critics, Johnson has no objection to a moderate punishment of Falstaff, particularly if its aim is to reform the knight, who, as we have seen, is viewed as a "thief and a glutton, a coward and a boaster." Although likeable, Falstaff should not be esteemed, and therefore any attempt to encourage this comic genius to reform his way of life is admirable. But sending Falstaff to the Fleet disturbs Johnson: "I do not see why *Falstaff* is carried to the Fleet. We have never lost sight of him since his dismission from the king; he has committed no new fault, and therefore incurred no punishment; but the different agitations of fear, anger, and surprise in him and his company, made a good scene to the eye; and our authour, who wanted them no longer on the stage, was glad to find this method of sweeping them away" (4:354; 7:522).

What could Falstaff have done to deserve imprisonment, what new crime could he have committed in the twenty lines of text that elapsed since he was banished? Shakespeare wanted first to show the knight's consternation at his punishment and then to clear the stage quickly of this bulky distraction. A convenient stage device, the imprisonment of Falstaff undermines the careful distinction developed in the play between crimes of weakness and those of malice, between Falstaff and Prince John, with Prince Hal poised between the two.

The issue at hand may become clearer by comparing Johnson's view of the conclusion to that of a modern editor. The new Arden edition cites with approval the words of its predecessor, which appeared in 1923. The following passage constitutes the Arden position for the last half century: "Falstaff's ultimate disgrace and punishment have gained for him much undeserved commiseration; the punishment . . . temporary imprisonment in the Fleet and banishment from court—was not exceptionally severe. Queen Elizabeth inflicted similar sentences upon favourite courtiers and court ladies who incurred her displeasure. To Shakespeare's contemporaries, the King's treatment of Falstaff would not appear harsh."[21] In taking the two punishments as one, in inextricably linking the banishment and the imprisonment, these twentieth-century editors beg the question. When the king forbade his friend within ten miles of his person, is there any indication that this punishment was felt by "Shakespeare's contemporaries" to be insufficiently harsh? Moreover, are we to believe that to Elizabethans there was no appreciable difference between banishment and incarceration?

Most modern commentators are not interested in the distinction between the two punishments because they follow Shakespeare himself, who, as Johnson points out, wants to sweep the Falstaffians from the stage in order to focus upon the political figures, the Lord Chief Justice, Prince John, and King

Henry V, those who represent the power and might of the Tudor dynasty. But even in political terms, the conclusion is lame and impotent. What sort of a ruler is a king who makes no distinction between crimes worthy of imprisonment and vices deserving of exile? To return to Tillyard's position, what sort of respect is aroused by a king who first banishes a man and then a moment later allows his Lord Chief Justice to imprison him? Or, to return to the opposition to Tillyard represented by Leech, is it satisfactory to say that the audience understands the necessity of imprisoning Falstaff but cannot agree with Prince John's pleasure at the removal of all the Falstaffians, all those who inspired our merriment throughout both parts of the play and who constitute the "people" of the play? The difference between Johnson's reading of the play and that of these modern critics is that the former formulates himself in moral terms and the latter ignore him, restricting themselves to historical and political terms. But my contention is that Johnson points to a personal/moral issue that is inseparable from the historical/political dilemma of *Henry IV*.

Johnson's objection to the conclusion of *Henry IV* is not essentially didactic: he is not castigating Shakespeare for a lack of declamatory speeches concerning the appropriate vices and virtues. Rather, Johnson employs moral terms to characterize a problem about the form of the conclusion. Once understood in structural, not didactic, terms, this position raises a new question for modern Shakespeareans. What kind of political doctrine is represented by a Tudor dynast who is incapable of distinguishing between vice that arises from malice and that which springs from frailty? Johnson's objection points to the neglect of the ethical dimension inherent in the modern political view of the conclusion.

The manner in which Johnson's moral position impinges upon the modern political one can be seen by considering Stephen Greenblatt's most recent version of his essay on *Henry IV* and *Henry V*, entitled "Invisible Bullets." A founder of the "new historicists," who employ historical investigation to locate materials that at once advance and undermine the established political position, Greenblatt demonstrates that Thomas Harriot's "Brief and True Report of the New Found Land of Virginia" (1588) provides a model for a concept of political language that is both orthodox and subversive. Greenblatt applies this model to *Henry IV* and *Henry V*. The conflict between these two elements is more marked in certain circumstances: "This exposure is most intense at moments when a comfortably established ideology confronts unusual circumstances, when the moral value of a particular form of power is not merely assumed but explained." But the difficulty with these explanations is "not that they are self-consciously wicked . . . but that they are dismayingly moral."[22] Since morality exposes but also covers up the problem, Greenblatt turns to linguistic analysis. But, as we shall see, he finds the same difficulty that Johnson located in moral terms.

Turning to the protagonists, Greenblatt asserts that "Hal is a juggler," a conniving hypocrite, and that the "power he both serves and comes to embody is glorified usurpation and theft." As a "juggler" he is finally identified with the playwright himself. The problem is that Hal will eventually become the king, the orthodox establishment, and must therefore juggle with the subversive nature of Falstaff: "This staging of what we may term anticipatory or proleptic parody is a major structural principle of Shakespeare's play. Its effect is not . . . to ridicule the claims of high seriousness but rather to mark them as slightly suspect and to encourage guarded skepticism," a skepticism that is finally rejected with the imprisoning of Falstaff.[23] Greenblatt concludes by considering the end of *Henry V,* the "language lesson" that Hal gives the French princess, the very same scene that troubled Johnson so much that he concludes his remarks on *Henry V* by pointing out that "the great defect of this play is the emptiness and narrowness of the last act" (4:487; 8:566). Although the result is "the apparent subversion of the monarch's glorification," Greenblatt points out "it is not at all clear that *Henry V* can be successfully performed as subversive." The dramas are thus seen to end with an ambiguous combination of orthodoxy and subversion. But, for Greenblatt, the subversive element only becomes apparent to modern audiences when they are provided with the appropriate historical, linguistic materials, which point up the double-sided aspect of Elizabethan political language. "There is subversion, no end of subversion, only not for us."[24] Yet Johnson experienced the same phenomenon, though he couched it in moral terms, examined structural properties, and was unlikely to have been familiar with the historical materials referred to by Greenblatt. In short, Johnson has located in the text the subversion that Greenblatt asserts is only available to post-Elizabethans in materials outside of the plays.

The reason that Johnson is able to locate the problem within the structure of the dramas is that he approaches it not in ideological but in moral terms. For him, the playwright's conclusion must do justice to the context, which encourages discrimination among his characters. Similarly, Johnson, in judging the conclusion, feels compelled to explain the basis of his assessment. The critic is morally obliged to make explicit his interpretation and judgment of the work of art. What precisely is meant by interpretation and judgment will be clarified in the next two chapters, where the principles of Johnson's summary statements will be examined.

The moral imperative that Johnson applies to Shakespeare he also applies to himself as a critic. Insisting that the specific problem of Falstaff's punishment be related to the general conception, the body politic, Johnson provides particulars in the *Notes* to exemplify his generalizations in the *Preface*. On the level of literary theory, I believe that we need to follow Johnson's example. It will not do to conclude that the status quo and its opposition are left in free play in Shakespeare's Henriad, like ignorant armies of ideology. Literature and criticism create contexts that require development, modification, even contradiction of ideology. The ethical imperative insists that the particular affect the general at all levels, that the individual, the nonconformist, the Falstaffian, influence the nature of ideology, from that of the Tudor dynasty to that of modern democracy. Literature and literary analysis are thus seen not merely as a result of but as one of the forces that contribute to the hegemony of ideology.

The ethical dimension is accordingly fundamental to the procedure of this chapter. Studying theory in relation to practice reveals important new insights. The section of the *Preface* that had been taken on its own as representing traditional didacticism is understood, when related to the *Notes*, as a formulation of an ethical question. Distinguishing between didacticism and morality enables us to understand how Johnson formulated an innovative reading of *Henry IV* within the theoretical terms available to him in the eighteenth century.[25] If our analysis of Johnson's criticism can be considered metacriticism, the metacritic is morally obliged to make explicit the basis for his or her assessment and interpretation of the relationship between theory and practice.

All critics formulate themselves in terms that are limited by their historical epoch; great critics occasionally arrive at insights that point beyond the terms of their era. Literary criticism as a separate discipline rests upon such insights and must dedicate itself to a method of retrieving them. As Johnson provided quotations from the texts of others to illustrate his definitions in the *Dictionary*, so the *Notes* exemplify and clarify the generalizations of the *Preface*. This study follows in Johnson's tradition. Each chapter concludes with an axiom of literary criticism derived from Johnson's interpretation of one of Shakespeare's plays. Theory and practice are deliberately intermingled so that my principles can be evaluated in relation to my perceptions, for one final criterion of any literary critical generalization must be whether or not it helps to further an understanding of literature. Morality, the most basic and continuous element of Johnson's criticism, one linking theory and practice, becomes important for me because it also mediates between criticism and ideology.[26] Unlike didacticism, morality involves a decision about how literary meaning relates to the human predicament. The next chapter demonstrates that Johnson added a summary statement at the end of all but two of the plays to make explicit his assessment of the relation between theory and practice, to delineate precisely where abstract ideas touched the earth.

CHAPTER TWO

Critical Editing of
Troilus and Cressida

In the *Preface* Johnson announces that instead of following the customary procedure of locating passages deemed particularly worthy of praise or blame,
he will append to each play a summary statement or "stricture," a term defined in the *Dictionary* as a "slight touch upon a subject, not a set discourse."
These comments—ranging in length from a few paragraphs to a few pages—
consist of a brief interpretation and a concise judgment of the literary merit
of the drama. To the modern reader, these strictures seem out of keeping
with the neutral and scholarly notes. This distinction is particularly marked
in modern anthologies where the notes are taken out of context and printed
as isolated, miscellaneous remarks. But in fact the combination of scholarly,
textual analysis and interpretive, evaluative commentary is characteristic of
Johnson's criticism.

Readers whose familiarity with Johnson derives from Boswell's *Life* assume that Johnson had strong views about most matters, particularly literary
ones, and that he seldom hesitated to make his opinions known. But the
relationship between polemics and analysis in his criticism is less familiar to
the general reader and is taken for granted by specialists. We all know the
most famous Johnsonian dicta: the description of *Lycidas* as "easy, vulgar, and
therefore disgusting," the dismissal of *Gulliver's Travels* as merely a story of

little and big people, the definition of a romance as a tale consisting of "a hermit and a wood, a battle and a shipwreck," and the definition of oats as that which is fed to horses in England and to the people in Scotland. It is often forgotten, however, that these remarks occur in contexts that are scholarly, critical, and textual—the *Lives* of Milton and Swift, *The Rambler,* and the *Dictionary.*

The last-mentioned is particularly exemplary of my point. Printed throughout the nineteenth and twentieth centuries without the illustrative quotations, the *Dictionary* could be made to appear to be an exercise in eccentricity, a compilation of opinionated definitions and quirky etymologies. When reunited with its "text," the *Dictionary* illustrates an important critical principle. For instance, the entry for "fall" includes 65 definitions and 145 illustrative quotations. Each definition has then an average of 2 passages enabling the reader to test the accuracy of the definition. Johnson makes his own view explicit and provides the reader with grounds for refutation. This principle is maintained in the edition of Shakespeare's plays; indeed, as Sherbo has demonstrated, these two great projects interact with one another.[1] Of the 145 quotations mentioned above, 20 are from Shakespeare.

In fact, in his edition of Shakespeare Johnson further refined this principle. The strictures provide an explanation and justification for the textual decisions made in the notes. However, since most of the notes involve restoring passages emended by previous editors, the modern reader is at a particular disadvantage because the standard edition of Johnson's Shakespeare reproduces only Johnson's notes, not those of others included in Johnson's text and not Johnson's text of the plays. The text of the plays is important because Johnson often prints notes offering a possible emendation of his own or justifying an emendation of another editor while leaving the original unchanged.[2] The suggestion is that understanding why various editors wanted to change a passage removes the need for change. This technique involves what could be called a "double hermeneutic": the artistic goal of Shakespeare (one hermeneutic) and the critical goal of Johnson or any other editor (another hermeneutic) together provide the basis for understanding and making bibliographic decisions about the text.[3] My aim is to demonstrate that the editor needs to make clear to his reader the critical premises, the interpretive bases, for his decisions and to provide the textual variants that constitute grounds for refutation, because interpretation is not only a descriptive but also a judgmental act. Bibliography, like criticism, is a teleological endeavor, and Johnson's stricture functions to articulate and assess the nature of Shakespeare's artistic goal.

INTERPRETIVE JUDGMENT IN THE STRICTURE

In order to show how the stricture functions for Johnson as an editor, I shall compare his text to previous ones and to an adaptation involving changes made as a result of interpretation. *Troilus and Cressida* is selected because it was adapted to the Restoration stage by John Dryden, whose version is regularly cited in Johnson's notes. Characteristically, Johnson makes his assessment and interpretation of *Troilus and Cressida* explicit in his stricture.

> THIS play is more correctly written than most of *Shakespeare's* compositions, but it is not one of those in which either the extent of his views or elevation of his fancy is fully displayed. As the story abounded with materials, he has exerted little invention; but he has diversified his characters with great variety, and preserved them with great exactness. His vicious characters sometimes disgust, but cannot corrupt, for both *Cressida* and *Pandarus* are detested and contemned. The comick characters seem to have been the favourites of the writer; they are of the superficial kind, and exhibit more of manners than nature, but they are copiously filled, and powerfully impressed.
>
> *Shakespeare* has in his story followed for the greater part the old book of *Caxton*, which was then very popular; but the character of *Thersites*, of which it makes no mention, is a proof that this play was written after Chapman had published his version of *Homer*. (7:547; 8:938)

The interpretive purport of this stricture becomes clear in reference to Dryden's *Troilus and Cressida*, the only version of the play performed during the eighteenth century. Although Johnson himself could not have seen the play (its last eighteenth-century performance was in 1733, before his arrival in London), he read it carefully, a fact made clear in his first note.[4] Indeed, Johnson's stricture is, in large part, a response to Dryden's preface to his version of *Troilus and Cressida*. For example, Dryden believes *Troilus and Cressida* to be an early work because the language is more "obscure" than that of the later plays, but Johnson finds it "was more correctly written than most of Shakespeare's compositions." Furthermore, to Dryden's objection that "Cressida was false, and is not punish'd," Johnson replies that the condemnation is appropriate to her sins, and among the characters that Dryden considered "left unfinish'd" are some that Johnson applauds as the finest achievement of the play. Finally, Johnson's explanation that the sources for Shakespeare were Caxton and Chapman is in direct response to the conclusion of Dryden's prologue:

> My faithfull Scene from true Records shall tell
> How *Trojan* valour did the *Greek* excell;

> Your great forefathers shall their fame regain,
> And *Homers* angry Ghost repine in vain.
> (Dryden, p. 250)

The general opinion alluded to here is that Homer sided with the Trojans and Caxton, in *The Recuyell of the Historyes of Troye*, with the Greeks. Unlike Shakespeare, whose source favored the Greeks, Dryden promises to set the historical record straight by consulting Homer. But Johnson points out that the presence of Thersites makes clear that Shakespeare was familiar with Homer.

Johnson's reason for qualifying some of Dryden's assertions should not be seen as an attack on the great Restoration writer; he had the highest regard for "the father of criticism" and respected his version of *Troilus*. Moreover, Johnson refers to Dryden's *Troilus* as an "alteration"; an imitator himself, Johnson recognizes that the alterer has a kind of license not accorded to the editor. Not an edition of Shakespeare, Dryden's drama is consulted as a form of literary criticism because the changes made are informed by an interpretation that helps Johnson clarify his own interpretive principles.

In general terms, the difference between Dryden and Johnson can be seen by turning to the comic characters. Johnson focuses on the amalgam of Greek and Trojan as representing the double or evenhanded position he believes is representative of Shakespeare's attitude toward the war. Favoring the Trojans, Dryden emphasizes the tragic love of Troilus and Cressida. Accordingly, Dryden made one important change in and one addition to the plot. Instead of betraying Troilus, as in the original, Cressida follows her father's instructions and only pretends to be interested in Diomedes, who then treacherously tells Troilus that Cressida has been unfaithful, causing the latter's suicide. A new scene is created in which Hector and Troilus draw swords in a quarrel over the possible return of Cressida to the Greeks. In responding to the imitator's view of *Troilus and Cressida*, Johnson makes clear in his stricture that the interpreter must decide whether Shakespeare favored one side or remained above the fray.

INTERPRETING AND EDITING

In order to establish the interpretive foundation for his edition, Johnson mentions Dryden at the outset.

> TROILUS. The *Greeks* are strong, and skilful to their strength,
>   Fierce to their skill, and to their fierceness valiant.

> But I am weaker than a woman's tear,
> Tamer than sheep, fonder than ignorance;
> Less valiant than the virgin in the night,
> And skill-less as unpractis'd infancy.

> Mr. *Dryden*, in his alteration of this play, has taken this speech as it stands, ex-
> cept that he has changed *skill-less* to *artless*, not for the better, because *skill-less*
> refers to *skill* and *skilful.* (7:410; 8:909)

In his *Dictionary*, Johnson distinguishes between these two words: "skilful" is
a positive term, while "artful" is more ambiguous, partaking at once of skill
but also of cunning and artifice. Dryden's choice of "artless" furthers his
aim. Reversing the first two scenes, Dryden opens with the Greek council,
where Ulysses delivers his famous "degree" speech and parodies Achilles.
The Restoration audience is introduced to Ulysses' artfulness, his clever-
ness and cunning, before the entrance of Troilus in order to emphasize the
contrast between the artful Greek and the artless Trojan.

But Shakespeare, as Johnson points out, emphasizes skill, not art, in this
speech; his Troilus reflects on the Greeks' ability at warfare, their physical
prowess, not their intelligence or guile. Dryden has radically altered the distinction Shakespeare has drawn between the Greeks and the Trojans. For the
Elizabethan playwright, the physical prowess of the Greeks is set off against
the personal sensitivity of the Trojans. For the Restoration adaptor, Greek
guile contrasts negatively with Trojan candor. Realizing that the evenhand-
edness of the original has been altered by Dryden, Johnson reprints at the
beginning of the play the following note by Pope: "Mr. *Dryden* thinks this one
of the first of our authour's plays: but on the contrary, it may be judged from
the fore-mentioned preface that it was one of his last; and the great number of
observations both moral and politic, (with which this piece is crowded more
than any of his) seems to confirm my opinion. Pope" (7:409). We are hereby
warned against taking at face value Dryden's denigration of the language of
the original. Johnson sees Dryden's negative assessment of the original as a
strategy for justifying his alterations. But because Dryden takes a clear position on the critical issues of the drama, Johnson continually refers to him.
For example, Ulysses' degree speech contains a textual crux that Johnson resolves in a way suggestive of the equivalent passage in Dryden. The original
reads as follows:

> ULYSSES. When that the General is not like the hive,
> To whom the Foragers shall all repair,
> What honey is expected?

Warburton suggests an emendation, believing that the sentence does not make sufficiently clear that the "General" and the "hive" are of different "degrees." Johnson, however, believes that no alteration is necessary: "The meaning is, *When the General is not* to the army *like the hive* to the bees, the repository of the stock of every individual, . . . *what honey is expected?* what hope of advantage? The sense is clear, the expression is confused" (7:430; 8:914). Here we see manifested a basic principle of Johnson's edition of Shakespeare: a steadfast refusal to emend or accept changes made by past editors when the original text can be explained by analyzing and explaining Shakespeare's artistic goals.[5] Sharing with Dryden an interest in the ultimate goal of the drama, Johnson consistently opposes the alterations made by previous editors.

Indeed, Dryden's rendition of the above-cited image may have helped Johnson:

> ULYSSES. For when the general is not like the Hive
>   To whom the Foragers should all repair,
>   What Hony can our empty Combs expect?
>   (Dryden, p. 253)

Clearly, an analogy is drawn between the general with his army, on the one hand, and, on the other, the hive with its bees: if each member of the group abides by his degree, his station in life, the community will integrate its members in an organized fashion. But Dryden goes one step further, adding the image of "empty Combs," which modifies the focus of the trope, shifting the emphasis from the organization of the hive to the honeycombs. Johnson stands firmly between Warburton and Dryden, refusing to get entangled in the eighteenth-century editor's unnecessary emendation and resisting the Restoration critic's addition of a socioeconomic element.

Maintaining a position between the bibliographer's neglect of artistic goals and the adaptor's license to change the text, Johnson establishes his editorial posture. In the debate, in act 2, about whether or not to return Helen, the Restoration Troilus explains his attitude in the following terms.

> TROILUS. We turn not back the Silks upon the Merchant
>   When we have worn 'em: the remaining food
>   Throw not away because we now are full.
>   If you confess 'twas wisedome *Paris* went,
>   As you must needs, for you all cry'd, *Go, go!*
>   If you'll confess he brought home noble prize,
>   As you must needs, for you all clapt your hands,

And cry'd *Inestimable!* why do you now
So underrate the vallue of your purchase?
(Dryden, pp. 266–67)

These nine lines are a conflation of twenty-one in Shakespeare (2.2.68–89); Johnson's note on this passage demonstrates his familiarity with Dryden. Shakespeare's Troilus refers to the "silks," not, as in Dryden, as "worn," but as "soil'd," in the quarto and as "spoil'd" in the folio. Printing the quarto version in his text, Johnson records the folio alternative in his note and explains that he prefers "soil'd" to "spoil'd" because Troilus's point is not that Helen is ruined or spoiled but that she is used or worn. Further evidence of Dryden's influence on Johnson in this same speech can be seen in the commentary on Troilus's phrase "Why do you now the issue of your proper wisdoms rate, and do a deed that fortune never did," which is paraphrased by Johnson as follows: "*Why do you, by censuring the determination of your wisdoms, degrade* HELEN, *whom fortune has not yet deprived of her value, or against whom, as the wife of* PARIS, *fortune has not in this war so declared, as to make us value her less*" (7:450; 8:918). Dryden's notion that you "underrate the vallue of your purchase" has been an important factor in Johnson's editorial decision.

But bibliographic considerations are not therefore neglected. Unlike Warburton, who printed the folio version without informing the reader that there was an alternative, Johnson provides both versions and offers a critical justification for favoring one over the other. Moreover, his paraphrase of this passage includes the term "fortune," which Dryden omitted in order to de-emphasize the implication that, while at the moment in the ascendancy, Helen could, in the future, fall, as indeed she does. Preparing us for the fact that circumstances will turn on Helen and the Trojans, Johnson reinforces Shakespeare's two-sided view of the Trojans.

Dryden, on the other hand, influences his audience to sympathize more with the Trojans by placing Pandarus on a level with Ulysses. Changing the placement of the scene in which Ulysses and Nestor decide to rig the lottery from the end of act 1 to the middle of act 2 highlights how Pandarus aids a warrior to reach his beloved while Ulysses urges a warrior back to the battlefront. Moreover, Dryden has changed the plot so that Pandarus, unlike Ulysses, is successful: since the Restoration Cressida remains faithful to Troilus, Pandarus's goal can be said to have been achieved, while Ajax is unable to goad Achilles out of his tent. Trojan values are seen as more fundamental than those employed by Ulysses and Nestor.

In fact, Dryden demotes Greek passion and makes few distinctions among the Greeks, enabling Johnson to show that Shakespeare's distinction is more subtle. In the original, the second act ends with the scene in which Nestor and Ulysses compliment Ajax on his humility while, in asides, remarking on his pride. Johnson uses a remark by Theobald to remind us that the stirring up of Ajax is for the purpose of reawakening Achilles' military valor:

AJAX. I will kneel him, I'll make him supple—
NESTOR. He's not yet through warm: force him with praises; pour in, pour in; his ambition is dry. (7:462)

Theobald points out that the beginning of Nestor's speech has, in the past, been erroneously assigned to Ajax: "Ajax is feeding on his vanity, and boasting what he'll do to *Achilles. . . . Nestor* and *Ulysses* slily labour to keep him up in this vein" (7:462). But the ploy misfires, because they equate Achilles' pride with Ajax's. While Johnson encourages us to discriminate among the Greeks, Dryden replaces this scene with a quarrel between Ajax and Achilles, which is aptly commented on by Thersites:

THERSITES. Fools
ACHILLES. I can brook no comparison
AJAX. Nor I
ACHILLES. Well *Ajax*
AJAX. Well *Achilles.*
(Dryden, p. 286)

These Restoration Greek warriors mirror one another's foolish pride; the differences of degree found in the original have been eliminated. Dryden gives less attention to the nuances of Greek pride because it is military in nature, and he is interested in the emotions aroused by love.

POLITICS AND HISTORY

In Dryden's act 3, the change in focus from history to politics becomes clear. The Restoration drama begins the act with the soliloquy of Thersites, which in Shakespeare is found in the middle of act 2, after Hector has agreed to defend Helen and before Nestor and Ulysses bait Ajax. In both versions, Thersites begins by denouncing Ajax and Achilles; then, in a passage cut by Dryden, he calls upon the "Gods" to deprive the Greeks of "that little, little less than little wit from them that they have; which short'arm'd ignorance itself knows is so abundant scarce, it will not in circumvention deliver a fly from a spider, without drawing the massy irons and cutting the web." Johnson explains that this last image means "*without drawing their swords to cut the web. They use no means but those of violence*" (7:455; 8:919). Dryden omits this curse upon violence in general, leaving Thersites to conclude by wishing upon everyone "a Pox," the Restoration equivalent of the Renaissance "Neapolitan boneache." While Shakespeare's Thersites curses all lovers and warriors, Dryden's cynic condemns Achilles and Ajax to the fate of love, the "Pox," because they fight "for a Cuckold's Queen." The original invective against war of all kinds has been transformed into one against conflicts over love. In this way, Dryden prepares his audience for the conclusion of act 3, the quarrel between Hector and Troilus, his one addition to the plot. This scene is particularly significant because it involves an intermingling of the love plot and the military action, elements that in Shakespeare are related but separate.

Shakespeare's reason for maintaining the separation of the two strands of the action is made clear in Ulysses' famous speech beginning "Time hath, my lord, a wallet at his back," a speech removed by Dryden. Johnson indicates in no uncertain terms that he considers this address to be significant: "This speech is printed in all the modern editions with such deviations from the old copy, as do exceed the lawful power of an editor" (7:484; 8:925). I know of no other instance in his entire edition of Shakespeare when Johnson comes down so hard on all of his predecessors. Clearly, he wants his reader to pause and digest this speech, the result of his scholarly and critical labor. We discover the reason for the severe tone of this note when Johnson records in this forty-five-line passage six variants between the quarto and folio, not one of which is mentioned by Warburton (see Johnson 7:484–85 and Warburton 7:434–35). Here Johnson takes a clear, judgmental stand, because this speech forms the basis of his interpretation.

Johnson recognizes that Ulysses is trying to raise Ajax's perspective above the level of the immediate cause to that of history. What will posterity say, Ulysses implies, about Ajax's behavior in the war with Troy? Dryden, on the other hand, considers a political question: how war threatens the stability of the family, the basis of the state.

Consistent with his view of the domestic scene as the microcosm of the body politic, Dryden begins act 4 with a scene in which Troilus and Cressida together lament their imminent separation from one another. Shakespeare, by contrast, begins with a truce when Aeneas, Paris, and Diomedes discuss Helen, a scene that demonstrates how war debases love and courtliness. Diomedes tells Aeneas that as soon as the truce ends, he will seek Aeneas's life. Aeneas replies, "And thou shalt hunt a lion that will fly with his face backwards. In humane gentleness, welcome to Troy" (4.1.20–21). Even the courtly Aeneas loses his temper when goaded by the brash Diomedes.

In a conversation later on in this same scene, Diomedes again insults the Trojans. When Paris asks who deserves Helen, Menelaus or himself, Diomedes replies without hesitation: "Both merits pois'd, each weighs no less nor more, be he as he, which heavier for a whore." As with others of Diomedes' salacious terms, Johnson, instead of disapproving, explains them in detail. The reference is to a wager, "that is, *for a whore* staked down, *which is the heavier?*" (7:493; 8:927). Here we find a particularly instructive example of how Johnson's critical acumen prevents the need for emendation. In his note to this passage, Johnson records a variant in the quarto and then paraphrases the folio version that he leaves unchanged. Ironically, Johnson seems so much to have grasped the purport of the passage that the modern Arden editor uses a term from Johnson's paraphrase to emend the passage.[6] Diomedes' language calls attention to the fact that the Trojans cannot escape the taint of Helen, whose unfaithfulness contributes to the descent of Troilus and Aeneas to her level. Dryden's attempt to demonstrate "how Trojan valour did the Greek excel" entails altering both Diomedes' part with regard to Cressida and the cutting of this scene. Johnson, on the other hand, makes certain that his readers understand that Diomedes' terms, however exaggerated, are not wholly inappropriate to Helen and the Trojans.

Nevertheless, Shakespeare does distinguish the Greeks, particularly Diomedes, from the Trojans. Giving Cressida over to the protection of Diomedes, Troilus proclaims that if Diomedes treats her "fair" he shall have the right to ask mercy in battle. Characteristically, Diomedes replies that the lady's physical charms are sufficient claim to his protection, thus angering Troilus:

> TROILUS. *Grecian,* thou dost not use me courteously,
>   To shame the zeal of my petition to thee
>   In praising her.

Johnson employs Warburton's explanation of what Troilus is saying: "Grecian, you use me discourteously. . . . You should not shame the *zeal* of it, by promising to do what I require of you, for the sake of her *beauty:* when, if you had good manners, or a sense of a *lover's* delicacy, you would have promised to do it, in compassion to his *pangs* and *sufferings*" (7:504). Troilus is shown to be a more delicate, courteous, and admirable character than Diomedes, but within twenty lines of this speech, we see Cressida greeting the Greeks with endearing kisses, giving us reason to wonder if Troilus's delicacy is inappropriate.

In the Restoration play, this conversation between Diomedes and Troilus takes place after Troilus has overheard what he believes to be Cressida's pledge of love to Diomedes. But because this version omits the scene of Cressida being greeted by the Greeks—Pandarus mentions it in a humorous fashion, minimizing the intimacy of the Greeks—and because the audience knows that Cressida is only feigning love on orders from her father, Diomedes' words have no applicability to Cressida. Indeed, at the end, Dryden makes Diomedes the villain of the play: refusing to admit in the presence of Troilus that Cressida has not succumbed to his desire, he is the cause of Cressida's suicide. Greek treachery and discourtesy cause the death of the heroine. In Shakespeare, as Johnson helps to make clear, the Trojans' respect for the conventions of romance is at once poignant and futile.

At this point, we see an apt illustration of the difference between Theobald's and Johnson's uses of Dryden. In the middle of act 4 of the original drama, when Ajax and Hector are about to begin their duel, Aeneas explains that Hector will allow the Greeks to decide the conditions of the combat.

> AGAMEMNON. Which way would *Hector* have it?
> AENEAS. He cares not; he'll obey conditions.
> AGAMEMNON. 'Tis done like *Hector*, but securely done,
>   A little proudly, and great deal misprizing
>   The Knight oppos'd.

Johnson first reproduces Theobald's justification of his emendation: "It seems absurd to me, that *Agamemnon* should make a remark to the disparagement of *Hector* for pride, and that *Aeneas* should immediately say, *If not* Achilles, *Sir, what is your name? To Achilles* I have ventur'd to place it; and consulting *Mr. Dryden's* alteration of this play, I was not a little pleas'd to find, that I had but seconded the opinion of that Great Man in this point. Theobald" (7:508). Johnson's own comment, made after the above note, might serve as a motto for his entire edition of Shakespeare: "As the old copies agree, I have made no change" (7:508; 8:930).

In this instance, Theobald is referring to act 4, scene 2 of the Dryden, in which the Greeks snub Achilles; in Shakespeare, this event happens in the middle of act 3. In addition to reordering the sequence of events, Dryden also changes the response of Achilles, who blurts out angrily, "I'le do something: But what I know not yet" (Dryden, p. 316). In the original version, Achilles returns to his tent. Theobald is concerned with explaining the speech immediately following, in which Aeneas defends Hector to Achilles. On this point, moderns are divided; the Arden text follows Theobald, and the Variorum is with Johnson. But, in referring to Dryden, Theobald overlooks the

fact that the Restoration warrior is at this moment prevented from returning to the battlefield by a letter from Polixene engaging him to keep his oath
against fighting the Trojans. In this way, Dryden emphasizes the corruption
of Achilles, who is, in some sense, consorting with the enemy. Theobald
finds it "absurd" for Hector to be insulted by Agamemnon, who is of all the
Greeks the least tainted and most dignified, less proud than Achilles and less
discourteous than Diomedes.

Johnson, on the other hand, realizes that Shakespeare deliberately reserved
this insult for the most respected of the Greeks, signaling to the audience
that Hector's chivalry is one of the key elements contributing to the defeat of
Troy. Theobald's use of Dryden at this point is inappropriate for, as Johnson
suggests, here is where Shakespeare and Dryden part company, the former
identifying with the Trojans and the latter refusing to take sides. Delighted
at seconding the opinion of the "Great Man," Theobald is equidistant from
Dryden and Johnson, both of whom understand that an interpretive matter
is here at issue: whether the audience is guided toward a political conclusion,
the doom of the Trojan state, or toward a historical one, how Greeks and
Trojans each contribute to the destruction of a civilization.

INTERPRETATION AND BIBLIOGRAPHY

Combining bibliographical and critical skills, Johnson avoids pedantry. Consider, for instance, Achilles' characterization of Thersites as a "crusty batch
of Nature." "Batch," Johnson comments, "is changed by *Theobald* to *botch*,
and the change is justified by a pompous note, which discovers that he did
not know the word *batch*. What is more strange, *Hanmer* has followed him.
Batch is any thing *baked*" (7:518; 8:932). On this occasion, apparently, Theobald did not consult the work of the "Great Man." Had he done so, he would
have found in act 4, scene 2, that Agamemnon refers to Thersites as "thou
crusty batch of Nature" (Dryden, p. 322). Once again, moderns are divided
on this point, the Arden editor siding with Theobald and the Variorum editor
with Johnson. But Johnson is annoyed that Theobald refused to recognize
that "batch" was a current term, one that Dryden deemed appropriate in the
same context. The description of Thersites is important because, near the
end of the drama, we may be tempted to adopt his attitude toward the other
characters. Here, although their ends are different, the paths of Dryden and
Shakespeare coincide. For Dryden, Thersites' Greek position must be seen
to be distorted, for he is of the batch who slaughtered the Trojans. For Shake-

speare, Thersites must be seen as unable to transcend that batch of Greeks and Trojans at war whom he comments upon with such contempt.

In Shakespeare this scene takes place at the beginning of act 5; by relocating it in the middle of act 4, Dryden accords it less prominence. In fact, the change in the treatment of Thersites presents an important clue to the difference between the conclusions of the Restoration and Elizabethan dramas. In a note on Thersites' catalog of maladies at the beginning of act 5, Johnson suggests the significance of Thersites in Shakespeare's *Troilus*.

> PATROCLUS. Male varlet, you rogue? what's that?
> THERSITES. Why, his masculine whore. Now the rotten diseases of the south, guts-griping, ruptures, catarrhs, loads o'gravel i' th'back, lethargies, cold palsies, raw eyes, dirt-rotten livers, wheezing lungs, bladders full of imposthume, sciatica's, limekilns i' th' palme, incurable bone-ache, and the rivell'd fee-simple of the tetter, take and take again such preposterous discoveries. (7:518–19)

Pointing out that "this catalogue of loathsome maladies ends in the folio at *cold palsies*," Johnson goes on to remark that "the retrenchment was in my opinion judicious." Then, in what appears to be an afterthought, he adds: "It may be remarked, though it proves nothing, that, of the few alterations made by *Milton* in the second edition of his wonderful poem, one was, an enlargement of the enumeration of diseases" (7:519; 8:933). Here we have a rare glimpse of Johnson's thinking process as an editor. "Has Shakespeare overdone it with Thersites' disease catalog," Johnson wonders, "or did he know what Milton came to discover, how some repetition was appropriate for the Renaissance audience?" In doubt, Johnson prints the quarto version, the longer one, against his own preference, probably because he suspected that his audience, like Shakespeare's, needed the extra emphasis. Given both versions, we can decide which better furthers the goal of demonstrating that Thersites cannot maintain the necessary balance between slander and satire, rationalization and reason.

Dryden also recognized the central role of Thersites: although he pruned most aspects of Shakespeare, Thersites' part was expanded. On the battlefield in the last act, he is challenged to a duel three times, one more time than in Shakespeare. It might be maintained that the effect is merely to make emphatic what is implicit in Shakespeare, a warning of the audience against wholesale adoption of Thersites' viewpoint. But Dryden makes a major modification in what Shakespeare would have us accept with qualification. One of Johnson's variorum techniques is instructive on this point. Near the end of the original play, Thersites delivers his last soliloquy, which will be cited in full to clarify the comment that follows.

> THERSITES. Now they are clapper-clawing one another, I'll go look on. That dissembling abominable varlet, *Diomede*, has got that same scurvy, doating, foolish knave's sleeve of *Troy*, there, in his helm; I would fain see them meet; that, that same young *Trojan* ass, that loves the whore there, might send that *Greekish* whore-masterly villain with the sleeve, back to the dissembling luxurious drab, on a sleeve-less errand. 'O'th'other side, the policy of those crafty swearing rascals, that stale ole mouse-eaten dry cheese *Nestor*, and that same dog-fox *Ulysses*, is not proved worth a black-berry.—They set me up in policy that mungril cur *Ajax*, against that dog of as bad a kind, *Achilles*. And now is the cur *Ajax* prouder than the cur *Achilles*, and will not arm to-day: whereupon the *Grecians* begin to proclaim barbarism, and policy grows into an ill opinion. (7:536–37)

As a gloss to this speech, Johnson reproduces Theobald's suggestion for an emendation. Noting that Thersites' claim that Ulysses and Nestor were "swearing rascals" is untrue, Theobald alters the term and explains his reason: "What, or to whom, did they swear? I am positive, that *sneering* is the true reading. They had collogued with *Ajax*, and trim'd him up with insincere praises, only in order to have stirr'd *Achilles's* emulation. In this, they were the true sneerers; betraying the first, to gain their ends on the latter by that artifice. Theobald" (7:537).

Without adding any comment, Johnson prints "swearing" in the text, implicitly rejecting Theobald's substitution, "sneering." Leaving Theobald's comment without his emendation demonstrates the use of bibliographic skill for critical purposes. The reader of Johnson's edition learns from Theobald's note that Thersites' observations are not completely accurate and from Johnson's text that Shakespeare wished to make precisely that point about Thersites. Dryden alters this soliloquy, omitting the false accusation against Ulysses and Nestor, leaving Thersites to rail against war in general. The Restoration playwright wants us to see Thersites' cynicism as itself a part of the war at which he rails. The waste of war, the central point of Thersites' speech, is also one of Dryden's main points, although the Restoration playwright makes cynicism serve the purposes of tragedy: "The *Trojans* make the *Greeks* retire, and *Troilus* makes *Diomede* give ground and hurts him, Trumpets sound. *Achilles* Enters with his *Myrmidons*, on the backs of the *Trojans*, who fight in a Ring encompass'd round: *Troilus* singling *Diomede*, gets him down and kills him; and *Achilles* kills *Troilus* upon him. All the *Trojans* dye upon the place, *Troilus* last." (Dryden, p. 352).

In Shakespeare's *Troilus,* only Hector is killed on stage; in the Restoration version, Hector's death is reported by Agamemnon after the above massacre, emphasizing that with the death of Hector so ends Troy. The final speeches of the two versions are therefore markedly different. Dryden's Ulysses begins by hailing Agamemnon as "truly Victor now" and ends with a heroic couplet.

> Then, since from homebred Factions ruine springs,
> Let Subjects learn obedience to their Kings.
> (Dryden, p. 353)

Even Ulysses finds victory bittersweet. And while he gestures toward Agamemnon, the audience beholds the pile of corpses, on the top of which is Troilus. Dryden has altered Shakespeare's "Master-Stroke" in accord with his interpretation, manifested most clearly in the character of Thersites, who is appropriately returned to present the epilogue. Explaining that he has come back "to huff out our play," Thersites decides to continue railing because

> If guilty, yet I'm sure o th' Churches blessing,
> By suffering for the Plot, without confessing.
> (Dryden, p. 354)

In addition to alluding to the Gunpowder Plot, Thersites refers to the play that has just ended; Dryden implies that only total cynicism like Thersites' could reject sympathy for Troilus, the hero of the tragedy. The waste of war leads to a lack of discrimination, to wholesale slaughter, and to attitudes that preclude a distinction between Diomedes and Troilus or between Cressida and Helen.

But Shakespeare sees Thersites not as a result but as a cause of the war: Greek cynicism helped destroy Troy. Accordingly, the Renaissance drama concludes, not with Thersites, but with Pandarus. Having been rejected by Troilus, who tells him to "live with thy name," the pander of panders bemoans his lot—"Why should [traitors' and bawds'] endeavour[s] be so lov'd, and performance so loath'd?" He concludes by asking the audience for their tears of sympathy and, failing to receive that, threatens to "bequeath you my diseases." Pandarus is singled out by Johnson, in his stricture, as one of those "vicious" characters who may "disgust but cannot corrupt" us because he is "detested and contemned" (7:547; 8:938). Another victim of the war, Pandarus manifests a characteristic kind of psychological wound in Shakespeare's *Troilus.* He has been reduced to a "broken lacquey, ignominy and shame," much as the speaker of this phrase, Troilus himself, has descended to desperately searching for death and as Cressida has now become a mere "drab." Ironically, the war caused by desire for Helen has resulted in the loss of the lovable and loving elements in Pandarus, Troilus, and Cressida, a procedure reminiscent of what happens to Falstaff in 2 *Henry IV.*

While Dryden brings us to mourn the loss of the Trojans, Shakespeare shows us how Trojan courtesy, no less than Greek valor, has contributed to the war that takes its toll on both sides. In addition to Hector and the city of Troy, the Trojans lose the heart of their civilization, their spirit of chivalry. Greek victory is at the price of what they fought for, the beauty and civilization of Troy. Shakespeare presents us with a historical view of war in which both sides lose. Dryden concludes with political tragedy: Cressida remains faithful, and Troilus, instead of rejecting his friend Pandarus and seeking death in war, kills Diomedes and is himself killed by Achilles. Pandarus's paradoxical epilogue is replaced by Thersites' one-sided cynicism, which, like the war machine itself, grinds up everything in its path. The Restoration Troilus and Cressida are innocent victims who, unlike their Elizabethan counterparts, never succumb to bitterness and corruption. Dryden's reader feels that somehow the peaceful and organized world, Ulysses' beehive, should reserve a place for Troilus and Cressida. The commonwealth, Dryden concludes, must protect such citizens as the protagonists if it is to sustain itself.

Johnson uses Dryden as a literary critical touchstone because the coherence of his drama derives from an artistic goal, an assessment and interpretation of *Troilus and Cressida.* It is the teleological nature of Johnson's commentary on Shakespeare that distinguishes his edition from that of his predecessors.

Moral judgments are inherent in this procedure because, for Johnson, no goal, literary or literary critical, can be justifiably pursued unless it forwards the common good. The innovative significance of the stricture should now be clear. Major and minor textual problems, from matters of punctuation to readings of entire passages, appear in an entirely different light when seen in terms of an explicit evaluative goal. A great interpretive editor of Shakespeare's plays, Johnson continually replaces emendations with the original text and provides textual variants, opening up the possibility for variations in the text and alternative readings of the text. Here we see the function of the double hermeneutic: the editor's presentation of the basis for his interpretation of the artistic aim of the drama provides not only the grounds for refuting the editor but also the means for generating other editions, new approaches to Shakespeare. Johnson's polemicism is not an eccentric posture but a critical principle. In the next chapter, we shall see how this editorial principle affects his concept of the history of criticism.

CHAPTER THREE

History of Criticism in *Twelfth Night*

In his *Proposals for an Edition of Shakespeare's Dramas*, Johnson asserts that some "authors are often praised for improvement, or blamed for innovation, with little justice, by those who read few other books of the same age" (7.54). Focusing upon other editors' notes included in Johnson's edition will enable us to consider the relation between Johnson and his predecessors. Chapter 2 provided a number of instances when Johnson's comments were elicited by the remarks of other editors. In fact, his edition is, in this sense, an abbreviated history of criticism.

Twelfth Night exemplifies quite explicitly how the stricture provides the grounds for the history of criticism implicit in the *Notes*. In this regard, it may prove helpful to compare Johnson's editorial technique to that of another editor using similar principles. H. H. Furness's *New Variorum Edition of Shakespeare's Twelfth Night* (1901) is selected for two reasons. First, my other chapters examine Johnson's *Notes* in relation to Restoration, eighteenth-century, romantic, and twentieth-century commentary; this one places Johnson in a Victorian context. The *Twelfth Night* new variorum is particularly appropriate because Furness, himself a Victorian, was able to include material from the whole period. Second, assessment of how Johnson is treated by Furness will highlight the distinctive nature of Johnson's variorum technique. In reproducing past commentary and relating it to present commentary, the variorum is also a history of criticism.

It should be emphasized at the outset, however, that the goal and scale of Johnson's and Furness's projects were vastly different. Johnson was preceded by a handful of editors—Rowe, Pope, Theobald, Hanmer, and Warburton—whose texts dated from the previous fifty years. Furness lists thirty-five editors whom he consulted from the period 1765 to 1900 (*NV,* pp. 419–20). Moreover, Johnson, unlike Furness, does not record all the textual variants from the quartos and folio. Nevertheless, both share a commitment to providing the reader with a summary of past commentary on the specifics of the text.

Since Furness has no equivalent of the stricture, we begin with Johnson's explanation in the *Preface* of how his innovative editorial technique is related to the assessment of his predecessors. The problem with individual notes is that "interruption refrigerate[s] the mind": "Parts are not to be examined till the whole has been surveyed; there is a kind of intellectual remoteness necessary for the comprehension of any great work in its full design and its true proportions; a close approach shews the small niceties, but the beauty of the whole is discerned no longer" (7:111). Johnson is announcing that in place of the differences of opinion between his predecessors over small, sometimes petty matters, he will keep the whole in mind when analyzing the parts. In other words, his assessment of previous editorial decisions will be informed by the judgmental interpretation presented in the stricture. Furness, on the other hand, instead of presenting his own position seeks to blend his opinion with that of the majority to form a consensus view. My contention is that Furness's method distorts the critical historical tradition and that we should therefore follow Johnson's example, making plain the critical precepts that form the basis for our perspectives upon the history of criticism.

INSIDE AND OUTSIDE THE LOVE CIRCLE

Johnson is first referred to by Furness in a note on the opening speech by the duke:

> "If musike be the food of love, play on,
> Give me excesse of it: that surfetting,
> The appetite may sicken, and so dye."

Johnson begins his note on this passage by reproducing Warburton's comment, and Furness follows his example.

> Warburton: There is impropriety of expression in the present readings of this fine passage. We do not say, *that the appetite sickens and dies thro' a surfeit;* but the subject of that appetite. I am persuaded, a word is accidentally dropt; and that we should read, and point, the passage thus: "that, surfeiting The app'tite,

Love may sicken, and so die."—Johnson: It is true, we do not talk of the *death of appetite*, because we do not ordinarily speak in the figurative language of poetry; but that *appetite sickens by a surfeit* is true, and therefore proper.—Mrs. Griffith (p. 119): The duke is made to wish his passion were extinct; which, I believe, the most unhappy lover never did. We wish to remove every uneasy sensation it afflicts us with, by any means whatever, sometimes even by death itself; but never by extinction of the affection.—W. A. Wright. Compare *Ant. & Cleop.*, II, V, 1: "Give me some music; music, moody food of us that trade in love." (*NV,* p. 8)

Concluding that most editors believe that the duke wishes to be rid, not of his appetite for love, but of his love for Olivia, Furness offers the following alternative: "Music . . . [is] not that on which love feeds, but, that which feeds love; in this sense, Orsino says in effect: Give me excess of music, let it feed love beyond measure, even to a surfeit of itself; so that when it has done all that it can, and love is full-fed, the appetite or desire for music sickens and ceases" (*NV,* p. 8). The duke is sick, Furness explains, neither of the appetite for love nor of Olivia but of the music upon which love feeds. Furness, however, agrees with Warburton, Griffith, and the nineteenth-century commentators that no lover ever wished to rid himself of the appetite for love. But that is precisely what Johnson's note implies, namely, that Orsino wants to be free, not only of Olivia, but also of the appetite for love. Why, during the period covered by Furness, does Johnson alone entertain the possibility that Orsino wishes to be free of the desire to love? Furness does not consider this question because all the other critics find it inconceivable that love, which for them is the subject of *Twelfth Night,* could be referred to by one of the main characters in the opening speech of the drama as a sort of disease.

Most nineteenth-century commentators believe that Orsino dwells in the realm of romantic love and is therefore incapable of wishing away that appetite. The reason for this assumption becomes clear in another textual crux in this same speech.

That straine agen, it had a dying fall:
O, it came ore my eare, like the sweet sound
That breathes upon a banke of Violets
Stealing, and giving Odour.
(*NV,* pp. 5–9)

The problem concerns the word "sound," which Pope altered to "south" and was so printed in all subsequent eighteenth-century editions. Although "sound" is in the folio, Pope believed that Shakespeare had originally intended "south-wind," which was then pronounced "sou-wind" and thus became easily, but erroneously, "sound." In the eighteenth century, "south" was preferred to "sound" because only the former could be understood to imply both smell and sound. Nineteenth-century editors printed "sound," and Furness summarizes their reasons: "The difficulty here, where sound is said to give forth an odour, is parallel to that where Hamlet speaks of 'taking arms against a sea of troubles,' and is due, I think, to the thick-coming fancies of poetic imagination rather than to a common confusion of ideas, or to a blameworthy mixture of metaphors" (*NV*, p. 12).

Understood as in love or lovesick, Orsino can be expected to speak in imaginative or poetic terms. Most eighteenth-century editors, like Warburton, were troubled by the indecorum of language. But Johnson departs from his predecessors, defending Orsino on the grounds that he speaks "the figurative language of poetry." Johnson prints "south," probably unaware that it was an emendation, for he develops a new interpretation of the duke, which becomes apparent in his comment on the following conversation.

> CURIO. Will you go hunt, my Lord?
> DUKE. What *Curio?*
> CURIO. The Hart.
> DUKE. Why so I do, the noblest that I have.

Presenting the prevalent Victorian position, Furness explains "Hart" by quoting from Petrarch. Johnson, however, refers us to the story of Acteon: "This image evidently alludes to the story of *Acteon,* by which *Shakespeare* seems to think men cautioned against too great familiarity with forbidden beauty. *Acteon,* who saw *Diana* naked, and was torn in pieces by his hounds, represents a man, who indulging his eyes, or his imagination, with the view of a woman that he cannot gain, has his heart torn with incessant longing" (2:355; 7:311). Although it is another typical Renaissance love posture, this one places more emphasis on the dangers of love. Johnson sees the duke, not as a man in love, but as one toying with the fashionable postures of love and aware of the perils of such postures.

This view leads him to part company with Furness and most nineteenth-century commentators on the character of Viola. After her first speech, Johnson remarks that "*Viola* seems to have formed a very deep design with very little premeditation: she is thrown by shipwreck on an unknown coast, hears that the prince is a batchelor, and resolves to supplant the lady whom he courts. . . . Viola is an excellent schemer, never at a loss; if she cannot serve the lady, she will serve the Duke" (2:357–58; 7:312). The nineteenth-century commentators are disturbed by the characterization of Viola as a "schemer." R. G. White asserts that "if there ever were an ingenuous, unsophisticated, unselfish character portrayed, it is this very Viola,—Dr. Johnson's 'excellent schemer,' who, wretched and in want, forms that 'very deep design' of supplanting a high-born beauty, of whom she never heard, in the affections of a man of princely rank, whom she has never seen" (*NV*, p. 27). Furness feels that the defense of Viola is so important that he reproduces a lengthy extract from *Fraser's Magazine* (1865) that concludes that Viola is wholly without "traces of design, or intrigue, or endeavour to use opportunities for her own advantage" (*NV*, pp. 29–30).

Instead of investigating whether or not Johnson's view of Viola is part of an alternative interpretation of *Twelfth Night*, Furness looks for critical consensus on discrete textual "points." Consider, for instance, the following words addressed by Orsino to Cesario:

> Deerre Lad, beleeve it:
> For they shall yet belye thy happy yeeres,
> That say thou art a man: *Dianas* lip
> Is not more smooth, and rubious: thy small pipe
> Is as the maidens organ, shrill, and sound,
> And all is semblative a woman's part.
>
> (*NV*, p. 56)

The comment in the new variorum on the last two words is as follows: "Johnson: That is, thy proper part in a play would be a woman's. Women were then personated by boys" (*NV*, p. 56). Furness records Johnson's remark without comment because in fact in Shakespeare's day women's parts were played by men. But why does Johnson record the obvious? Pointing to the convention of the drama serves to break open what might be called, in reference to the Victorian notion, the magic circle of love. Alluding here, not merely to the Viola/Cesario disguise within the play but also to the boy actor playing the part of Viola, a fact outside the context of the drama, Johnson wants his audience to be on both sides of the love circle. Most nineteenth-century critics, however, were not interested in this double perspective and therefore passed up the opportunity to break the spell of the magic circle. Furness reproduces Johnson's note but does not consider why Johnson chose to interrupt his reader at this point: individual interpretations that fall outside *the* tradition are not pursued.

NEGLECT OF DIFFERENCE

Indeed, role-playing, particularly as it involves deception and lying, is not pursued by nineteenth-century critics of *Twelfth Night*. Near the end of act 1, Olivia defends the clown against Malvolio, occasioning Feste's exclamation, "Now Mercury indue thee with leasing, for thou speak'st well of fooles" (1.5.95–96). The term "leasing" is explained in the new variorum as follows:

> Heath (p. 187): Olivia had been making a kind of apology for fools; and the Fool in recompense prays Mercury, the god of cheats and, consequently, of liars, to bestow upon her the gift of leasing, or lying; humorously intimating that, whoever undertook the defense of fools would have plentiful occasion for that talent.—Knight: Is it not rather,—since thou speakest the truth of fools (which is not profitable), may Mercury give thee the advantageous gift of lying?—R. G. White: As Olivia undertakes the defence of his calling, the Clown prays Mercury, the god of liars, to enable her to push her defence beyond the bounds of truth. "Leasing" appears to have been used to convey the idea of falsehood without malice. It was measurably synonymous with "gabbling," which is apt to run into lying. "Gabbynge, or lesynge, *Mendacium, mendaciolum*."—*Prompt. Parv.* [But "Gabbing" in the *Prompt.* has in it no trace of *gabbling*. That there is a difference between *lying* and *leasing* seems clear; possibly, about the same as between *lying* and *fibbing*. In a letter written by Robert Armin, and printed in the *Introduction* to his *Nest of Ninnies* (p. XVI, ed. Sh. Soc.), we find, "It is my qualitie to add to the truth, truth, and not leasings to lyes." Heath has given, I think, the best interpretation of the passage; Dr. Johnson has a note to the same effect—ED.]. (*NV*, p. 73)

Established gradually, the difference here between the eighteenth- and nineteenth-century is finally very marked. An eighteenth-century commentator, Heath equates "leasing" with "lying," as does Johnson: "*May* Mercury *teach thee to lye, since thou liest in favour of fools*" (2:368; 7:313). The other commentators included in the note, all nineteenth-century editors, subtly modify the meaning of the term "leasing" until it becomes, not lying, but fibbing. Furness shows a gradual modification that masks the fact that a marked change has occurred: eighteenth-century lies have dwindled to harmless fibs. Although Heath and Johnson have no difficulty in accepting the possibility that Olivia may adopt a role altogether contrary to her real self, Furness and most of the other commentators wish to avoid any suggestion that the heroine is lying or insincere. Yet Furness believes that, but for the slight refinement of "lie" to "fib," he is in agreement with Heath. Johnson's development of this slight difference into an alternative interpretation of the comedy is, as may be expected, neglected by Furness.

At the end of act 1, Olivia soliloquizes about Cesario, "I do I know not what, and feare to finde mine eye too great a flatterer for my minde." Furness first cites Johnson's paraphrase of this line: "I believe the meaning is; I am not the mistress of my own actions; I am afraid that my eyes betray me, and flatter the youth without my consent, with discoveries of love." He then catalogs five later editors who develop an alternative, which is summarized as follows: " 'My mind will be unable to resist the too favorable impression which my eyes have received' " (*NV,* p. 94). The nineteenth-century commentators believe that Olivia admits that the emotional aspect of love overpowers any rational faculty; Johnson sees an Olivia who wonders about the depth of the love she has expressed. Unlike Furness's Olivia, who reflects upon the consequences of having fallen in love, Johnson's heroine meditates about how romantic gestures can be deceptive.

In act 2, Johnson shows how the perils of courtship approach evil. Upon realizing that Olivia's ring is a love-token, Cesario/Viola remarks:

Poore Lady, she were better love a dreame:
Disguise, I see thou art a wickednesse,
Wherein the pregnant enemie does much.
How easie is it, for the proper false
In womens waxen hearts to set their formes.

Johnson explains "pregnant enemie" as "the dexterous fiend, or enemy of mankind" and "proper false" as " 'how easy is disguise to women!' how easily does *their own falsehood,* contained in their *waxen,* changeable *hearts,* enable them to assume deceitful appearances" (*NV,* p. 104). Viola's disguise can be dangerous and even the occasion of evil. Furness, however, employs comments from the next century to alter the tone. "Pregnant enemie" means, not the enemy of mankind, but "quick-witted, alert, ready," and "proper false" suggests that women's hearts are not deceitful but are "easily *impressible*" (*NV,* p. 104). Johnson's danger and evil have been replaced by impressionableness and folly, the relatively harmless errors of lovers.

However, it would be inaccurate to conclude that Johnson is insensitive to the love element in *Twelfth Night.* Furness makes clear that it is precisely in this regard that Johnson's commentary is superior to that of Warburton. In act 2, the duke tells Cesario what to say to Olivia.

Tell her my love, more noble than the world
Prizes not quantitie of dirtie lands,
The parts that fortune hath bestow'd upon her:
Tell her I hold as giddily as Fortune:

But 'tis that miracle, and Queene of Iems
That nature prankes her in, attracts my soule.

Furness reproduces Johnson's rebuttal of Warburton:

> prankes her in] Warburton: What is "that miracle and queen of gems," we are
> not told in this reading. Besides, what is meant by "nature pranking her in a
> miracle"? We should read, "That nature pranks, *her mind*"—i.e. what "attracts
> my soul" is not her "fortune," but *her mind*, "that miracle and queen of gems
> that nature pranks," i.e. sets out, adorns.—Johnson: The "miracle and queen of
> gems" is her *beauty*, which the commentator might have found without so em-
> phatical an enquiry. As to her mind, he that should be captious would say, that
> though it may be formed by nature, it must be "pranked" by education. Shake-
> speare does not say that nature pranks her in a miracle, but in the miracle of
> gems, that is, in a gem miraculously beautiful. (*NV*, p. 146)

Johnson demonstrates that Warburton is being needlessly obscure in suggesting that the duke is moved by Olivia's mind. Orsino is not a Neoplatonist;
he is attracted to her outward beauty. Furness lets Johnson speak for him,
because beauty, not mind, is the focal point of this love play. But Johnson
reproduces Warburton's note on "mind," not merely to contradict him, but
to show that beauty is enhanced by mind: beauty "may be formed by nature"
but "must be pranked by education." Education, we shall see, for Johnson
includes an awareness of the role-playing involved in courtship and of the
perils of such disguises.

HUMOR AND ROLE-PLAYING

Johnson's sense of humor emerges as he differs from the Victorian view of
the gulling of Malvolio. One of the most hilarious moments is the steward's
struggle with the clue, MOAI:

> MALVOLIO. M. But then there is no consonancy in the sequell that suffers
> under probation: A. should follow, but O. does.
> FABIAN. And O shall end, I hope.
> TOBY. I, or I le cudgell him, and make him cry O.

Johnson suggests that Fabian's "O" refers to a "*hempen collar*," but Furness
adds that "the jesters never intended to carry their joke as far as 'a hempen
collar'" (*NV*, p. 171). The nineteenth-century critics are anxious to play
down the hatred expressed toward Malvolio because they see the comedy
here as fun at the expense of folly, not a pointed satire of the steward. Not

surprisingly, this difference in attitude toward Malvolio is directly related to differences in interpretation of *Twelfth Night*.

For Johnson, Malvolio's flaw resides in his hostility to role-playing in the courtship ritual. For instance, Olivia, even in her most passionate moments, is capable of wordplay, a talent that Johnson notices with his characteristic mixture of admiration and consternation.

> VIOLA. Madam, I came to whet your gentle thoughts
>   On his behalfe.
> OLIVIA. O by your leave I pray you.
>   I bade you never speak againe of him;
>   But would you undertake another suite
>   I had rather heare you, to solicit that,
>   Then Musicke from the spheares.
> VIOLA. Deere Lady.
> OLIVIA. Give me leave, beseech you: I did send,
>   After the last enchantment you did heare,
>   A Ring in chace of you.

Warburton asserts that "heare" must be "here," not "hear," but Johnson replies that "hear" is no more "nonsense than the emendation." Furness explains that Warburton and Mason were led astray by the folio's "heare," which they erroneously took to be "here," instead of "hear" (*NV*, pp. 191–92). But it seems to me that more is at stake than a misunderstanding of the orthography of the first folio. "Hear" was avoided by Warburton and Mason probably because it involves a pun on the "musike from the spheres." Johnson, in his inimitable surly manner, insists on explaining the pun because it demonstrates Olivia's playfulness, her sense of humor and awareness of her own role-playing even in the midst of a love dialogue.

The element of conscious disguise is reinforced in the 1765 text when, in this same speech, Olivia says, "cyprus, not a bosom, Hides my poor heart," and Johnson explains that "*a cyprus* is a transparent stuff" (2:404).[1] At the same time, Johnson continually emphasizes that the love felt by Olivia is genuine.

> VIOLA. By innocence I sweare, and by my youth,
>   I have one heart, one bosome, and one truth,
>   And that no woman has, nor never none
>   Shall mistris be of it, save I alone.

save I alone] Johnson: These three words Sir Thomas Hanmer gives to Olivia probably enough.

Furness disagrees, adding, "very improperly, I think.—ED" (*NV,* p. 198). Johnson is willing to entertain the possibility that Olivia might declare her love for Cesario, a notion with which we would expect Furness to agree. But the new variorum editor believes that the demure Olivia is not so pert and forward; Johnson views the heroine as merely adopting the role of demureness with Orsino and that of forwardness with Cesario.

But while Viola and Olivia manipulate language to suit their changing moods and postures, Malvolio, according to Johnson, is manipulated by his own words. At the height of his "Midsummer madnesse," the steward explains how he sees Olivia's signs of love for him.

> I have lymde her, but it is loues doing, and loue make me thankefull. And when she went away now, let this Fellow be look'd too: Fellow? not *Malvolio,* nor after my degree, but Fellow.
> 78. lymde] Johnson; That is, I have entangled or caught her, as a bird is caught with birdlime. [Compare, *Much Ado,* III, i, 109: 'Shee's tane (*limed,* in the Qto) I warrant you, We have caught her Madame.']
> 78. loues . . . loue]. See II, V, 161. R. G. White with plausibility conjectured that we should have read *Love's* and *Love.*—Innes: It may be, however, that Malvolio thought it more becoming to adopt the pagan adjurations of the court, in lieu of his previous puritanism.
> 80. Fellow?] Johnson: This word, which originally meant companion, was not yet totally degraded to its present meaning; and Malvolio takes it in the favourable sense. (*NV,* p. 222)

This note exemplifies how Johnson's notes are digested into the fabric of the new variorum. The overall impression created by the above catalog is that, entering for the first time the realm of love, the puritanical Malvolio uses somewhat inappropriate language; like all novices, he makes some serious blunders. As they appeared in his own edition, Johnson's comments present, not a man in love, but one unsuccessfully attempting to present himself as such. In imagining his courtship of Olivia, he is unaware of the negative connotations of the terms of his "endearment."

Furness wants us to smile with Malvolio, but Johnson points to more biting satire against a character who approaches evil. For instance, when Toby exclaims at the steward, "Hang him foul collier," Johnson explains, to the consternation of the nineteenth-century editors, that "the devil is called 'Collier' for his blackness" (*NV,* p. 226). Yet when Sir Andrew makes a theological reference in his letter of challenge, Johnson is shocked: "Farewell, and God have mercie upon one of our soules. He may have mercie upon mine, but my hope is better, and so looke to thy selfe." After paraphrasing the line—"We may read, '*He may have mercie upon* thine, *but my hope is better.*' Yet the passage may well enough stand without alteration"—Johnson comments that "it were much to be wished that *Shakespeare,* in this and in some other passages, had not ventured so near profaneness" (2:417; 7:320–21). Furness suggests that Johnson has missed the humor here. But Johnson believes that since Ague-cheek is *not* certain of victory, the humor derives from doubt as to whether he is wishing mercy to Cesario or himself. Johnson's objection concerns, not the humor, but the religious doctrine of mercy that should be extended to one's opponent. It is precisely the comedy that reveals the lack of mercy. The new variorum neglects an important new question. Why does Johnson object to the suggestion that Sir Andrew is irreligious while making a point of a similar kind of behavior in Malvolio?

Furness proceeds by way of textual cruxes, a procedure that eventually undermines his position. When asked by Cesario to make peace for him with his opponent, Toby refers to Cesario as a "firago." Johnson says "*Virago* cannot be properly used here, unless we suppose Sir Toby to mean, I never saw one that had so much the look of a woman with the prowess of man" (2:420; 7:321). Furness cites Victorians who insist that Toby could not know that Cesario was really a disguise for Viola and who point out that "firago" probably is derived from "fire-eater." Although a fiercer term, "firago" sacrifices the suggestion in "virago" of the woman in the man, deemphasizing the deliberate reference to "supposes."

Emphasizing the many forms of disguise in the play, Johnson is the first editor to explain Feste's reference to affection as a foolish form of disguise. Early in act 4, the clown, thinking Sebastian is Cesario, addresses him in the following terms:

SEBASTIAN. I prethee vent thy folly some-where else, thou know'st not me.
CLOWN. Vent my folly: He has heard that word of some great man, and now applyes it to a foole. Vent my folly: I am affraid this great lubber the World will proue a Cockney.

Here we see both the advantages and the disadvantages of the new variorum method. The crux here is the phrase "great lubber of the World." Furness first produces Johnson's note—"that is, affectation and foppery will overspread the world"—then cites eight commentators dating from 1807 to 1883, and concludes with his own definition: "If the affected misapplications of terms becomes widespread, it will show that the world is nothing but a foppish cockney" (*NV,* pp. 250–51). Although the distinction between Johnson and Furness here seems minimal, some commentators in between had very different views, the most prominent being R. G. White, who changes "lubber world" to "lubberly word: that is, *vent*, which, in the sense of utter, was affectedly used in S's day." Some editors, between 1807 and 1883, attempted to alter "world" to "word" so that Feste's accusation of foppishness applied, not to all the world, but only to those who used such words as "vent." Furness rejects these emendations because "lubber the world" is in the first folio, the only authorized text, and there is no evidence that in Shakespeare's day "vent" was considered a term of affectation. But why for nearly the whole of the nineteenth century did editors try to avoid the reading acceptable to Johnson? Victorian critics had difficulty accepting that the idea of affectation and disguise pervaded the world of *Twelfth Night* because such a view called into question the sincerity of the main characters in the play.

Ironically, one result of such a view is that Johnson explains a pun that the Victorians refused to accept. Speaking to Sebastian of Toby's challenge to him, Olivia remarks that "he started one poore heart of mine." Johnson speculates that there might "be an ambiguity intended between 'heart' and *hart*," but Furness cites two nineteenth-century commentators who oppose this suggestion and concludes that "it is not a quibble, nor even a play on the words; these imply consciousness, or, at least, intention; but I believe that it was an unconscious adoption by Olivia of both significations of the word" (*NV*, p. 256). In the previous note, Furness agreed with Johnson that "lubber the world" is to be preferred to "lubberly word," but, unaware of the interpretative implication that deliberate affectation pervades the drama, he now opposes the suggestion that Olivia is consciously playing upon the term "heart." Johnson, we recall, was the first to point out that "hart" in act 1 is related to the story of Acteon; here, in act 4, he wonders if Olivia feels that in loving Sebastian, whom she believes to be Cesario, she is risking the fate of Acteon. Victorian critics are committed by their interpretation to reject the suggestion that characters deeply involved in the love plot could be deliberately employing puns that indicate an awareness of the masks of love games.

THE PROBLEM OF MALVOLIO

The major difficulty with the Victorian view of the main characters as being serious and straightforward is that Malvolio presents himself in just this way and is ridiculed for it. Here an important ramification of Johnson's interpretation becomes clear. After Feste has impersonated Sir Topas for Toby's exquisite enjoyment, the latter compliments the clown, who replies, "Nay I am for all waters" (4.2.65). Again, the difference between the effect of Johnson's note in his own edition and that in the new variorum is instructive. In his own text, Johnson corrects Warburton: "*Nay, I am for all waters*] A phrase taken from the actor's ability of making the audience cry either with mirth or grief [Warburton]. I rather think this expression borrowed from sportsmen, and relating to the qualifications of a complete spaniel" (2:429; 7:322). Omitting Warburton but citing Johnson, along with a number of other editors, Furness concludes in agreement with Malone: "Whatever the origin of the phrase, be it to fish in all waters, or to swim in all waters, or to drink all liquors, . . . Feste means he can turn his hand to anything" (*NV*, p. 265). In this way, the new variorum obscures the fact that Johnson's explanation was to eliminate Warburton's reference to acting, a surprising and crucial factor in assessing the major textual problem in this famous scene.

Uncharacteristically, Johnson rejects the reference to acting, because he does not want us to be distracted from the moral lesson inherent in the comedy.

> CLOWN. But as well! then you are mad, indeede, if you be no better in your
> wits than a foole.
> MALVOLIO. They have heere propertied me.

Once again, the distinction between the appearance of Johnson's note in his own edition and that in the new variorum is significant. The reader of the 1765 edition saw the following at the bottom of the page.

Propertied me.] They have taken possession of me as of a man unable to look to himself.

Here the Clown in the dark acts. two persons, and counterfeits, by variation of voice, a dialogue between himself and Sir *Topas*—I will, *Sir, I will*, is spoken after a pause, as if, in the mean time, Sir *Topas* had whispered.

Tell me, are you not mad, or do you but counterfeit?] If he was not mad, what did he counterfeit by declaring that he was not mad? The fool, who meant to insult him, I think, asks *are you mad, or do you but counterfeit?* That is, *you look like a madman, you talk like a madman: Is your madness real, or have you any secret design in it?* This, to a man in poor *Malvolio's* state, was a severe taunt.

Vice was the fool of the old moralities. Some traces of this character are still preserved in puppet-shows, and by country mummers. (2:430–31)

The unmistakable impression received from Johnson's edition is that Malvolio is severely taunted by Sir Topas, who despises the steward and treats
him in a way reserved for the figure of vice in the old morality plays. Each
of the above four notes is included by Furness, but they are combined with
others' notes and comments in such a way as to modify the tone and change
the focus. For instance, Malvolio's claim that they "have propertied me" is
paraphrased by Johnson as "they have taken possession of me," but Furness
comments on the reference to stage props. Johnson here stresses the moral
significance of the gulling, his belief that Malvolio is ridiculed for his vice; the
nineteenth-century critics break the illusion in order to lighten the burden
of pain and evil.

Even when the devil is referred to, the Victorians see no allusion to evil, a
fact borne out by the new variorum's note on the final line of the scene, Feste's
"Adieu good man diuell," where the history of editorial egos is manifest.

> Johnson: This line has neither rhyme nor meaning. I cannot but suspect that
> the fool translates Malvolio's name, and says, "Adieu, good man *mean-evil*"—
> M. Mason (p. 120): I believe, with Johnson, that this is an allusion to Malvolio's
> name, but not in his reading, which destroys the metre. Read—"Adieu, good
> *mean-evil*," that is, *good Malvolio*, literally translated.—Malone: The last two
> lines of this song have, I think, been misunderstood. They are not addressed in
> the first instance to Malvolio, but are quoted by the Clown, as the words "ah
> ha!" are, as the usual address in the old Moralities to the Devil. We have in *The
> Merry Wives*, "No *man* means evil but the *devil*," [V, ii, 15]; and in *Much Ado*,
> "God's a good man," [III, v, 37]. A recurrence of the same word, instead of a
> rhyme, is hardly a sufficient reason for a change, especially in a song like this,
> which is sung by Feste in the mere exuberance of his high spirits. If the words
> apply to Malvolio, however vaguely, well and good; too close an application was
> hardly to be desired. To imply that Malvolio is the Devil in a play, is to imply
> that Feste himself is the Vice,—hardly a more creditable character. For Feste's
> purpose, it is sufficient that the Song, taking up Malvolio's last words, ends with
> bidding him adieu—ED.]. (*NV*, p. 273)

Aside from Furness's specious argument—if Malvolio is the devil, then Feste
is the vice, which leaves out of account the fact that the clown, unlike the
steward, consciously disguises himself—it is clear that what Johnson sees as
a moral issue in a play about disguise and affectation the others view as a jest
in a love drama. For Johnson, Malvolio's unwillingness to accept role-playing
is a serious shortcoming.

JOHNSON'S DOUBLE PERSPECTIVE

At the conclusion of the play, the results of the differences between our editors can be seen by comparing their notes on the famous phrase "a natural perspective," which the duke utters upon seeing together for the first time Viola and Sebastian: "One Face, one voice, one habit, and two persons, / A natural Perspective, that is, and is not." Furness cites three commentators before Johnson—Warburton, Tollet, and Capel—who believe that the phrase refers to "an appearance of nature's forming that seems a body and is none." Johnson's version is found in the middle of two pages of small print—"A 'perspective' seems to be taken for shows exhibited through a glass with such lights as make the pictures really protuberant. The Duke therefore says, that nature has here exhibited such a show, where shadows seem realities; where that which *is not* appears like that which *is*." This note is followed by two nineteenth-century ones, suggesting that the allusion is to a mirror or "optical glasses" that produce strange, distorted, and unexpected images. Finally, Furness offers his own version: "By '*natural* perspective' Orsino means that an effect has been produced by nature which is usually produced by art" (*NV*, pp. 299–300). The progress of this note is a microcosm of the history of commentary on *Twelfth Night*. Before Johnson, literal or realist readings predominate: the duke is confused but will soon see clearly and understand that Viola has a twin brother. After Johnson, figurative readings come to the fore: the replica of Viola, which seems natural and alive, is associated with productions of art. Johnson maintains elements of both but agrees with neither: "Nature has here exhibited such a show where shadows seem realities; where that which *is not* appears like that which *is*." This sentence deliberately seeks a middle ground between reality and art, between what is and what is not. Characteristically, Johnson becomes a point of transition in the movement toward the realm of "art," which for Furness is the final goal of *Twelfth Night*. But the new variorum does not eliminate Johnson's interpretation: the reader finds Johnson's stricture in an appendix entitled "Criticisms." Here, separated from the text of the drama, major critical differences are recorded, graphically illustrating how in the new variorum interpretation is divorced from editorial decisions.

JOHNSON AND THE TRADITION

The "Criticisms" section of the new variorum appendix is divided into two parts, one devoted to general remarks and the other to assessments of the main characters. Johnson's voice is again muffled by a consensus of others. After Pepys's and Dounes's brief diary accounts of Restoration performances, Johnson's remarks, the only ones from the eighteenth century, appear: "This play is in the graver part elegant and easy, and in some of the lighter scenes exquisitely humorous. *Aque-cheek* is drawn with great propriety, but his character is, in great measure, that of natural fatuity, and is therefore not the proper prey of a satirist. The soliloquy of *Malvolio* is truly comick; he is betrayed to ridicule merely by his pride. The marriage of *Olivia,* and the succeeding perplexity, though well contrived to divert on the stage, wants credibility, and fails to produce the proper instruction required in the drama, as it exhibits no just picture of life" (*NV,* p. 378).

This paragraph is followed by selections from fifteen critics, writing from 1811 to 1887, who, with the exception of Hallam, share the belief that the mood of *Twelfth Night* is romantic or pastoral because it is most essentially about love. Again, Johnson's comment stands out from the others. Indeed, the lone dissenting voice, Hallam believes *Twelfth Night* falls well below the achievement of *Much Ado:* "Viola would be more interesting, if she had not indelicately, as well as unfairly towards Olivia, determined to win the Duke's heart before she had seen him. The part of Sebastian has all that improbability which belongs to mistaken identity, without the comic effect for the sake of which that is forgiven in Plautus and in *The Comedy of Errors*" (*NV,* p. 379). Johnson faces both of these issues. Viola's artful scheming is not indelicate, and Sebastian's improbability does not render the drama a failure. Aside from a few unsuccessful scenes, *Twelfth Night* is, for Johnson, full of episodes that are "elegant and easy" and "exquisitely humorous," terms of high praise. Not sharing with the Victorians the assumption that love is the subject, Johnson avoids Hallam's problem by seeing the drama as concerned with a different topic, one particularly pertinent to Malvolio.

MALVOLIO'S PRIDE

Analyzing how Johnson's view of Malvolio relates to the section of Furness's critical appendix devoted to the steward, we shall see why his important insight is neglected. Johnson's position—that Malvolio's soliloquy is "truly comick; he is betrayed to ridicule merely by his pride"—is omitted from the new variorum, which begins with Lamb's remarks. The eight entries in this part of the appendix cover the period from 1823 to 1896. Lamb initiates the tradition that Malvolio is "a sort of Puritan," a position shared by all nineteenth-century commentators except one, who insists that he is a philistine. But whatever the term, all agree that Malvolio's problem stems from a lack of a sense of humor. "Neither buffoon nor contemptible," he is not "moved to any cheerfulness by any innocent jest" (*NV,* pp. 396, 397). Our attitude toward Malvolio should accordingly be a mixture of pity and scorn: "We may pity him,—in some measure respect him,—but we *must* laugh at him" (*NV,* p. 399).

Predictably, most of these nineteenth-century commentators feel uneasy with the final treatment of Malvolio. Russell (1884) asserts that the "cruel joke" is "for the Nineteenth-century carried too far to be entirely funny" (*NV,* pp. 400–401). And this judgment is borne out by Lamb, who confesses that it has "a kind of tragic interest," and by Archer, who characterizes Malvolio's "punishment" as "excessive, to the point of barbarity" (*NV,* p. 400). Although Johnson is satisfied at Malvolio's being ridiculed for his "pride," most commentators in the following century see him as a figure of folly, not vice, who is teased for humorlessness, not pride.

To understand Johnson's position we need to consider how his attitude toward Malvolio relates to his general view of *Twelfth Night.* Refusing to participate in the conventional games, rejecting any suggestion that he, like the others, adopts the disguises and ruses of courtship with the same contempt that he has for the carousing of Toby and his companions, Malvolio is finally shown to have been, like the other main characters, playing a role. Hissing at the end, "I'll be revenged on the whole pack of you," he ceases to play the part of the steward, of one who is "ever controlled, with an austere regard." His pride, Johnson suggests, consists in the belief that he alone does not "prepare a face to meet the faces." Insisting that he is what he appears to be, scorning affectation and disguise, Malvolio evades the game element of the ritual of courtship. Not merely a humorless philistine or a grave puritan, the steward, in his self-love, approaches vice, for he feels superior in one respect to all, even Olivia. Malvolio's final exit is to Johnson comic, not tragic, because it constitutes a change in posture, the unmasking of the one person in the play who believes he never dons a mask. The other characters let him go off in a huff because he considers himself above the need to wear a mask that the others adopt to protect their vulnerable inner beings. Such a view of Malvolio, however, only furthers the difficulties presented by this character for those who see *Twelfth Night* as a play about love. For, in the end, the lovers seem to care less about Malvolio than he does about them.

TELEOLOGY IN THE HISTORY OF CRITICISM

Pursuing the interpretive goal of critics, comparing Johnson's overall view with that of Furness leads to modern criticism of *Twelfth Night*. How do our contemporaries confront the problem of the final treatment of Malvolio? To answer this question we need to return for a moment to a textual crux in act 5. In explaining the phrase "natural perspective," Johnson differs from both the eighteenth- and nineteenth-century commentators by combining the literal and figurative readings. In 1975, the editors of the Arden text explained the same phrase as follows: "The Duke refers to an artificial 'perspective' . . . or distorting glass, which, by optical illusions, can make one picture or object appear like two or more; the same effect, he says here, is now produced by nature, without the operation of art."[2] This position is reminiscent of that of Furness; indeed, it could be demonstrated, but it would take us too far afield, that the modern position derives from the new variorum.

Nevertheless, the present-day position develops beyond the Victorian one. While for Johnson the duke means that "nature presents the unreal as if it were real," the modern editor believes that Orsino is pointing out that an artistic device is usually responsible for the sort of display that is here produced by nature. The difference is one of emphasis: Johnson stresses the end, the picture itself, and the modern editor points to the means by which the picture is created. Shifting the focus from end to means is how modern critics attempt to reconcile us to the conclusion of *Twelfth Night*. In reply to "Johnson's objection to Olivia's marriage, and some modern critics' dissatisfaction with Viola's," the modern editors cite the following resolution: "The ending takes little account of the reason for particular attachments; it is, on the contrary, a generalized image of love. . . . The union of lovers in *Twelfth Night* is more a freezing of the moment of romantic contemplation, before the practical business of marriage."[3]

We are asked to see the end of *Twelfth Night* from the viewpoint of Shakespeare, not from that of the participants. Marriage is a conventional way of distancing the audience from the "particular attachments," the ends, in order to emphasize the means, the moment of "romantic contemplation." Johnson calls our attention, however, not to the act of freezing but to the frozen moment. "Romantic contemplation" might apply to Viola but not to Sebastian and Olivia. When juxtaposed with the position of Johnson, these modern editors' views raise a new problem. Even if the final marriages are merely a device of closure, a means of producing a verbal icon, the problem is in characterizing that final image. A perspective on the history of criticism, however, suggests a way of combining elements of Johnson and the critical tradition of the nineteenth and twentieth centuries.

Since Johnson stands alone in the new variorum in complaining of the treatment of Sir Andrew Aguecheek, this issue may enable us to see his uses and limitations from a modern point of view. Johnson disapproves of this element of the comedy because Sir Andrew is marked by "natural fatuity" and is therefore "not the proper prey of a satirist." The singularity of this assessment is underlined by the fact that Lamb, whom we would expect to be as sensitive as anyone to the victimization of innocence, finds sheer delight in the episode.

> Few now remember Dodd. What an Aguecheek the stage lost in him. . . . In expressing slowness of apprehension, this actor surpassed all others. You could see the first dawn of an idea stealing slowly over his countenance, climbing up by little and little, with a painful process, till its cleared up at last to the fulness of a twilight conception,—its highest meridian. He seemed to keep back his intellect, as some have had the power to retard their pulsation. The balloon takes less time in filling than it took to cover the expansion of his broad moony face over all its quarter with expression. A glimmer of understanding would appear in a corner of his eye, and for lack of fuel go out again. A part of his forehead would catch a little intelligence, and be a long time in communicating it to the remainder. (*NV*, pp. 406–7)

Lamb presents us with a marvelous verbal description of what Johnson calls "natural fatuity." But he delights in it, and Johnson disapproves. It seems to me that here Johnson is impeded by his didacticism, which equates Malvolio and Aguecheek. In performance and on the written page, Aguecheek is not a hapless victim but a hilarious fool. If we view these two characters in terms other than those of vice or evil, one problem is obviated. Malvolio refuses to accept what Sir Andrew is incapable of grasping. The former's willfulness is more serious because it involves belief in his inherent superiority; the latter suffers from ignorance and stupidity. But Shakespeare excludes both from marriage because the process of courtship—disguise and role-playing—functions properly only if one is able to accept that wooer and wooed, oneself and others, wear masks.

The duke, Olivia, Viola, Sebastian, are all unmasked at the end; they and their mates must accept that each is not what they seemed to be. Andrew and Malvolio are, respectively, incapable of and unwilling to accept their own unmasking. Shakespeare's satire against them is neither moral nor romantic. The point is not that they are evil or incapable of love, but that they are

unable or unwilling to manipulate courtship conventions, the process of falling in love. *Twelfth Night,* in my view, ends with the marriage ritual to show
that love in marriage cannot be achieved without unmasking the wooers. The
illusions and disguises of this game can serve their ultimate purpose only if
they are at last seen for what they are, courtship rites. The abrupt and improbable quality of the conclusion of *Twelfth Night* serves to emphasize that
the comedy finally isolates, neither love nor evil, but the ability to manipulate
the courtship conventions. Johnson's objection to the marriage at the end
represents a mimetic blindness to a formal device; he is unable to see that the
contrived closure forwards his own idea that the play is about the process of
falling in love, not love.[4] Here we see a negative example of Johnson's editorial principle. Because his position on these characters is made explicit and
related in the stricture to his interpretation of the play, we are able to assess
and discriminate among the elements of his position.

On the other hand, the concept of critical consensus based on interpretation that remains implicit leads to marginalization of Johnson's insight that
is important for nineteenth- and twentieth-century critics. We must abandon the belief in a critical consensus, of *the* tradition. The history of literary
criticism, an important element of the art of the variorum editor, is limited by
the historian's view of the literary work. Like criticism, the history of criticism is a teleological endeavor; we will better advance our understanding of
it by following Johnson's example in the stricture, by admitting to our own
and attending to others' interpretive goals.[5] Johnson's characteristic polemicism, the judgmental aspect of the stricture, functions not only for criticism
but also for the history of criticism. As we shall see, an editor's interpretation
can point to issues beyond the realm of the literary.

CHAPTER FOUR

Feminist Satire
and Bibliographic Ideology
in *The Taming of the Shrew*

The predominant view of Johnson as the moralist of his age has led to his being separated from the great satirists of the era, particularly Pope. The derision and ridicule of Pope's irony are thought to be alien to the sober moralist who has been called by one critic the "satirist manqué."[1] Elsewhere I have suggested that in *The Vanity of Human Wishes* and in the *Life of Pope* Johnson is capable of creating his own penetrating satire and of understanding that of Pope. Here my point is to demonstrate that Johnson makes explicit, in his notes to *The Taming of the Shrew*, the goal of the satire implicit in Pope's edition of the comedy. Johnson's sense of humor becomes a focal point in this chapter. The mirror that Johnson tells us Shakespeare held up to nature could, under certain circumstances, be what Swift called a "glass" of satire.[2] And satire, while seen by most eighteenth-century writers to bolster an orthodox position, can from a modern perspective point to subversion. Recently, Robert Weimann remarked that "the role of mimesis in the ideological function of the Shakespearean text has hardly been considered."[3] This chapter will demonstrate how an eighteenth-century mimetic concept of satire bears upon modern feminist concerns with ideology. Dramatic irony is the means by which theory and practice, ideology and bibliography, are linked: Johnson's sense of comedy enables him to relate literature to the human condition. My conclusion is that theoretical and ideological issues cannot be divorced from practical and textual concerns.

During the middle of the eighteenth century, the printed text of *The Taming of the Shrew* differed markedly from the one with which we are familiar today: Pope first found some interludes and an epilogue involving Christopher Sly, which Johnson retained and, by way of his interpretation of the play, explained. In 1773, George Steevens marginalized this material derived from a "bad" quarto; subsequent editors have either cut or placed these scenes in appendixes. The bibliographical issue is relatively straightforward: almost all editors agree that the original had some equivalent of these scenes since the interludes are easily accommodated in the "good" or folio text and the epilogue helps resolve a technical problem.[4] Nevertheless, the material that Pope and Johnson provided is no longer to be found in modern texts, because most editors now believe that these scenes from the "bad" quarto are probably not by Shakespeare.[5] However, modern editors give no indication *in the text* that the original version may well have contained some interludes and an epilogue.

Indeed, few spectators and critics know that most editors agree that the play was probably originally structured as a play-within-a-play, with Christopher Sly commenting at regular intervals and at the end. Stage productions, so far as I can ascertain, never presented a version of these scenes, because during the time when Pope and Johnson printed their texts, the Christopher Sly material was cut.[6] This bibliographical blindness, the general lack of awareness that the original *Shrew* was quite possibly a play-within-a-play with a vocal spectator on stage, resulted, in my view, from an implicit ideological commitment inherent in the orthodox antifeminist reading of *The Taming of the Shrew*. My conclusion is that editors must face the ideological issues at the heart of bibliographical decisions. Pope and Johnson, obviously not feminists, come to their views by way of an eighteenth-century conception of satire. But to understand this matter, we need to turn to the textual and staging history of *The Taming of the Shrew*.

SLY ON STAGE

Although *The Taming of the Shrew* was a popular play during the eighteenth century, what Johnson and his contemporaries saw was only part of what we witness on the stage today. In fact, Shakespeare's drama was not restored until 1844. In 1754, Garrick presented *Catherine and Petruchio*, which dominated the stage for the remainder of the century. Garrick continued the tradition begun by John Lacey who, in *Sauny the Scott; or, The Taming of the Shrew* (published in 1735 but apparently performed since the beginning of the eighteenth century), eliminated both the Christopher Sly material and the subplot concerned with the wooing of Bianca. By 1716, the story of Christopher Sly cut by Lacey formed the basis of two plays at the rival theaters, Drury Lane and Lincoln's Inn Fields, each of which omitted the story of the courtship of the two sisters. These plays, both entitled *The Cobbler of Preston*, employed the scenes with Sly, particularly the induction, to present political satire related to the Rebellion of 1715: Sly, a cobbler, falls into a drunken stupor, is dressed up as a Spanish lord, and awakens believing that he is "but a Pretender" (p. 93).

By the middle of the eighteenth century, the Sly *Shrew* plays were separated from those containing Catherine and Petruchio.[7] Garrick's play does maintain the rudiments of Shakespeare's main plot, but with one significant change. Once it is clear that her father is determined to marry her to Petruchio, Catharine asserts, "I'll marry my revenge, but I will tame him" (p. 199), a point she reiterates later on in the same scene, vowing to "tame this haggard" (p. 200). This theme of double shrew taming is commented upon by the servants, who remark that "he is more shrew than she" and that "he kills her in her own humor" (pp. 209, 212). At the conclusion, the main characters are so completely aware that each is imitating the behavior of the other that Petruchio presents the final speech (spoken by Shakespeare's Katherina) while holding her hand.

SLY AS SATIRICAL MIRROR

The stage tradition, as we have mentioned, must be distinguished from that of the printed text, particularly during the eighteenth century. In 1773, the interludes and epilogue that Pope originally printed and Johnson kept were removed by George Steevens, who had been unable to find the source for Pope's additions. Although this source has since been located, modern readers will find these scenes only in the appendixes of learned editions. It is perhaps misleading to refer to this material as discrete scenes since in all it amounts to less than twenty lines. But its structural significance is not negligible. Instead of the Christopher Sly who comes on for the induction and then is removed or remains silent, we have a small audience on the stage interrupting the action and commenting upon it during and after the performance.

This modification in the form of the drama had a different meaning in the eighteenth century than it may have for us. The most important remarks in Johnson's day are those of Richard Hurd, who, in 1751, pointed out that Christopher Sly represents Shakespeare's class satire: "He would expose, under the cover of this mimic fiction, the truly ridiculous figure of men of rank and quality, when they employ their great advantages of *place and fortune*, to no better purposes, than the soft and selfish gratification of their own intemperate passions: Of *those*, who take the mighty privilege of *descent* and *wealth* to lie in the freer indulgence of those pleasures, which the beggar as fully enjoys, and with infinitely more propriety and consistency of character than their *Lordships*" (*SCH* 3:420–21).[8] Hurd characterizes the "privilege of descent and wealth" by using "epicurean," not in a strict philosophical sense, but as a pejorative term for aristocratic sensual indulgence. It is "my Lord," we are reminded by Hurd, who decides to divert himself by deceiving Sly into believing that he is an aristocrat. But Shakespeare, according to Hurd, arranges the satire so as to reflect upon the lord: "For the whole was written with the best design of exposing that monstrous Epicurean position, 'that the true enjoyment of life consists in a delirium of sensual pleasure.' And this, in a way the most likely to work upon the great, by shewing their pride that it was fit only to constitute the summum bonum of one 'No better than a poor and loathsome Beggar'" (*SCE* 3:423–24).[9] Hurd believes that the comedy results from Sly's mimicry of the ways of the lord; the self-indulgent aristocrat is thus presented with an embarrassing caricature of himself, a beggar enjoying lordly epicurean pleasures. Indeed, Hurd emphasizes the pictorial element of the satire by comparing it to the art of painting. Painters are said to have damaged their craft by presenting "the rich or noble Connoisseur" with what he "demands"; Shakespeare, on the other hand, has painted the picture of an aristocrat who is satirized by being shown to have commissioned what is, in fact, a parody of the aristocrat's self-indulgence. Predictably, the dramas of the day which presented Christopher Sly made use of this device for purposes of social and political satire.

TWO SHREW TRADITIONS

When Johnson came to edit *The Taming of the Shrew*, there were two "shrew" traditions, one concerning the Christopher Sly material, which was employed as a kind of sociopolitical satirical mirror, and the other centering on the Katherina and Petruchio story, which concludes with a marriage truce. Hurd's idea of the mirror brings to mind one of the most famous passages of the *Preface:* "This therefore is the praise of Shakespeare, that his drama is the mirrour of life; that he who has mazed his imagination, in following the phantoms which other writers raise up before him, may here be cured of his delirious extasies, by reading human sentiments in human language; by scenes from which a hermit may estimate the transactions of the world, and a confessor predict the progress of the passions" (7:65). Of course, Johnson here uses the image of the mirror in a more general sense than does Hurd, but Johnson makes specific application of this notion to *The Taming of the Shrew.* In fact, Johnson regards both of the traditions, Sly's mirror and the taming of Katherina, as pertinent to Shakespeare's play. The concluding comment on the *Shrew* is unusual in that it begins by reprinting an essay from the *Tatler,* followed by a comment: "It cannot but seem strange that *Shakespeare* should be so little known to the authour of the Tatler, that he should suffer this Story to be obtruded upon him, or so little known to the Publick, that he could hope to make it pass upon his readers as a novel narrative of a transaction in *Lincolnshire;* yet it is apparent, that he was deceived, or intended to deceive, that he knew not himself whence the story was taken, or hoped that he might rob so obscure a writer without detection" (3:99; 7:351).

Since Johnson believes that Shakespeare's *Taming of the Shrew* is the source of this story in the *Tatler,* a summary of it may help us understand what he considers essential in the original version. Mr. Tatler's story contains the elements familiar to us: a young woman of "imperious temper" marries a man who takes her home, not in a coach and six, but on a "Skeleton of a Horse." At home, they are greeted by the dog, which, when commanded to open the gate, looks up and wags its tail. "The Master, to shew the Impatience of his Temper, drew a Pistol and shot him dead." After the couple have settled into their home, the husband proposes at a party that the men shall send for their wives, who are in a room above playing cards. The guests' wives reply that they will "come by and by." But the host's wife "no sooner heard her Husband's Desire whispered" than "the Cards were clapp'd on the Table, and down she comes with, My Dear, would you speak with me" (3:97–99).

But the essay also refers to an eighteenth-century aspect of the shrew tradition: the mirror technique used in the Sly material. Appropriately, these references frame the tale: prior to the courtship, we are told that the bridegroom, "though a Man of the most equal Temper, . . . had artificially lamented to her that he was the most passionate Creature breathing. By this one Intimation, he at once made her understand Warmth of Temper to be what he ought to pardon in her, as well that he alarmed her against that Constitution in himself" (3:97–98). Similarly, the tale concludes with a reminder that the bridegroom had artificially assumed a shrew role to mirror the bride's behavior: "He receives her in his Arms, and after repeated Caresses tells her the Experiment, confesses his Good Nature, and assures her, that since she could now command her Temper, he would no longer disguise his own" (3:99). We may surmise that for Johnson the mirror technique of the Sly material is as familiar an element of the shrew story as is the subduing of the shrew. Here we can see Johnson combining the stage history with the written tradition, one of many instances that could be cited to demonstrate that Johnson's insensitivity to dramatic performance has been exaggerated.

Johnson's final comment, however, relates the Sly material and the main plot to the subplot, the courtship of Bianca: "Of this play the two plots are so well united, that they can hardly be called two without injury to the art with which they are interwoven. The attention is entertained with all the variety of a double plot, yet is not distracted by unconnected incidents" (3:99; 7:351). Here Johnson parts company with Garrick and with the acting tradition of the play that dominated the London stage throughout the eighteenth century. Indeed, Brian Morris, the Arden editor of *The Taming of the Shrew*, has gone so far as to suggest that in his appreciation of the "double plot" Johnson began the modern tradition of commentary on Shakespeare's drama: "Of all the post-Shakespearian adaptations of *The Shrew* only Lacey's *Sauny the Scott* has any use for the subplot, with its disguises and intrigues. The verdict of the theatre seems to have been that it is inferior, detachable and dispensable. . . . Not until the Victorian period . . . was it restored to performance. Yet, almost alone among the early critics, Dr. Johnson recognized that it is essential to Shakespeare's purposes" (p. 109). In fact, this 1981 Arden edition cites Johnson's view of the two love plots and concludes that "modern critics concur, virtually with one voice" (p. 110). Yet Morris and Johnson make opposite decisions concerning the Christopher Sly material. While Johnson prints the interludes and the epilogue from the "bad" quarto, Morris, like other moderns, follows the folio and relegates the other scenes to an appendix.[10]

MIRRORING AND MANNING THE HAGGARD

I shall compare Johnson's edition to Morris's edition, because the Arden editor presents without qualification the position for male supremacy that is generally accepted—although with some hesitation—by modern scholarly editors. For instance, the Oxford editor believes that *The Shrew*, essentially a farce based on the orthodox position, is least successful at the end when it presents the orthodox doctrine in a straightforward manner. Similarly, the Cambridge editor accepts the traditional view but feels obliged to add that the difficulty we have with this position is the fault not of Shakespeare but of his age.[11] Although critics have contested the orthodox position, as we shall see shortly, most scholarly editors accept it. Modern editors have thus prevented reconsideration of the Pope-Johnson text. Understanding the nature of the critical difference between these two eighteenth-century editors and modern ones reveals the problems that result from separating editorial-textual matters from critical-interpretive ones.

Morris begins by relating the two plots with Christopher Sly's scene. "The most obvious link is between Sly's assumption of a new personality and Katherina's translation into a loving wife" (p. 115). The "three-fold structure of induction, plot, and subplot" is seen by Morris to involve the main issue of *The Shrew*, the "process of change, metamorphosis, and transformation." We are advised to keep in mind that "Elizabethan educationists were less concerned with liberating the pupil's consciousness by encouragement to free-ranging enquiry than with inculcating an approved body of knowledge in the context of a serenely accepted social order" (p. 129). But education in *The Shrew*, we are informed, is not of the formal kind; Petruchio "is the teacher, Katherina is his pupil. His task is to inculcate such knowledge and instil such behaviour as will fit her to take a useful place in the existing society" (p. 131). At the beginning of act 2, Katherina presents herself as a typical shrew, but Petruchio eventually forces her to change permanently. Her sister, Bianca, is Katherina's foil. Both are surrounded by disguise and deception, but Bianca remains unchanged while Kate becomes a different person.

Still, we must remember, according to Morris, that love in marriage, not change, is the ultimate message of *The Shrew*. "Romantic love" relates "the passion of Lucentio for Bianca with the Katherina-Petruchio plot" (p. 142). Moreover, the induction "offers an extensive and subtle parody of all the play's attitudes to love. . . . It looks like a version of the traditional quarreling between Noah and his wife in the Moralities," thus satirizing Katherina before her transformation. This theme of love in marriage reaches a "climax" in the final scene of the play. Katherina's obedience speech, Morris assures us, is "meant to be a final statement on the subject of love and marriage": what she says is that "the wife is vassal to the husband, the husband is vassal to the prince, the prince is vassal to God, the only Lord of Creation." This view is described as "completely in accord with normal Elizabethan opinion on the rights and status of wives" (pp. 145–46).

Although this final speech is an affirmation of a commonplace, the final wager represents something more than obedience. Petruchio, in testing his wife, Morris explains, "is taking a risk . . . giving his wife the freedom to humiliate him." Grateful for the delicate way in which Petruchio has handled the situation, Katherina gives more than he asked; she "gives not only the duty of the Widow to Hortensio, but the duty of all wives to their husbands." This act of wifely love evokes an appropriate response from her husband: "Petruchio responds to this unsolicited act of love and generosity with one of the most moving and perfect lines in the play, almost as if he is lost for words, taking refuge in action: 'Why, there's a wench! Come on, and kiss me, Kate.' I believe that any actor striving to represent Petruchio's feelings at this moment in the play should show him as perilously close to tears, tears of pride, and gratitude, and love" (p. 149). Morris sees a resolution of the three structural units of the play—the induction, the main plot, and the sub-plot—in the notion of marital love, which is present from early on in the Bianca plot, parodied in the Sly material, and gradually realized in the main plot by way of Petruchio's education of Katherina. Yet Morris's final image— Kate, in an "unsolicited act of love and generosity," approaching Petruchio, who is near "tears of pride, and gratitude, and love"—is reminiscent of Gar-rick's conclusion to *Catharine and Petruchio,* where the husband, holding his wife's hand, utters her words, in a literal and figurative sense, of wifely sub-mission. The difference between the eighteenth- and the twentieth-century views concerns the means toward the same end. For Johnson and Garrick, Kate eventually recognizes herself in the mirror of satire; Morris believes that Petruchio, in his capacity as tamer, subdues the shrew and makes her as-sume the position of the Elizabethan wife. The question is, does Kate change because of her sense of humor, her ability to laugh at herself, or because of education by means of "the strap"? Both the Oxford and the Cambridge editors side with Morris in this respect.[12]

JOHNSON'S SATIRICAL MIRROR

Although Johnson does not mention the induction in his concluding remarks, his notes on specific expressions in this opening scene point to Sly's inability to see the irony directed against himself. Unlike his predecessors, Johnson explains Sly's first words, "I'll pheaze you, in faith." According to Johnson, the term "pheaze" means "to harrass, to plague"; he then goes on to remark that such phrases are "vulgarly used by persons of Sly's character on like occasions" (3:3; 7:342). While the modern editor attributes Sly's use of such phrases to his "drunken tongue" (p. 153), Johnson's point becomes clearer in another comment on this opening scene that has no equivalent in either the modern or previous eighteenth-century editions. When Sly asserts that his family members are "no rogues," Johnson remarks, "That is, no *vagrants*, no mean fellows, but Gentlemen" (3:3; 7:342). The reader begins to see that Sly is not merely a figure of low comic relief; his ignorance is functional, indicative of his pretensions above his station.

To reinforce this point, Johnson employs one of his variorum techniques: the inclusion of a predecessor's note which, in the context of Johnson's edition, takes on a new and extended meaning. For example, Sly's expletive "paucas pallabris" is glossed as follows: "*Sly*, as an ignorant Fellow, is purposely made to aim at Languages out of his Knowledge, and knock the words out of Joint. The *Spaniards* say, *pocas palabras*, i.e., few words: as they do likewise, *Cessa* i.e., be quiet. Theob." (3:3). In the context of his own edition, Theobald's note illustrated Sly's ignorance; surrounded by the comments of Johnson's edition, it points to Sly's social pretensions, especially when seen in conjunction with Johnson's use of Warburton for a similar purpose later on in the induction. Explaining what one of the aristocrats means when he says, in reference to Sly, that they will need "a little vinegar to make our devil roar," Warburton remarks that "to apply the gall and vinegar" to the devil is to make him "suffer some disgrace" (3:8). In the context of Johnson's text, this note about the farcical element of the morality play takes on a moral dimension. If Sly's assumption of upper-class manners mirrors the abuses of the aristocracy, his own pretentiousness represents how, to use Swift's terms, he sees everyone but himself in the glass of satire. As we progress through the notes, it will become clear that Johnson, unlike Morris, includes all of the Sly material and distinguishes himself from his contemporaries by explaining what Pope possibly took for granted: that the significance of this material relates to the notion of the glass of satire.

Johnson's most important comments in act 1 concern the character of Petruchio. The protagonist's explanation of what he wants in a wife appears strange to Warburton.

> PETRUCHIO. if you know
> One rich enough to be *Petruchio's* wife,
> (As wealth is burden of my wooing dance)
> Be she as foul as was *Florentius'* love,
> As old as *Sibyl*, and as curst and shrewd
> As *Socrates' Xanthippe*, or a worse,

> She moves me not; or not removes, at least,
> Affection's edge in me.
>
> (3:25)

"He tells you he wants money only," Warburton complains, "and, as to *affection*, he thinks so little of the matter, that give him but a rich mistress, and he will take her though incrusted all over with the worst bad qualities of age, ugliness and ill manners. Yet, after this, he talks of *Affection's edge* being so strong in him that nothing can abate it" (3:25–26). After reproducing Warburton's comment, Johnson explains that Petruchio tempers his monetary ambition with some irony: "Surely the sense of the present reading is too obvious to be missed or mistaken. *Petruchio* says, *that if a girl has money enough, no bad qualities of mind or body will* remove affection's edge; that is, hinder him from liking her" (3:26; 7:345). In contrast to Warburton, Johnson realizes that Petruchio is determined to engage both his pecuniary desires and his affection. Once he has decided that the girl is rich enough, he is determined to like her. Petruchio's claim to be solely interested in money is, as Morris points out, part of his assumed role. Johnson is the first editor to make clear that Petruchio is not eliminating affection as a criterion. It is not surprising that understanding the importance of the relationship between the two plots leads to the exposure of Petruchio's posturing, since the Bianca plot is almost entirely made up of games and stratagems involving role-playing.

In act 2, Johnson applies a similar kind of variorum technique to Katherina. Here the reader of the 1765 edition is confronted by Johnson's note juxtaposed with one by Warburton on the facing page, the left-hand note referring to a term applied to Kate and the right-hand one to Petruchio.

-hilding—] The word, *hilding*, or *hinderling*, is *a low wretch;* it is applied to *Catherine* for the coarseness of her behaviour

Beccare, *you are marvellous forward.*] We must read *Beccalare;* by which the *Italians* mean, thou arrogant, presumptuous man! the word is used scornfully, upon any one that would assume a port of grandeur. Warburton. (3:34–35)

Johnson again makes Warburton's scholarship serve his critical purpose. The coarse Katherina and the forward Petruchio complement one another. And since we know that the man's behavior is assumed, we may wonder what lies beneath the outward appearance of the shrew, a suspicion further reinforced by Johnson's comment on the first conversation between the two main characters.

PETRUCHIO. Alas, good *Kate*, I will not burden thee;
   For, knowing thee to be but young and light—
KATHERINA. Too light for such a swain as you to catch;
   And yet as heavy as my weight should be.
PETRUCHIO. Should *bee;*—should *buz.*—
KATHERINA. Well ta'en, and like a buzzard.
PETRUCHIO. Oh slow-wing'd turtle, shall a buzzard take thee?
KATHERINA. Ay, for a turtle, as he takes a buzzard.

(3:40)

Warburton has no comment on this passage, role-playing being again neglected in his edition. But Johnson and Morris, in the modern tradition,
attempt to explain this conversation: the crux is the last line, which Johnson
paraphrases as follows: "He may take me for a turtle, and he shall find me
a hawk" (3:40). Assuming that Katherina believes that Petruchio's label of
"turtle" refers to what lies beneath her mask, Johnson suggests that Kate is
saying that you may hope to find a turtledove beneath this hard exterior, but,
in fact, I am as hard within as without. Morris, on the other hand, reflects
on Kate's outward appearance and offers an alternate paraphrase: "The fool
will take me for a faithful wife, as the turtle-dove swallows the cockchafer"
(p. 207).

In this way, Morris eliminates any suggestion that the characters are aware
that the other is playing a role. In fact, as we shall see, Morris's conception
of the conclusion of the drama precludes the possibility that Katherina and
Petruchio suspect one another of role-playing, a characteristic they share
with Sly. But at the end of this act, Johnson prints an interlude that Morris
relegates to the appendix:

SLY. Sim, *when will the Fool come again?*
SIM. *Anon, my Lord.*
SLY. Give's *some more drink here—where's the tapster? here*, Sim, *eat some of these
   things.*
SIM. *So I do, my Lord.*
SLY. *Here*, Sim, *I drink to thee.*

(3:47)

However, Johnson's note on this scene suggests another view of the relationship between Sly and the characters he comments upon: "The fool, being
the favourite of the vulgar, or, as we now phrase it, of the upper gallery, was
naturally expected in every interlude" (3:47; 7:347). The conversation of
Kate and Petruchio has overtaxed Sly's limited mentality, and he requires

a "fool" for light relief. Sly provides, for Johnson, the vulgar response; his interlude warns the audience against his literalist response to the play.

In act 3, Johnson continues to guide his reader by showing how awareness of role-playing in others leads to admission of the same kind of behavior in oneself. First, Bianca is wooed by Lucentio, who uses "dog latin" to express his love and is told "presume not . . . despair not." Then, Hortensio presents a musical love letter that employs the figure of the gamut, eliciting the following response from Bianca: "Call you this Gamut? tut, I like it not; Old fashions please me best; I'm not so nice to change true rules for odd inventions." Johnson is followed by modern editors in accepting Theobald's emendation of "old inventions" to "odd inventions." What is odd and fantastical in Hortensio's behavior is his attempt to win a woman by conventional means alone, by way of outward fashion, for while Lucentio frankly admits to Bianca that he is disguised as Cambio, Hortensio does not reveal his true identity to Bianca. Hortensio assumes that Bianca will be won by his musical wit, a new fantastical fashion, and accordingly, loses her. Lucentio, by contrast, uses his new-fangled Latin to present himself. But Hortensio had already made a similar kind of mistake with Kate. When instructing her on the guitar, he attended to the "frets" upon the instrument instead of the fretful player and she "broke his head."

When, in this same scene, Petruchio appears in his eccentric garb for the wedding, his appearance represents a parody of Hortensio's separation of the outward fashion from the inner man. Kate had anticipated such behavior in her bridegroom, whom she called "mad-brain Rudesby, full of spleen." Johnson explains that "spleen" here means "*full of* humour, caprice, and inconstancy" (3:51; 7:348). To ensure that the reader does not miss the significance of Petruchio's whimsical manner of dress, Johnson reproduces Warburton's note on the servant's hat: "*An old hat, and* the humour of forty fancies *prickt up in't for a feather*] This was some ballad or drollery of that time, which the Poet here ridicules, by making *Petruchio* prick it up in his foot—boy's old hat for a feather" (3:53). In Johnson's *Dictionary* "prick" is "to dress oneself for show." Petruchio's and his servant's appearances represent a deliberate toying with ephemeral and capricious fashions, those odd ways that Hortensio failed to use successfully in his courtship of Bianca.

The difference between the two editors becomes clear at the taming school, where the modern editor attends to Petruchio's words, while Johnson invites us to compare the responses of Kate and Hortensio. Morris finds Petruchio's soliloquy "central to the play" because "in it he describes openly to the audience his plan to subdue Katherina precisely as a falconer tames a wild bird."

Moreover, the plots are here united because, according to Morris, Bianca also has need of the taming school.

At this point, Johnson prints one of the Sly interludes, appendicized by Morris, in which the tinker, discovered asleep, is taken off to be dressed in his own clothes for the conclusion of the drama. As the play approaches its conclusion, Sly, the vulgar observer, is replaced by the more sophisticated Hortensio, who will, until Sly returns at the end, supply the obvious or literal view for the audience. To emphasize this turning point, Johnson interrupts his reader to indicate that this interlude is probably where the "fifth act begins," that is, it represents a clear division between what has happened and what is to come.

For Johnson, Hortensio serves throughout the taming scene as a sort of parodic choral figure. At table the famished Kate refuses, at first, to thank Petruchio for the meat; then, upon seeing that he will send it away, she relents. But Petruchio urges Hortensio to eat the meat, and he replies, "Signior Petruchio, fy, you are to blame." Johnson uses a quotation to explain Petruchio's point of view: "All my labour has ended in nothing, or proved nothing. We tried an experiment, but it sorted not" (3:73). Hortensio is outraged because Kate did, after all, say thank you. He fails to understand that, for Petruchio, the point was to teach her to express her gratitude upon first receiving the food, not to prevent its removal. However, Hortensio is less dense than Sly. When the haberdasher arrives, Petruchio expresses his disapproval of the hat Kate has chosen.

> KATHERINA. I'll have no bigger, this doth fit the time:
>   And gentlewomen wear such caps as these.
> PETRUCHIO. When you are gentle, you shall have one too,
>   And not 'till then.
> HORTENSIO. That will not be in haste.
>
> (3:74)

Hortensio recognizes that the shrew still needs more taming, but Johnson employs Warburton's comment to suggest a more refined view of Petruchio's lesson: "*Shakespear* has here copied nature with great skill. *Petruchio*, by frightening, starving and overwatching his wife, had tamed her into gentleness and submission. And the audience expects to hear no more of the *Shrew:* When on her being crossed, in the article of fashion and finery, the most inveterate folly of the sex, she flies out again, though for the last time, into all the intemperate rage of her nature. Warburton" (3:74). This note, combined with two of Johnson's own remarks, makes clear that his point is not merely that Petruchio is taming Kate but that, in insisting upon minute details, he is mirroring her feminine concern about fashion and finery. Petruchio's use of the term "Censor" is explained by Johnson as a vessel formerly used in "barbershops," and, concerning Petruchio's reference to the tailor as "thou thimble," Johnson explains that "the taylor's trade having an appearance of effeminacy, has always been, among the rugged *English*, liable to sarcasms and contempt" (3:75). Johnson glosses the terms of "fashion and finery" to demonstrate that Petruchio is mirroring "the most inveterate folly" of Kate's sex.

The importance of the distinction between taming and mirroring becomes clear in the next scene where Petruchio insists that Kate concede that the sun is the moon. Hortensio is perplexed by this absurd request, but when Kate finally accedes to her husband's command, Hortensio announces, "Petruchio, go thy ways, the field is won." But Petruchio is not yet finished, and now Hortensio is utterly lost. In reply to Petruchio's insistence that Kate address Vincentio as a woman, Hortensio exclaims, "A will make the man mad, to make the woman of him." Yet here Kate, undaunted, begins to wax enthusiastic, referring to Bianca's father-in-law as this "young budding virgin." Johnson's note at this point is important; it derives, as he indicates, from Pope, and it has no equivalent in Warburton's or Morris's edition: "In the first sketch of this play, printed in 1607, we find two speeches in this place worthy preserving, and seeming to be of the hand of Shakespear, tho' the rest of that play is far inferior. Pope" (3:83).

Like Pope, Johnson reproduces these lines but relegates them to the margin because their textual source is suspect. Nevertheless, the reproduction of Pope's note indicates that Johnson also believes them worthy of preserving. Significantly, these speeches continue the mirroring technique.

> [PETRUCHIO.] Fair lovely maiden, young and affable,
>   More clear of hue, and far more beautiful
>   Than precious fardonyx, or purple rocks
>   Of amethysts, or glistering hyacinth
>   —Sweet Catharine, this lovely woman—
> KATHERINA. Fair lovely lady, bright and crystalline,
>   Beauteous and stately as the eye train'd bird;
>   As glorious as the morning wash'd with dew,
>   Within whose eyes she takes her dawning beams,
>   And golden summer sleeps upon thy cheeks.
>   Wrap up thy radiations in some cloud,
>   Lest that thy beauty make this stately town

Uninhabitable as the burning zone,
With sweet reflections of thy lovely face.

(3:83)

These lines further the view that Kate is not physically subdued but par-
ticipates willingly in Petruchio's mirroring, enthusiastically entering into the
spirit of it. To complement Petruchio's role reversal, his assumption of the
part of the whimsical, domineering wife, Kate plays the dominated husband
who humors his shrewish wife. Such a ploy is beyond the capacity of Hortensio, because it requires the participants' knowledge that each is assuming
the traditional role of the other. Far beyond the stage of tamer and tamed,
Kate and Petruchio can play this game only if they are conscious that each is
mirroring the other.[13]

TWO DIFFERENT ORTHODOX VIEWS OF THE CONCLUSION

The readers of the 1765 and 1981 editions of *The Shrew* have therefore been
guided by their editors to approach the last act with different attitudes. Johnson's reader sees that the characters are finally aware of one another's role-
playing in the main plot as well as the subplot. Morris's reader understands
that Kate has finally been subdued physically. These two conceptions of how
the shrew is tamed lead to different ways of staging the conclusion. Johnson
includes an epilogue with Sly, which Morris places in an appendix. In this
scene, the tinker awakes, believing that the play he has seen is a dream. When
his companion Sim suggests he quickly find his way home before his wife
curses him for sleeping away the night, Sly replies: "*Will she? I know how to
tame a* Shrew. . . . *I'll to my Wife, and tame her too, if she anger me*" (3:97). Sly's
assertion that the play is about a literal, physical taming of the shrew makes
the audience think twice before adopting such a view. The epilogue enables
Johnson to suggest that Kate has learned control by seeing her own behavior imitated by Petruchio. Marginalizing this epilogue, Morris furthers his
reading of the drama as a sophisticated version of Sly's position. Clearly, the
textual question concerning the Sly material cannot be separated from interpretive issues. Because Sly's response represents a parody of the "manned
haggard" position, many difficulties are obviated by cutting down his part
and appendicizing the interludes and, most important of all, the epilogue.
On the other hand, Sly's interludes and epilogue further Johnson's belief
that the shrew changes as a result of seeing what Sly cannot—her own image
in the mirror of satire.

But the Sly material adds a dimension to the drama not considered even by Johnson. Here, we need to consider the modern critical debate concerning *The Shrew*. The key elements of this controversy can be seen by briefly outlining Coppelia Kahn's response to Robert Heilman. In the introduction to his edition of *The Shrew* (1966), Heilman began by pointing out that for "three hundred years Shakespeare's *Taming of the Shrew* was generally accepted as being about the taming of a shrew," that is, a "manning the haggard." But moderns have objected to this position: "After three centuries of relative stability, then, Petruchio has developed rather quickly, first from an animal tamer to a gentleman-lover who simply brings out the best in Kate, and then at last to a laughable victim of the superior spouse who dupes him." But Heilman claimed that this recent development involved a movement "away from the text." We are urged to recognize that the courtship of the two central characters is "a process that is farcically conceived and that never wholly loses the markings of farce." Understood in these generic terms, the play, according to Heilman, provides no evidence to support the modern "Katolatry which . . . reveals the romantic tendency to create heroes and heroines by denying the existence of flaws in them by imputing all sorts of flaws to their families and other associates" (p. 160). The conclusion of *The Shrew* was taken in literal terms. "The play gives no evidence that from now on she will be twisting her husband around her finger. The evidence is rather that she will win peace and quiet and contentment by giving in to his wishes, and that her willingness will entirely eliminate unreasonable autocratic wishes in him. But after all, the unreasonable and the autocratic are his strategy, not his nature; he gives up an assumed vice, while Kate gives up a real one." Heilman concluded that Shakespeare's achievement resides in having realized some character development—Kate's transformation from shrew to dutiful wife—in a farce.[14]

In 1975, Coppelia Kahn responded to Heilman. Agreeing that the comedy is a farce, Kahn argued that its purpose is to exaggerate "ludicrously the reach and force of male dominance and thus pushes us to see this wish for dominance as a childish dream of omnipotence." Believing that the drama is a satire on Petruchio, Kahn began with Kate's father, who values money above his daughter's happiness in marriage. Turning then to Petruchio, Kahn asserted that he is the shrew of the play: "If Petruchio were female, he would be known as a shrew and shunned accordingly by men." His attempt at physically taming his wife was characterized as shocking. "Petruchio reduces Kate to an animal capable of learning only through deprivation of food and rest, devoid of all sensitivity save the physical. The animal metaphor shocks us and

I would suggest was meant to shock Shakespeare's audience, despite their respect for falconry as an art and their reverence for the great chain of being emphasized by E. M. W. Tillyard." When Kate finally succumbs and begins to humor her husband, we witness "her realization that the power struggle she had entered into on Petruchio's terms is absurd." For Kahn, Kate's final speech, although "perfectly orthodox," takes on irony in dramatic context: "It fairly shouts obedience, when a gentle murmur would suffice." Kahn therefore concluded that although Kate "seems to be the most vocal apologist for male dominance, she is indeed its ablest critic." [15]

In the past fifteen years, this critical controversy has remained unresolved. In fact, most recent commentary involves gathering new evidence for either side. Those favoring Heilman's position turn to Elizabethan literature on marriage to demonstrate that neither Baptista's nor Petruchio's attitude toward Kate is unusual or shocking. Those sympathetic to Kahn find motifs in the drama to further document their belief that male dominance as a concept is being satirized.[16]

The ideological element at the basis of this disagreement becomes clear in a recent essay by Joel Fineman. Analyzing the language of the play, Fineman argued that the war of words between Petruchio and Kate is analogous to the theoretical difference between Lacan and Derrida. The question for Fineman becomes "what kind of language is it . . . that woman speaks, and in what way does it differ, always and forever, from the language of man." The answer, we are informed, is the language of Petruchio who, "assimilating to himself the attributes of Kate, will hold his own lunatic self up as mirror of Kate's unnatural nature." In addition to isolating the mirror technique, Fineman also recognized that the irony of the drama turns on Sly. When Sly wishes that the play were over so that he can go home to bed with his wife, we are informed, "The joke here is surely on Sly, for the audience knows full well that the consummation Sly so devoutly desires will never be achieved." But Fineman concluded that Petruchio uses the language of women to silence Kate and that the subversive deconstructive theory of language is the necessary other, the female aspect, of the Lacanian male-oriented system. Like Kahn, Fineman expressed dissatisfaction with this final notion that the feminine is subsumed by the masculine: "There is no compelling reason . . . why readers or critics of master literary texts should in their theory or their practice act out what they read." [17] The final submission of Kate has been taken to the level of theory: the concept of subversion is itself tamed, for Derrida's subversive, feminine theory is subsumed by Lacan's masculine, psychological conception.

Here we see on a theoretical level the result of bibliographic blindness. All of the modern critics that I have consulted accept that the authoritative text is that which omits the Sly material after the induction; most seem unaware that there ever were in Shakespeare's version some interludes and an epilogue. Hence, the critical debate has been artificially confined—one might say tamed—in a constructed text that purports to be "natural," untouched. It would surely advance the feminist position to know that the taming plot was probably intended as a play within the play, a part of the joke on Sly. By way of his evaluative interpretation, Johnson is the first to articulate the subversive nature of the satirical mirror. For us, this notion can have far-reaching consequences. Is the entire concept of a hierarchy in marriage being satirized? Does the spectacle of the mirror technique on the stage suggest the means by which husband and wife can subvert the marital hierarchy?

This matter comes to the fore by means of the mirror of satire, because satire by its very nature calls for change, ranging from the reforms of the sinner to those required of the state. As a moralist Johnson focuses upon the former; feminism is more concerned with the latter. But the principle of irony can apply to ideology, because satire in its most radical form can constitute subversion. Dramatic irony has exposed the ideological bases of bibliographic decisions: here we see how the most literal element of the text bears upon the loftiest abstractions about the human condition. To accept the referential nature of literary interpretation is to confront the dilemma of the major ideological differences between critics, particularly those from separate historical periods. In analyzing this problem, we need to move to the level of literary theory. In the next chapter I will suggest how mimeticism, an outmoded theory based upon an outmoded ideology, can bear upon the concerns of modern critics and theoreticians.

CHAPTER FIVE

Mimetic Theory in *King Lear*

Samuel Johnson the literary critic is usually characterized as judicious, commonsensical, above all rational. But these terms do not seem appropriate to his comment on the death of Cordelia: "I was many years ago so shocked by *Cordelia's* death, that I know not whether I ever endured to read again the last scenes of the play till I undertook to revise them as an editor" (6:159; 8:704). In addition to being deeply personal, this response leads Johnson to formulate a new question about *King Lear.* How would the survival of Cordelia detract from the purpose of this tragedy? Modern critics do not even entertain such a question, because it is assumed that concern for the survival of the virtuous daughter was one of the factors motivating Nahum Tate's alteration of the end of the drama. My contention is that Johnson's question, only superficially related to Tate, comes in a literal and figurative sense from the heart of mimeticism and that modern formalist and postformalist positions do not constitute a satisfactory reply. Specifically, the concept of time—the time that elapses between Edmund's confession and Cordelia's death—cannot be accounted for by either theory. Formalism and postformalism flatten out time into a spatial component, removing the question. Mimeticism accepts time but cannot understand the function of this live toad in an imaginary garden. This question can be resolved only by combining elements of both the eighteenth and twentieth-century literary theories.

Juxtaposing these literary methodologies separated by two centuries, I shall illustrate how a dialogue can be instituted between modern theoreticians and an adherent of an outmoded literary theory. Contending that mimeticism permits the expression of critical anxiety about the death of Cordelia that is repressed by modern theory, I conclude that we must appropriate from mimeticism if we are to come to terms with the end of *King Lear*.

Like his remarks on the other plays, Johnson's comments on *Lear* have been treated in a miscellaneous manner, but in this instance the reason involves, in addition to the general neglect of Johnson's interpretation, the widely held belief that Johnson preferred Tate's *Lear* to Shakespeare's. A rudimentary examination of Tate's drama in relation to Johnson's notes to *Lear*, however, reveals that, far from disapproving of the Elizabethan version, Johnson influenced the gradual return to the eighteenth-century stage of Shakespeare's *King Lear*.

EIGHTEENTH-CENTURY VIEWS OF "KING LEAR"

In Johnson's day, Shakespeare's *Lear* was never presented on stage; Nahum Tate's version appeared in London from 1681 to 1838.[1] Although Tate's *Lear* dominated the British stage for a century and a half, few today have read the play. Most of us know about the radical change to the conclusion: the seventeenth-century poet laureate has the dubious distinction of ending with Lear giving Cordelia as a bride to Edgar. But the changes that Tate made were far more extensive; in fact, he transformed the original tragedy into a political drama about the family as a microcosm of the state. The general nature of his alterations should be kept in mind if we are to understand the view of *King Lear* current when Johnson began to edit the play.

Apart from the modification to the language that can only be fully appreciated by reading the play, the following changes in the action should be kept in mind: (1) Cordelia is indifferent to Lear at the outset because she is in love with Edgar; (2) when rejected by Burgundy, Cordelia remains without a husband; (3) the part of the fool has been eliminated; (4) Gloucester and Cordelia plot to restore Lear to the throne, are imprisoned by Edmund and rescued by Edgar; (5) a love scene between Edmund and Regan is interrupted by the peasants, who, enraged by the blinding of Gloucester, have begun an uprising; (6) instead of attempting suicide, Gloucester despairs, but is encouraged by Edgar; (7) when Edmund's hired assassins come to murder Lear, Edgar, Albany, and Lear kill them. (8) Albany returns the crown to Lear, who awards Queen Cordelia to Edgar in the presence of Kent and Gloucester.[2]

Tate begins, not with the division of the kingdom, but with Edmund's soliloquy, which provides us with a convenient passage to present as a sample of Tate's diction.

BASTARD. Thou, Nature, are my goddess; to thy law
My services are bound. Why am I then
Deprived of a son's right because I came not
In the dull road that custom has prescribed?[3]

This brief summary makes clear that Tate altered the beginning and middle as well as the end of the play. Twenty-one years after the Restoration, Shakespeare's tragedy was converted into a story of how order is restored and tragedy avoided when the monarch returns to his throne: the successful love relationship of Cordelia and Edgar makes clear that political stability promotes and is reinforced by domestic harmony. The villains of the play, Goneril, Regan, Cornwall, and Edmund, place their individual ambition above the good of the family and the commonwealth; Tate suggests that in comparison to their crimes, Lear's initial error of handing over the kingdom to his evil daughters in a fit of temper is a venial sin. The Restoration drama is designed for an end different from that of Shakespeare, and the decision to conclude by saving Lear and Cordelia is in accord with that end.

Of course, Shakespeare's *King Lear* was available to those readers who had access to the printed text, but most critics preferred Tate's play. In 1710, Charles Gildon gave his wholehearted approval to Tate's revision, for "the King and *Cordelia* ought by no means to have dy'd" (*SCH* 2:258).[4] In 1711, Joseph Addison, on the other hand, asserted that "*King Lear* is an admirable Tragedy . . . as *Shakespeare* wrote it; but as it is reformed according to the chymerical Notion of poetical Justice in my humble Opinion it has lost half its Beauty" (*SCH* 2:273).[5] But Addison was clearly in the minority at this early point in the eighteenth century. His opinion had no immediate effect on stage managers or critics. For instance, Lewis Theobald, writing four years later, argued in favor of Tate's conclusion: "Virtue ought to be rewarded as well as Vice punish'd; but in their [Lear's and Cordelia's] Deaths this Moral is broke through" (*SCH* 2:306).[6] The didactic function of Tate's *King Lear* is nowhere made clearer than in Thomas Cooke's remarks of 1731. Summarizing the Restoration play, Cooke characterizes the "moral inferences" of the conclusion.

Edmund, Cornwall, Goneril, and *Regan* are disloyal to their Prince, undutyful to the Parents, and every Way false to their Trust. Their Crimes are attended with so many horrid Circumstances that their Punishment is scarcely adequate to their Guilt. *Lear* and *Gloucester* had offended, but more to Appearance thro an

Error of the Judgement than the Will; they are punished. They are made sensible
of their Errors, and are placed in a State of Tranquillity and Ease agreeable to
their Age and Condition, with *Kent* (whose Loyalty remained unshocked to the
last), rejoicing at the Felicity of *Edgar* and *Cordelia*, whom they had wronged, and
who forsaked them not in the Hour of Distress, and who cherished a virtuous
Love each for the other. (*SCH* 2:467)[7]

Cooke goes on to explain that few sermons provide such a vivid example of
Cordelia's belief that "there are Gods, and Virtue is their Care," citing the
words of Tate's *Lear*.

By 1740, however, critical interest began to shift from the conclusion of
the play to the storm scene. Quoting from the Tate text, William Smith, in his
discourse on the sublime, pointed to the reciprocal relationship between internal and external, between introspection and description, in Lear's speech
to Kent (3.4.24–36): "The Miseries and Disorders of *Lear* and *Edgar* are then
pointed with such judicious Horror that every Imagination must be strongly
affected by such Tempests in Reason and Nature" (*SCH* 3:98).[8]

In 1747, a disagreement arose about how the stage presentation of the beginning of the play affected one's understanding of the central issue being
presented. Samuel Foote believed that Garrick's Lear overemphasized the
feelings of filial ingratitude and was therefore not sufficiently regal: "The
Desire of Royalty, then, is the Point that distracts *Lear's* Judgment" (*SCH*
3:213).[9] Taking the opposite view, an anonymous commentator defended
Garrick: "There is not a single word mention'd (except once) in the first and
second Scene of his Madness that has the least Relation to Royalty. It is evidently the Usage of his Daughters that continually rankles in his Mind" (*SCH*
3:265). This reviewer goes on to advise Garrick to abandon Tate and present
the original version: "Why will you do so great an Injury to *Shakespeare* as to
perform *Tate's* execrable Alteration of him? Read and consider the two Plays
seriously, and then make the Publick and the Memory of the Author some
Amends by giving us *Lear* in the *Original, Fool* and all" (*SCH* 3:267). This
statement in 1747 represents a turning point in the eighteenth century in
two related respects: once the question was raised as to whether the central
issue of the play is domestic or political, producers and stage managers attended less to the end and more to the body of the play, thereby beginning
the gradual process of restoring more and more elements of Shakespeare to
the stage.

In 1748, Peter Whalley used a speech from the Elizabethan *Lear* as part
of a detailed defense of Shakespeare's language. Instead of characterizing
the style as original but unpolished or natural but unlearned—the sorts of

terms used to defend Tate's linguistic alterations—Whalley saw the language as metaphoric but carefully wrought, not "founded upon Truth and Reason, [but] parallel to many of the stoical Extravagancies of *Lucan*" (*SCH* 3:285).[10] And in 1748, John Upton produced a Shakespearean grammar to prevent assumptions about "what Shakespeare *ought* to have written [and] to discover and retrieve what he *did* write" (*SCH* 3:308).[11] It is significant that Upton's citations from *Lear* are mainly from the middle three acts. In this same year, Samuel Richardson made clear his preference for Shakespeare's conclusion.

Two years later, Arthur Murphy expressed his disapproval of the "unskilful alteration" of *King Lear* (*SCH* 3:375), and, in the same year, Thomas Edwards made a textual discovery which had important implications. Edwards exposed Warburton's error with regard to the following passage:

LEAR. Know that we have
    divided in three our kingdom; and 'tis our fast intent
    To shake all cares and business from our age
    Confering them on younger strengths.
                              (1.1.36–39)

Substituting "first" for "fast," Warburton explains that "first" is "as *Shakespeare* wrote it": "That the *first* reason of [Lear's] abdication was the love of his people, that they might be protected by such as were better able to discharge the trust; and his natural affection for his daughters, only the *second*" (*W* 6:5). Edwards points out, however, that "fast" is "not an interpolation of Mr. Lewis Theobald" but is in the earliest version of the play and means "*determined resolution*" (*SCH* 3:404–5).[12] Johnson and most modern editors agree with Edwards. Warburton, operating in the tradition derived from Tate, assumed that Lear's primary concern was political, not domestic. By 1750, however, this Restoration reading of *Lear* was being seriously questioned. For example, to Joseph Warton's assertion that Lear's madness is the result of "the loss of royalty" (*SCH* 4:78),[13] Arthur Murphy replied, "This notion is not only fundamentally wrong but also destructive of the fine pathetic that melts the heart in every scene. . . . The behaviour of *Lear's* children is always uppermost in the thoughts of the aged monarch" (*SCH* 4:95).[14]

In 1756, David Garrick staged at Drury Lane his revised version of Tate's *Lear*. Aside from the reinstatement of Shakespeare's words, one structural alteration is very important. Edmund and Regan cease to have the prominence they had in Tate. Instead of beginning the drama with Edmund's soliloquy, Garrick returns to the original opening scene, where Lear divides up his kingdom. Moreover, Garrick removed Regan and Edmund's love scene in the grotto. The overall effect of these changes is to give less emphasis to politics and political manipulations and more to the relationship between Lear and his daughters. As is well known, Johnson was a good friend of Garrick; they had come to London together in 1737, and Johnson had been working on Shakespeare since at least as early as 1745. Surely, their many conversations during this period must have touched upon the one's editorial problems and the other's acting and directing concerns. But we can only speculate as to who influenced whom and to what extent. We can, however, be certain that Johnson's edition of *Lear* did influence George Colman when he revised Tate for a production first presented at Drury Lane in 1768. Colman quotes from Johnson's Shakespeare at length in his *Preface* to this, the first production of *Lear* since 1681 to remove the love of Edgar and Cordelia, one of the most prominent of Tate's additions. In fact, Colman is reported to have considered adding the fool and concluding with the deaths of Cordelia and Lear (*SCH* 5:295).[15] Instead, he compromised, keeping Tate's conclusion but for the marriage of Edgar and Cordelia. Not surprisingly, the play failed, being neither Shakespeare nor Tate. But this attempt to return to Shakespeare's *Lear*, however abortive, was, in large part, a result of Johnson's edition of *King Lear*.

THE DOMESTIC POLITICIZED

When Samuel Johnson began to edit *King Lear*, probably in the period from 1745 to 1765, attention was shifting from political to domestic discord in the play. Playwrights and producers were gradually restoring Shakespeare's language and structure to the stage but recognized that their audiences would not accept the deaths of Cordelia and Lear. Johnson's position derives from both the critical and the theatrical traditions; indeed, he is the first to recognize that Lear's problem stems from attempting to resolve a domestic problem by political means.

Johnson's general practice of making explicit in the final stricture what remains implicit throughout the notes is once again illustrated in *King Lear*. The stricture begins with high praise for *King Lear*: indeed, it would be hard to find a more commendatory summary anywhere in his edition of Shakespeare's plays. This laudatory beginning must have been particularly startling to readers in Johnson's day, since it concerned a tragedy that had not been presented on the stage for nearly a century. Of Johnson's paragraph of praise, the following is a fair sample: "The tragedy of *Lear* is deservedly celebrated among the dramas of *Shakespeare.* There is perhaps no play which keeps the attention so strongly fixed; which so much agitates our passions and interests our curiosity" (6:158; 8:702). To further bolster his high assessment, Johnson goes on to defend the play against an objection raised to Lear's initial behavior: "On the seeming improbability of *Lear's* conduct it may be observed, that he is represented according to histories at that time vulgarly received as true. And perhaps if we turn our thoughts upon the barbarity and ignorance of the age to which this story is referred, it will appear not so unlikely as while we estimate *Lear's* manners by our own. Such preference of one daughter to another, or resignation of dominion on such conditions, would be yet credible, if told of a petty prince of *Guinea* or *Madagascar*" (6:158; 8:703).

Since the historical age of the drama is "barbaric" and the setting a petty principality, Lear's treatment of his daughters becomes believable. This approach to the tragedy focuses upon the domestic dilemma; for this reason, Johnson makes clear that he sides with Murphy in the disagreement previously discussed: "It is disputed whether the predominant image in *Lear's* disordered mind be the loss of his kingdom or the cruelty of his daughters. Mr. *Murphy*, a very judicious critick, has evinced by induction of particular passages, that the cruelty of his daughters is the primary source of his distress, and that the loss of royalty affects him only as a secondary and subordinate evil; He observes with great justness, that *Lear* would move our compassion but little, did we not rather consider the injured father than the degraded king" (6:159–60; 8:704–5). For Johnson, the tragedy engages the interest of the general reader because, although few of us can identify with the dilemma of a degraded king, most care about the suffering of an injured father. Here the critic and scholar in Johnson merge in a characteristic way. The question concerning the improbability of dividing up a kingdom becomes a secondary scholarly issue, one having to do with primitive political customs, because the primary critical issue concerns the relationship between father and daughter. But in order to understand Johnson's unique rendering of this position, we need to consider some of his notes to the play.

In the scene early in act 1 when Lear divides up his kingdom, Johnson opposes Warburton on the question of "fast/first intent," a decision that, as we have seen, is based upon the belief that family concerns are more important than political ones.[16] Johnson reinforces this point by way of a variorum technique. A few lines later in the same scene, Cordelia remarks, "Sure I shall never marry like my sisters," a phrase that perplexed editors until Pope restored the continuation from the quarto, "To love my father all," a phrase that gives renewed emphasis to Cordelia's role as wounded daughter. Following Pope, Warburton includes the phrase, because without it he believes the "sense" would be incomplete. In Johnson's edition, however, following soon after the long note opposing Warburton, the sentence serves as further evidence that the disagreement between Lear and Cordelia is domestic rather than political.

But Johnson does not reject the political element; in fact, he sees it as an important part of Lear's tragic situation. Near the end of this same fateful scene, Johnson makes a comment that constitutes the basis of an innovative reading of *King Lear:* "*Lear,* who is characterized as hot, heady and violent, is, with very just observation of life, made to entangle himself with vows, upon any sudden provocation to vow revenge, and then to plead the obligation of a vow in defence of implacability" (6:12; 8:663). Family matters have the force of public edicts. This king has yet to learn that on occasion his role as a ruler must be subordinated to his duty as a father. Johnson is *not* agreeing with Tate's view of *Lear* as a political play; nor is he arguing that it is a domestic tragedy. Rather, he sees the play as the tragedy of a man who must learn to distinguish between his roles as father and as king. Throughout most of the drama Lear attempts to employ political means to resolve domestic problems. For this reason, Johnson indicates at the outset that, although politics is an important facet of Shakespeare's *King Lear,* Tate's conclusion, the return of the throne to the king, cannot resolve the problem of the Shakespearean tragedy.

Yet Johnson favors the conclusion of Tate's *King Lear.* A careful examination of Johnson's statement about the end of the play reveals that his view cannot be adequately understood in such bald terms as for or against Tate's *Lear.* The pertinent passage in the stricture begins with a discussion of the notion of poetic justice. After summarizing Addison's argument against and Dennis's in favor of poetic justice, Johnson adopts an uncharacteristically ambivalent position. Instead of deciding for or against poetic justice, he concludes that compliance with the doctrine is unlikely to make a drama any worse. He then turns to *Lear,* focusing upon the death of Cordelia: "In the present case the publick has decided. *Cordelia,* from the time of *Tate,* has always retired with victory and felicity. And, if my sensations could add any thing to the general suffrage, I might relate, that I was many years ago so shocked by *Cordelia's* death, that I know not whether I ever endured to read again the last scenes of the play till I undertook to revise them as an editor" (6:159; 8:704). Few sentences in the canon employ the word "I" five times. Furthermore, the other element of Tate's conclusion, the marriage of Edgar and Cordelia, which must have been most prominent on the stage, is not recommended or even mentioned. My point is that Johnson does not wish to promote Tate's resolution, which he knew involved far more than saving Cordelia. Rather, by expressing his visceral horror at the death of the virtuous daughter, Johnson asks how the survival of Cordelia would detract from the point of the play. His reference to Tate is an attempt to relate his "sensations" to the "general suffrage," a factor that helps to explain why Garrick and Colman, while restoring more and more of Shakespeare's original play, were nonetheless unable to stage the death of Cordelia. We misunderstand Johnson if we assume that his disapproval of the death of Cordelia constitutes an acceptance of Tate's *Lear*. On the contrary, Johnson has a profound respect for and understanding of Shakespeare's *Lear*, and his difficulty concerning the death of Cordelia is directly related to modern difficulties with this tragedy.

JOHNSON ON THE FOOL

Johnson's interpretation is firmly based upon deep sympathy for Cordelia. Since the part of the fool and that of Cordelia could easily have been assumed by the same actor and since Lear uses the term "fool" to refer to Cordelia, Johnson's sensitivity to the function of these two characters brings him closest to the modern position. Shortly after Lear deprives Cordelia of her dowry, Goneril begins to show her true colors, telling her youngest sister that she has received what she deserves. Cordelia replies, "Time shall unfold what plaited cunning hides, Who covers faults, at last with shame derides." Unable to suppress his feelings, Johnson resorts to French to express his indignation: "*Il rira bien, qui rira le dernier,*" a phrase he later deleted, probably because it misleadingly suggests that Cordelia is ultimately triumphant (6:17; 8:665).[17]

The most damaging of Lear's implacable vows is, of course, the banishing of Cordelia and Kent, by which he gives absolute dominion to Goneril and Regan. In Tate's drama Edmund, the main villain, is stunned by the beauty of Cordelia, a clear allusion to the tempter first beholding Eve in *Paradise Lost*. Johnson, on the other hand, makes clear that for Shakespeare the major sources of tragedy are Goneril and Regan whose malignancy, unlike that of Edmund, which stems from personal and political ambitions, is motiveless and inexplicable—sheer evil. Edmund becomes a figure of secondary importance who is viewed, not as a satanic rebel, but as one who has no concept of higher authority, an atheist. The longest note in Johnson's

edition on Edmund's soliloquy consists of Warburton's comment connecting Edmund's term "nature" with that employed in a Renaissance treatise
on atheism. Johnson employs his predecessor's historical research to demonstrate that Edmund should be seen, not as Tate's archenemy from within,
but as the disenfranchised outsider who is completely dependent for power
on the insiders, Goneril and Regan.

Not only does Johnson return the reader's attention to the two older sisters, but he also makes clear that their cruelty exceeds the requirements even
of their perverse desires. For instance, in the first act, when Goneril refers
to her father as an "idle old man," Johnson, with some hesitation, decides
to include a passage from the quarto, which Warburton omitted: "Now, by
my life, old fools are babes again; and must be us'd with Checks, as flatteries
when they're seen abus'd." Johnson explains the pun on "abus'd": "There
is a play on the words *used* and *abused*. To *abuse* is, in our authour, very frequently the same as to *deceive*" (6:30–31; 8:669). Johnson directs us to feel
that this daughter is abusing her father, particularly in view of the contrast-
ing references to Cordelia. For example, Kent speaks of his faith that the
youngest of the sisters will come to the aid of her father.

> KENT. I know, 'tis from *Cordelia*
>   Who hath most fortunately been inform'd
>   Of my obscured course, and shall find time
>   From this enormous state seeking to give
>   Losses their remedies.
>   (6:59–60; 8:676)

Admitting that this passage is "very obscure, if not corrupt," Johnson
nevertheless paraphrases it and explains that, in the past, it has been altered
or omitted: "This passage, which some of the editors have degraded, as spuri-
ous, to the margin, and others have silently altered, I have faithfully printed
according to the quarto, from which the folio differs only in punctuation"
(6:59; 8:676). Kent speaks from the stocks, where, as Lear's servant, he has
been placed by order of Cornwall, Regan's husband. Understandably, Kent
turns in hope of relief to Cordelia. Johnson recognizes the need to keep this
passage in the text because the audience must understand that Lear is now
ruled by those who do not love or even care about him: the only possibility
for rescue must come from Cordelia, who feels normal concern for her father
and who is, at the moment, beyond the clutches of Regan, Cornwall, and
Goneril.

At this point, however, Lear, unaware of the nature of his problem, seeks remedy by reminding Regan that he reserved to himself the respect due to a king. When this measure fails, Lear nears madness, and the fool becomes his guide. It has become a commonplace of modern criticism that the fool provides the key to understanding Lear on the heath. Johnson can be said to have begun this tradition by way of his continuous, careful attention to the words of the fool, a considerable accomplishment for one who never had the opportunity to see the character on the stage. Here it is particularly difficult to select passages that do justice to the accretive process experienced by the reader of Johnson's edition, but a few instances may suffice. First, consider the fool's explanation of why he accompanies Lear on the heath during the storm.

> But I will tarry; the fool will stay
> And let the wise man fly;
> The knave turns fool, that runs away;
> The fool no knave, perdy.
> (6:64; 8:678)

This passage was left unexplained until Johnson offered the following comment.

> I think this passage erroneous, though both the copies concur. The sense will be mended if we read,

> But I will tarry; the fool will stay,
> And let the wise man fly;
> The fool turns knave, that runs away;
> The knave no fool,—

> That I stay with the King is a proof that I am a fool, the wise men are deserting him. There is knavery in this desertion, but there is no folly. (6:65; 8:678)

The Arden editor quotes Enid Welsford's rejection of "Johnson's emendation." First, it should be made clear that Johnson does not emend the text; the change occurs only in the note and is another example of Johnson's use of suggested emendations to clarify, not to change, the text. These "changes" are seldom transferred to the text, because they serve as speculations to help the reader understand what is implicit in the original version. In this particular instance, the Arden editor has been so put off by what he erroneously considers to be an emendation that he fails to recognize that the following paraphrase of Kittredge's, which he accepts, is almost identical to Johnson's: "The fellow that forsakes his master is (from the point of view of the higher wisdom) a fool, since true wisdom implies fidelity; and the fool who, like me, remains faithful, is at all events, no knave."[18] Most modern editors, however, commend Johnson for his commonsense remarks on the fool. But it should now be clear that in Johnson's day such sense was quite uncommon; he is the first editor to understand that the fool offers, in his convoluted and paradoxical way, the common sense that Lear must acquire.

The manner in which Johnson distinguished himself from his predecessors can be seen in his difference of opinion with Warburton concerning the following passage:

> LEAR. You owe me no subscription; then let fall
>   Your horrible displeasure. Here I stand, your slave.

Warburton emended "slave" to "brave," explaining the meaning as "I defy your worst rage." Leaving the text unchanged, Johnson explained that "the meaning is plain enough, he was not their *slave* by right or compact, but by necessity and compulsion" (6:81; 8:683). Here we see how critical intelligence serves the textual editor. Believing that the intent is to enhance the bravery and heroism of the protagonist, Warburton alters "slave" to "brave." But Johnson sees that Lear is learning what the fool had explained earlier—that kings, like all other humans, are slaves to the rain. Johnson's bibliographic decision is based upon his understanding of the fool's view of Lear—there is more foolishness than bravery in defying the rain—an understanding that does not preclude the fool's anger at Lear's being thrust out into the storm.

Johnson's empathy with the protagonist who grasps only at an advanced age what most understand as youths—that he is vulnerable to the elements of nature—leads to an understanding of Lear's development on the heath.

> LEAR. In, boy, go first [*To the Fool.*] You houseless poverty—
>   Nay, get thee in; I'll pray, and then I'll sleep—.

Johnson remarks: "These two lines were added in the authour's revision, and are only in the folio. They are very judiciously intended to represent that humility, or tenderness, or neglect of forms, which affliction forces on the mind" (6:88; 8:685). "Affliction" and "mind" are the key terms here; Johnson demonstrates that by means of anguish Lear is learning. Again, this point does not seem particularly startling to us, but in Johnson's day such passages were left without comment, because at this time the middle of *Lear* was only beginning to be of interest. The modern notion that Lear's madness is the means by which he comes to understand what it is to be human begins with the commentary of Johnson.

But the most difficult problem concerning the function of affliction in *King*

Lear involves the blinding of Gloucester. Johnson's position has troubled many modern critics. The relevant passage should be cited in full, because, as with his comments on the death of Cordelia, Johnson's own carefully chosen words have been neglected.

> My learned friend Mr. *Warton*, who has in the *Adventurer* very minutely criti-cised this play, remarks, that the instances of cruelty are too savage and shock-ing, and that the intervention of *Edmund* destroys the simplicity of the story. These objections may, I think, be answered, by repeating, that the cruelty of the daughters is an historical fact, to which the poet has added little, having only drawn it into a series by dialogue and action. But I am not able to apolo-gise with equal plausibility for the extrusion of *Gloucester's* eyes, which seems an act too horrid to be endured in dramatick exhibition, and such as must always compel the mind to relieve its distress by incredulity. Yet let it be remembered that our authour well knew what would please the audience for which he wrote. (6:158–59; 8:703) [19]

The objection to the blinding of Gloucester is not framed in terms of in-decorum or immorality. By that criterion, the cruelty of Goneril and Regan to Lear could hardly be exceeded. Nor is the point that such actions should *never* be performed on the stage. The last sentence above makes clear that what audiences find acceptable is historicized: an unsuitable event in the eighteenth century may have been appropriate in Shakespeare's time.

Johnson's objection is that the repulsiveness of the blinding compels him to distract himself from the play, to "relieve his distress by incredulity." In-stead of contemplating the meaning of the action, he can only bear to witness it by reminding himself that it is not an actual blinding. The problem ad-dressed has to do, not with "neoclassical" rules of theatrical decorum, but with the concern of any theatrical director in any historical era: a stage action that forces the audience to relieve its anguish by ceasing to concentrate on the play is self-defeating. Even when the desired effect is that of shock, the psychological limitations of the spectators must be kept in mind, for noth-ing is served by losing the audience's attention. Johnson is pointing out that for the spectator of his day the dramatic representation of the blinding of Gloucester prevented contemplation of the meaning of the representation, and I can only add that my own experience at productions of *King Lear* con-firms this position.

Because Johnson's objection stems from his belief that the drama reaches, and sometimes exceeds, the limits of human endurance, he understands the significance of the subplot in relationship to the main plot. In fact, his sen-sitivity to the horror of the deed leads him to a new insight. Theobald had

remarked that the servants struck with horror at the blinding of Gloucester are of his retinue. But Johnson is the first to articulate a point accepted
by modern editors, that "it is not necessary to suppose them the servants of
Glo'ster; for *Cornwall* was opposed to extremity by his own servant" (6:105;
8:689). The unnaturalness of the blinding is in itself sufficient explanation
for the servants turning upon their master.

The pain and anguish of the ordinary man are now first understood by
Lear and Gloucester.

> GLOUCESTER. Let the superfluous, and lust-dieted man,
>   That slaves your ordinance, that will not see
>   Because he does not feel, feel your power quickly.

> *Lear* has before uttered the same sentiment, which indeed cannot be too strongly
> impressed, though it may be often repeated. (6:110; 8:691)

Clearly, Johnson relates the subplot and main plot by way of "affliction," the
one physical, the other psychological, both revealing human limitations and
needs. In fact, in his stricture, Johnson defends the double plot against the
traditional objection of his day: "the injury done by *Edmund* to the simplicity
of the action is abundantly recompensed by the addition of variety, by the art
with which he is made to cooperate with the chief design, and the opportunity
which he gives the poet of combining perfidy with perfidy, and connecting
the wicked son with the wicked daughters, to impress this important moral,
that villainy is never at a stop, that crimes lead to crimes, and at last terminate
in ruin" (6:159; 8:703–4). Like his remarks on the fool, these on the subplot
point to the fate of Cordelia.

THE DEATH OF CORDELIA

If, as I maintain, Johnson is the first editor to understand that Shakespeare's
King Lear shows how affliction leads Lear to discover the nature of his humanity, then why can he not accept the death of Cordelia? Moreover, since
Johnson recognizes that Goneril and Regan are more evil than Edmund,
what is the difficulty with a tragic conclusion in which the wicked triumph
over the virtuous? For Johnson, Cordelia comes in the end to represent the
message of the play. The last act brings to a culmination the protagonist's
acceptance of his own primal needs as a human being, a view that becomes
clear in the comment on Lear's words of comfort to Cordelia after they have
been captured by the enemy forces:

LEAR. No, no, no, no! come, let's away to prison;
   We two alone will sing, like birds i'th' cage.
   When thou dost ask me Blessing, I'll kneel down,
   And ask of thee Forgiveness. So we'll live,
   And pray, and sing, and tell old tales, and laugh
   At gilded butterflies; and hear poor rogues
   Talk of Court-news, and we'll talk with them too,
   Who loses and who wins; who's in, who's out;
   And take upon's the mystery of things,
   As if we were God's spies.

First, Johnson cites Warburton, who characterizes this speech as "an admirable description of the idle life of a coffeehouse politician" and suggests that the phrase "God's spies" should be understood as follows: "We will take upon us to interpret and judge of the designs of Providence in the various fortunes and revolutions of men and governments, as if we were placed for spies over God Almighty, to watch his motions." Johnson, on the other hand, sees this speech as advocating the viewpoint, not "over" God, but near him, like that of the angels: "I rather take the other meaning. As if we were angels commissioned to survey and report the lives of men, and were consequently endowed with the power of prying into the original motives of action and the mysteries of conduct" (6:144; 8:700).[20]

The difference between Warburton and Johnson could not be more clear-cut. Warburton believes that Lear is urging his daughter to join him in spying upon God and judging of the ways of Providence; Johnson believes that the king proposes the perspective of an angel in order to spy, not upon God, but upon man. For Johnson, Lear exhorts his daughter, not to question the ways of Providence, but to join him in adopting a spiritual viewpoint upon the material world. Following Johnson's reading, what does Lear mean by inviting Cordelia to join him in prison in order to survey the original motives of action and the mysteries of conduct? In turning toward Cordelia and away from Goneril and Regan, Lear indicates that he has ceased to have any interest in revenge or in the restoration of his political power. Having previously ranted and raved about ingratitude and injustice, Lear now accepts his unjust fate and seeks a relationship of love with his daughter beyond the limits of gratitude and justice. For Johnson, Lear has comprehended the heart of his own tragedy, which is less about a "degraded king" and more about an "injured father."

Johnson here goes one step beyond the innovative critics of his own age. The initial political discord that is merely a symptom of a domestic problem becomes, near the end of the play, a notion implicit in the action of the tragic protagonist. And it is this profound insight—innovative in his own day, even though generally accepted in our own—that redefines the difficulty with the death of Cordelia. Johnson is the first commentator to recognize that the death of Cordelia undermines the message of the play, for at the moment of her death Lear has learned to value her and the love that she represents above all else in the world. If the tragedy demonstrates that Cordelia's affection for her father is more important than anything else that preoccupied Lear throughout the drama, that notion is called into question by her death at precisely the point when Lear understands it.

Here Johnson raises the most difficult question that can be posed about *King Lear*. The issue does not concern the outmoded concept of poetic justice. Johnson does not defend the doctrine itself, and those familiar with the *Life of Addison* will know that Johnson, near the end of his life, came to attack it. But here he asks a question that is not doctrinaire. To return for a moment to the passage in the stricture concerning the death of Cordelia, I wish to rephrase Johnson's general observation into a question that can be posed to contemporary commentators. Johnson admits that it may be acceptable in drama for the wicked to prosper, because that constitutes a just representation of life. But, he continues, "I cannot easily be persuaded, that the observation of justice makes a play worse." The question this note leads me to raise is not why must Cordelia die but in what way would her survival detract from the tragic denouement. When formulated in these terms, the question offers a new perspective upon modern views of *Lear*.

A MIMETIC QUESTION FOR MODERNS

Since the amount of modern criticism on *King Lear* exceeds the material published in the three previous centuries, I have selected those readily available views that form the basis for the recent positions.[21] Maynard Mack's "Actors and Redactors" (1965) formulates what for moderns remains the central issue in *King Lear:* Is it possible "that something like the whole play might be actable and knowable if we were to come to it with other ends in view than rationalizing the irrational, regularizing the irregular, and unifying on a particular plan what cannot be unified on such a plan?"[22] Most modern commentators on *Lear* still seek to delineate a form or structure that is adequate to the irrational and the irregular; indeed, they part company with Johnson and the critics of his age who, in their view, were doomed by their aesthetic assumptions to rationalize and regularize. Thus moderns turn away from

eighteenth-century critics whose positions on *King Lear* are seen as epito-
mized by Tate, the regularizer of Shakespeare's language and rationalizer of
the conclusion of the drama.

Johnson, as we have demonstrated, clearly diverges from this tradition; his
question about the death of Cordelia stems, not from an attempt to regularize
or rationalize, but from one of the most widely accepted tenets of the literary
method of his day—mimeticism. Johnson's terms are Hamlet's: *King Lear*
must serve as a "mirrour" of some aspect of "nature." In what way, he urges
us to inquire, does the survival of Cordelia alter the natural referent in that
mirror?

Posing this mimetic question to modern commentators exposes the limitations of both positions and demonstrates that this great tragedy requires
a method that incorporates elements of the literary theories from both the
eighteenth and twentieth centuries. It is important to recognize that neither
eighteenth- nor twentieth-century critics refer to the specific reason for Cordelia's death: the fact that Edmund's confession of her sentence was too late.
This most tragic episode concerning time is the source of Johnson's agony,
though he is unable to express it in these terms. For moderns, however, the
agony is repressed. Indeed, the mimetic question has not before been posed
in our time because we have yet to understand the function of questions
derived from old and outmoded theories, those of "historical" interest.

The essays of the moderns, excluding those of the 1980s (to be discussed
shortly), can be divided into the secular and the religious. The problem had
been formulated earlier by A. C. Bradley: "The 'gods,' it seems, do *not* show
their approval by 'defending' their own from adversity or death, or by giving
them power and prosperity. . . . Let us renounce the world, hate it, and lose it
gladly. The only real thing in it is the soul, with its courage, patience, devo-
tion. And nothing outward can touch that."[23] For Bradley, the end of *Lear*
pointed beyond its own mortal, tragic dilemma. But the precise nature of
this ascension beyond this world was not made clear. In 1935, Enid Welsford explained that the "conflict of good and evil, of wisdom with folly," is
presented as a reversal of roles: "Kings and noblemen are turned into fools
and beggars," enabling the tragic hero to learn "that *in this world there is no
poetic justice.*" She concluded that "there is nothing contemptible in a motley
coat"; indeed, such a reversal of roles helps explain to us the Elizabethan
belief in the "Divine inspiration of madmen." *King Lear* moves beyond this
unjust world by presenting the fool as an inspired prophet: "Lear's tragedy is
the investing of the King with motley: it is also the crowning and apotheosis
of the Fool."[24]

In 1961, John Holloway presented a more overtly religious extension of Bradley's position. The drama represents the Elizabethan faith in the "universal cataclysm," the physical destruction of the mortal world that precedes the Day of Judgment. The action of *King Lear* is, according to Holloway, pervaded by the expectation, continually thwarted, that "since Nature is an order (though doubtless a stern one) release from suffering is at hand." But because the suffering continues, good cannot be said to triumph, even in the end; rather, "we are left with the spectacle of how suffering can renew itself unremittingly until the very moment of death." Order is restored, not by love, but by man returning to his duty. "To follow the master, to sustain the state, to bless one's child, to succour the aged and one's parents—this idea of being brought back to rectitude is what the play ends with." For Holloway, *Lear* employs suffering, the agony of the great cataclysm, to bring one to a sense of spiritual duty.[25]

Another regularly anthologized religious position is C. J. Sisson's "Justice in *King Lear*" (1962). Sisson demonstrated that dividing up one's inheritance before death was not uncommon in the Elizabethan period and that *King Lear* therefore has some historical validity and need not be seen as based upon a primitive, folkloric legend. Moreover, the drama, Sisson insisted, is not so far removed from Christianity as its pagan setting would suggest. Indeed, Lear is reformed by the "Christian concept of chivalry." Yet what the play tells us about divine justice, Sisson continued, is incidental and contradictory; the reason for this discrepancy is that "power and justice, human or divine, are none of them ultimately important after all." All attempts at balance between right and wrong, whether of man or God, are "mortal and fallible." For Sisson, one arrives by negatives at the proper Christian resolution: the recognition that the drama raises questions about divine justice in order to show that resolutions cannot be derived from the mortal, tragic world.[26]

Before moving on to some modern secular readings, we should pose Johnson's question to these twentieth-century religious interpretations: how would the survival of Cordelia detract from these views of *King Lear?* Welsford's notion of role reversal, the king in motley, is surely one with which Johnson would be in sympathy, for, as I have demonstrated, his notes continually clarify the essential sanity, goodwill, and intelligence of the fool's seemingly bizarre remarks. But the death of Cordelia does little to reinforce this role reversal. On the contrary, when, in the final act, Lear and Cordelia are taken prisoner, the king, in suggesting that he and his daughter go to prison together, is adopting the traditional posture of the fool—the neglected, isolated, mistreated man who sees the world more accurately than those in positions of power. Moreover, when, near the end of the play, Lear remarks, "And my poor fool is hang'd," whether he refers here to the fool as well as Cordelia or both, the association of motley and innocence is given further emphasis. When the king and his daughter have willingly accepted their motley role, what function is served by their death?

Similar difficulties arise when the question is posed in relation to the arguments of Holloway and Sisson. How would Holloway's concept of duty be in any way weakened by the survival of Cordelia? How does the murdering of Cordelia, the most dutiful daughter in the drama, further the doctrine of man's duty? Sisson, proposing that *King Lear* ends with Christian resolution because all mortal alternatives fail, neglects to consider the form of Christianity represented by Lear and Cordelia in submitting willingly and meekly to prison. Would not the survival of Cordelia in that posture have reinforced the Christian position? Surely, the lack of the possibility of Christian retirement for Lear and Cordelia is part of what troubles Johnson about the conclusion.

By way of transition to some readily available alternative positions, let us consider a well-known view that could be accommodated to either the secular or the religious reading. In "King Lear and the Comedy of the Grotesque" (1930), G. Wilson Knight pointed to a comic element in the drama which "treads the brink of tears." Knight finds that the "profound insight of the Fool" is that "he sees the potentialities of comedy in Lear's behavior." The grotesque humor is best illustrated by Gloucester's attempt to commit suicide by jumping from what he believes to be the cliff at Dover. The grotesque comedy of tragedy here and in Lear's last words of the play indicates "that all human pain holds beauty, that no tear falls but it dews some flower we cannot see." Johnson, it seems to me, would not contest the concept of grotesque beauty in *King Lear*, but he might retort that, since Lear and Cordelia, in the end, understand and express this notion, their continued existence, instead of their death, would better reinforce this theme.[27]

In an influential secular reading, "The Unity of King Lear" (1948), Robert Heilman asserted that unity is the key to understanding the play. Heilman began by relating the subplot to the main plot: "Lear, without questioning his own rightness, imposes his will upon others; Gloucester accepts the will of others without effactually questioning their rightness. Thus Lear and Gloucester are, in terms of structure, not duplicates, but complements: this is one key to the unity of *King Lear*." The central theme binding these two plots is, according to Heilman, the "symbolism of kinship." "Lear's tragic flaw is the whole being of Goneril and Regan. Lear makes a fatal error of understanding: then his essential method of thought is picked up by his daughters and made their way of life." In the end, Heilman asserts, "Family mediates between the soul of man and the community to which he belongs. . . . By being the father of Goneril and of Cordelia, Lear includes both of them within himself; we cannot then idly hate Goneril as evil but we must recognize the genesis of evil and hence modify our sympathetic identification with Lear so that it includes a sensitiveness to the spiritual trouble within him."[28] But is not this notion precisely what Lear manifests in kneeling down before and begging forgiveness of Cordelia and willingly sacrificing all political power to his elder daughters? Once again, we find that Lear and Cordelia, in the end, manifest in their conduct an understanding of the theme that is designed to encompass them. And the question that Johnson leads me to ask remains unanswered: How would the notion of the family of good and evil, of Lear spawning Goneril and Regan, on the one hand, and Cordelia, on the other hand, be undermined by Lear and Cordelia retiring to prison?

Another well-known secular reading, Jan Kott's "King Lear, or Endgame" (1964), takes the pessimism of the secularists to the farthest limits. In terms reminiscent of Knight, Kott argues that the "world of tragedy and the world of the grotesque have a similar structure." *Lear* is seen as containing ideas similar to those of Samuel Beckett. The process of the play, "the peeling of the onion," is the systematic destruction of all absolutes, until one comes to the core, unaccommodated man, represented by the fool. "The Fool appears on the stage when Lear's fall is only beginning. He disappears by the end of Act III. . . . A clown is not needed any more. King Lear has gone through the school of clown's philosophy. When he meets Gloucester for the last time, he will speak the Fool's language."[29] Kott's doctrine of the absurd is presented at the end of *King Lear* by Lear himself. Would the doctrine, then, not be better served by the survival of the protagonists?

Similarly, postformalist readings of the 1980s cannot face the mimetic question. In 1983, Stephen Booth declared that the proper attitude toward the death of Lear is represented by Kent, who sees it as a release, a form of relief. But Kent's speech, Booth neglected to mention, is in response to the sight of Lear holding the dead Cordelia in his arms; once she is gone, no one, including Tate himself, would argue that Lear has any reason for living.[30] And that is why Johnson focuses upon Cordelia; without her, Lear's existence is empty, a living death. Kent's words lead, not to the resolution of the question, but to a reformulation of it: why does Lear, having finally learned every lesson the play has to teach, end with a life not worth living?

In 1988 Stephen Greenblatt reformulated what he has called the "new historicist" position. Demonstrating that the Elizabethan political and religious authority ceased to validate exorcism in the church and removed it to the theater, Greenblatt argued that Shakespeare welcomed this development and deliberately pursued the notion of dramaturgical exorcism in *King Lear*. He concluded that the religious rite that appears on stage is emptied of its sacred significance: "Whereas before they had a literal, they now have a literary use and are as so many notes of remembrance unto us, that what they did signify in the letter is accomplished—with a drastic swerve from the sacred to the secular—in the theater." By not taking the position of religiosity, "[Shakespeare] writes for the greater glory and profit of the theater, a fraudulent institution that never pretends to be anything but fraudulent, an institution that calls forth what is not, that signifies absence, that transforms the literal into the metaphorical, that evacuates everything it represents."[31] If the end of *Lear* is designed to isolate the artificiality and emptiness of the theater, it still is not clear how Lear and Cordelia retiring together from public life would detract from this conception of absence and evacuation.

Modern commentators do not consider the question posed for me by Johnson's notes to *King Lear* because the mimetic terms—what does Cordelia's death mirror in nature?—are outmoded. Nevertheless, this question points to an issue that haunts moderns. The death of Cordelia remains a source of critical anguish, not merely because it is cruel and unjust, but, more important, because the explanations provided are less than satisfactory. On the stage, this event pushes the audience to—perhaps even beyond—its limits of endurance. The residue of gratuitous cruelty, of motiveless malignancy, cannot be fully expressed by modern criticism because formalist and postformalist methods have excluded from their repertoire referentiality. Mimeticism, on the other hand, emphasizing referentiality, is able to articulate the problem but not resolve it. My contention is that the resolution of the problem involves a combination of the two theories.

Before attempting my own formulation, I should make clear that this question formulated from Johnson's commentary is markedly different from that posed by Tate's *Lear*. To relegate Johnson's commentary to the realm of historical interest because he seems to favor the Restoration version is inaccurate and unjust. Tate, as we have seen, radically altered the play; even his conclusion involved, in addition to the survival of Lear and Cordelia, the marriage of Edgar and Cordelia. One can easily evade the problem about the end of *Lear* by pointing out that Shakespeare did not write a political play about the need to have a father/king at the head of the family/nation. The Elizabethan *King Lear* is the tragedy of a man who believes that he can use political means to achieve domestic control. Johnson advocates none of Tate's many and various alterations except for those related to the blinding of Gloucester and the death of Cordelia.

To respond to Johnson's question, we need to apply theoretical consider- ations to the text, for it seems to me that the end of Shakespeare's *King Lear* goes beyond the limitations of both Johnson's approach and those of the modern commentators. When Lear enters with Cordelia dead in his arms, we see before us a man who at last understands his own tragedy. Shakespeare's point is that the world does not wait for us to comprehend it; time and the unfolding of evil carry on even as we seek to understand them. *King Lear*, therefore, is a tragedy about the tragic possibility inherent in understand- ing tragedy. In that sense, *King Lear* contains a special tragedy for literary criticism. The time that it takes for ignorance (Lear) or innocence (Cordelia) to understand the nature of evil may be long enough for the venom to have entered the bloodstream.

The tragic concept of time lies outside the boundaries of modern ap- proaches. Locating structures or affective forms for the tragedy, these meth- ods seek to explain the tragedy by transcending the fate of the protagonists, but such a structural principle cannot account for the fact that the tragic pro- tagonist himself finally embodies the principle of his own tragedy. Time can- not be captured by formalist and postformalist spatial concepts, for it must be understood as a point of reference that eludes artistic form. *King Lear* explic- itly denies itself a resolution by way of a totalizing theme; Lear and Cordelia manifest every such possibility which with them suffers tragic death.

Johnson is confronted with a different but equally unresolvable problem, for, from his point of view, why would Shakespeare imitate a tragic dilemma of man if that representation does not aid our understanding or endurance of tragedy? To him, the death of Cordelia is an accident. *King Lear* demonstrates how evil gains ultimate control precisely by way of the protagonists' attempt to comprehend the evil at the heart of the tragedy. Understandably, Johnson was shattered by Shakespeare's conclusion, for with the death of Lear and Cordelia dies the mimetic reason for understanding tragedy. Johnson, how- ever, makes overt his struggle with the most difficult and important issue of *King Lear* that has been repressed by modern critics.

As a tragedy about the tragic possibility involved in understanding tragedy, *King Lear* is a form that subverts itself. This concept has a formalist and a mi- metic aspect. The form of the death of Cordelia images the idea of a tragedy about understanding tragedy. Mimeticism subverts this idea, referring us to the realm of relentless time where the critical procedure of analyzing *King*

Lear may result in an end like that of King Lear. For me, the profundity of *King Lear* resides in its dramatization of the fact that critical awareness cannot transcend this dilemma. No literary critical structure, no form of comprehension, can protect us from the fact that all kinds of human comprehension, including literary criticism, are time-bound and liable to be too late.

Modern commentators, however, have failed not only to explain the function of the conclusion but even to realize that such a question must be faced. They are content to assume that the form or affect of *King Lear* raises us above concern for its protagonists. Johnson's notes make clear that *King Lear* calls such an assumption into question. Although his insight is a great critical achievement that has been overlooked, my object is not to advocate a new mimeticism. My reading of *Lear* brings present-day and Johnsonian elements into a dialectical relationship that places the two theories in relation to one another. The discovery of the presence of the past, of the relevance to modern criticism of Johnson's notes on *Lear*, depends on the realization that Johnson's view was based not upon the political didacticism inherent in Tate's *Lear* but upon an important concept of mimeticism.

Johnson's visceral response to the death of Cordelia is a source of profound literary criticism: it suggests that great literature and great critics interact in ways that may be beyond the theoretical terms of their historical eras. The juxtaposition of two literary theories makes clear that the conclusion of *King Lear* causes insurmountable difficulties for each theory in isolation but can be resolved by combining elements of both. This analysis suggests that, as Ralph Cohen has demonstrated, literary theory is a genre that proceeds historically by recombining elements from the past.[32] Neglect of old theories produces a paucity of new ones. Literary critics need the help not only of predecessors in their own field but also of experts in other fields. We consider next how the art of interpretation commits literary criticism to a relationship with other humanistic disciplines.

CHAPTER SIX

Imagination in *The Tempest*

Historians of ideas have long distinguished the eighteenth century from romanticism on the basis of the imagination. Indeed, the "dissociation of sensibility" separating these two ages is seen, at least in part, as a move away from distrust of the imagination during the "Age of Reason" to a new celebration of its creative potential. Johnson's attitude toward the imagination is generally thought to be contained in the title of a famous chapter of *Rasselas*, "The Dangerous Prevalence of the Imagination." I have demonstrated elsewhere that, in the context of *Rasselas*, this notion needs to be qualified.[1] Here my interest is in how Johnson's critical conception bears upon the history of the imagination, an issue that will clarify the relationship between literary criticism and the history of ideas.

Coleridge, the great romantic theoretician, formulated his position with direct reference to Johnson. Not surprisingly, this issue is most manifest in critical comments on *The Tempest*. Shakespeare's drama of the imagination pertains not only to Johnson and Coleridge but also to the transition from the eighteenth century to romanticism. An examination of Johnson's *Notes* to *The Tempest* leads to a reassessment of the current view of the relationship between Johnson and Coleridge on this issue and points to a modification of our understanding of the move from the eighteenth century to romanticism. Since the imagination cannot be contained within any single discipline, it exemplifies the necessary interrelation of the humanities. In my conclusion, I will demonstrate that critical appropriation from another discipline—

in this instance, the history of ideas—involves a mutual responsibility. The critic needs to accept his partial dependency upon the experts in other fields, and those experts should be open to modifications in their field suggested by innovative literary criticism.

CHARACTERS VERSUS EVENTS

In his lectures on *The Tempest*, Coleridge distinguishes his own view of the dramatic imagination from that of Johnson and formulates the position that prevailed throughout the nineteenth century and is now taken for granted. Johnson's position is assumed to be typical of his age. It is therefore first necessary to understand that his view constituted an innovation in his day, a departure from the tradition begun in the Restoration. In an age when character criticism was coming to the fore, Johnson based his reading of the drama upon the action or events.

From the Restoration to the middle of the eighteenth century, the only version of *The Tempest* produced on the stage was the Dryden-Davenant play entitled *The Tempest; or, The Enchanted Island.*[2] The subtitle contains the key to this work. Operatic techniques are employed to transport the audience to a fanciful island marked by outlandish events and inhabited by two young couples (the courtship of two new characters, Dorinda and Hippolito, parallels that of Miranda and Ferdinand) who fall in love at first sight, having never before seen a member of the opposite sex. The dialogue between these two sets of lovers becomes the focal point of the comic opera. For instance, upon first seeing Miranda, Ferdinand exclaims that he could love the entire race of such creatures.

Interested in the unique effects produced by the spectacle of "real" people raised in a world different from ordinary reality, Dryden believes that Caliban speaks his own kind of language. In the *Preface to the Fables*, he agrees with the view attributed to Lord Falkland, Lord C. J. Vaughn, and Mr. Selden: "*That* Shakespeare *had not only found out a new Character in his* Caliban, *but had also devis'd and adapted a new manner of language for that Character*" (*SCH* 2:197). Given the fact that throughout the Restoration and the eighteenth century language was considered by its very nature to be referential, Caliban could have acquired a new manner of language only in a new kind of world.

Defining the nature of Caliban's speech became an important issue during the first half of the eighteenth century because the language of the indigene involves the question of referentiality, the relationship between *The Tempest* and what the critics of the time called reality or nature. In 1709, Nicholas

Rowe respectfully summarized his assessment of the Dryden-Davenant version: "This Play has been alter'd by *Sir William D'Avenant* and Mr. *Dryden;* and tho' I won't Arraign the Judgment of these two great Men, yet I think I may be allow'd to say that there are some things left out by them that might, and even ought to be kept in" (*SCH* 2:197–98). Rowe recognizes that the major problem with Shakespeare's *The Tempest* is the one that preoccupies most critics of this period, the relationship between "Magic" and "Truth": "I am very sensible that he does, in this Play, depart too much from the likeness to Truth which ought to be observ'd in these sorts of Writings; yet he does it so very finely, that one is easily drawn in to have more Faith for his sake than Reason does well allow of. His Magick has something in it very Solemn and very Poetical" (*SCH* 2:197).[3]

Rowe implies that one instance of the need to have faith beyond reason concerns the language of Caliban, whose speech, as Dryden pointed out, is of a new kind. Yet in 1710, Charles Gildon objected to the Dryden-Davenant version because it was much more extravagant than the original. Gildon was one of the first to point out that Shakespeare's use of magic and sorcery must be understood in terms of the general beliefs of the Renaissance audience: "Those who make this [the use of magic and sorcery] a Fault in our Poet know little of the Matter, for it is sufficient for him to go upon received Notions, no Matter whether Philosophically, or absolutely true, or not. *Shakespeare* liv'd in an Age not so remote from a Time in which the Notion of Spirits and Conjurors and the strange and wonderful Power of Magic, but that it was almost an Article of Faith among the *Many*—I mean not the very Mob, but Men of Figure and true Learning" (*SCH* 2:229–30). Gildon argues that for Shakespeare's audience the action of *The Tempest* was credible; the drama had, in its day, a kind of verisimilitude that no one would claim for the Dryden-Davenant opera. "Our Improvers," Gildon concludes, "have never been eminent for their Imitations of Nature in the *Drama*. Mr. *Dryden* had wandred too far in *Romance* to relish Nature or know how to copy her."[4]

In 1747, Warburton took this position one step further: "These two first Plays, *The Tempest* and the *Midsummer Night's Dream*, are the noblest efforts of that sublime and amazing Imagination, peculiar to *Shakespear*, which soars above the Bounds of Nature without forsaking Sense; or, more properly, carries Nature along with him beyond her established Limits" (*W* 1:3). In his edition of *The Tempest*, Johnson reproduces this headnote without comment, indicating his agreement. But Warburton created difficulties for himself by going on to explain, in a section omitted by Johnson, that "Shakespear hath very artificially given the air of the antique to the language of *Caliban,* in order to heighten the grotesque of his character" (*W* 1:19). Although remarking that Caliban's language contains "no new phrase or diction unknown to all others," Warburton was attacked by John Holt, who saw no element of the grotesque or the antique because "there is nothing obsolete in Phrase or Idiom" in Caliban's speech. On the contrary, Holt continues, "his Stile is peculiarly adapted to his Origin," and there is nothing "absurd, capricious or unnatural in his Character." Holt therefore concludes that the "traditionary Sentiment of Lord *Faulkland,* Lord Chief Justice *Vaughn,* and Mr. *Selden,* that *Shakespeare* had given a *new* Language to this new invented Character, will hold good" (*SCH* 3:346–47). Holt believes that Caliban's language is not a grotesque or antiquated version of that used by the other characters; it is different in kind: "His Language is finely adapted nay peculiarized to his Character, as his Character to the Fable, his Sentiments to both, and his Manners to all: his Curiosity, Avidity, Brutality, Cowardice, Vindictiveness, and Cruelty exactly agreeing with his Ignorance and the Origin of his Person" (*SCH* 3:344).[5]

Holt is one of the first to resort to character criticism to defend Shakespeare, a strategy that began to become more frequent during this period. In 1751 Thomas Gray pointed to the verisimilitude in Shakespeare's dramas, even in such "absurd stories as *The Tempest*": "I do not admit that the excellencies of the French writers are measured by the verisimilitude, or the regularities of their Dramas *only.* Nothing in them or in our own, even Shakespeare himself, ever touches us unless rendered *versimile,* which by good management may be accomplished even in absurd stories as *The Tempest,* the Witches in *Macbeth,* or the Fairies in the *Midsummer Night's Dream;* and I know not of any writer that has pleased chiefly in proportion to his *regularity*" (*SCH* 3:448).[6] Although Gray does not explain how the absurd story of *The Tempest* is made verisimilar, Joseph Warton does help clarify how Shakespeare naturalizes the unfamiliar. A friend of Johnson's, Warton also wrote for the *Adventurer.* His essay on *The Tempest* appeared on 25 September 1753, a time when Johnson was also contributing to the periodical. Possibly the two conversed about their essays; in any event, Johnson was surely aware of Warton's position. Warton finds that Shakespeare's excellence involves most importantly "consistency of his characters" (*SCH* 4:61).[7] For instance, although marked by "amazing wildness of fancy," Ariel's speech and actions are always appropriate to his personality. Similarly, Caliban, seen by Warton as a monster who speaks and acts in outlandish ways, remains consistent with his personality. Caliban's catalog of various ways to kill Prospero is explained by Warton as referring to the various chores and activities that are a part of Caliban's daily life.

To summarize the critical estate of *The Tempest* from the Restoration to the middle of the eighteenth century, the Dryden-Davenant opera that provided a convenient way around the major critical dilemma of the time gradually fell out of favor. Critics could not avoid the problem of how such a fanciful play could be rendered believable, of how to place the magic island in nature. The revival of interest in Shakespeare's *The Tempest*, particularly in the language of the original version, produced a major disagreement. Most followed the Restoration tradition that Shakespeare's imagination produced something new in kind, that Caliban spoke a language of his own. This explanation, as developed by Holt and Warton, was a version of character criticism, for it claimed that Caliban's language was to be understood as appropriate to his character. Warburton did not accept this position but offered no alternative. Johnson begins his edition with a portion of Warburton's headnote, announcing his position in the debate and implying that his notes will contain an alternative to the character criticism prevalent during his day.

But before turning to the notes, we should consider the passage in the *Preface* that is frequently cited as locating Johnson in the tradition of character criticism.

> Other dramatists can only gain attention by hyperbolical or aggravated characters, by fabulous and unexampled excellence or depravity, as the writers of barbarous romances invigorated the reader by a giant and a dwarf; and he that should form his expectations of human affairs from the play, or from the tale, would be equally deceived. Shakespeare has no heroes; his scenes are occupied only by men, who act and speak as the reader thinks that he should himself have spoken or acted on the same occasion: even where the agency is supernatural the dialogue is level with life. Other writers disguise the most natural passions and most frequent incidents; so that he who contemplates them in the book will not know them in the world. Shakespeare approximates the remote, and familiarizes the wonderful; the event which he represents will not happen, but if it were possible, its effects would probably be such as he has assigned; and it may be said, that he has not only shewn human nature as it acts in real exigences [*sic*], but as it would be found in trials to which it cannot be exposed. (7:64–65).

The terminology employed here is certainly reminiscent of that used by Holt and Warton. Like most critics of his era, Johnson believed that Shakespeare often succeeded in familiarizing the unfamiliar by way of his characters. But it is seldom noted that actions are linked with characters at the beginning and middle of the paragraph—as in "act and speak" and "natural passions and most frequent incidents"—until the "event" and "acts in real exigences [*sic*]" predominate. As we shall see in chapters 7 and 8, Johnson also emphasizes action over character in *Hamlet* and *Macbeth*. My contention here is that for Johnson the great achievement of *The Tempest* resides in the familiarization of events, not characters, and that this notion distinguishes Johnson's reading of *The Tempest* from that of his contemporaries and provides grounds for a reassessment of the relationship between Johnson and Coleridge on the imagination.

REFERENTIALITY AND DELUSION

In one of his lectures on *The Tempest*, Coleridge explains how his view of the imagination is to be distinguished from that of Johnson. A "romantic drama," *The Tempest* accentuates improbability and the need for the audience to exercise its imagination. The critical issue is what Coleridge calls dramatic "delusion." With reference to the famous section of the *Preface* where Johnson asserts that the audience of a drama never forgets that it is beholding a fiction, Coleridge remarks, "In evincing the impossibility of delusion, he [Johnson] makes no sufficient allowance for an intermediate state, which we distinguish by the term illusion."[8] Chapter 7 will show that Johnson has his own sophisticated concept of dramatic delusion. At this point we need to understand that, unlike Coleridge, Johnson does not think that dramatic delusion wholly eliminates reference to what Johnson calls reality or nature.

Coleridge, on the other hand, compares the intermediate state of illusion to a dream. Most modern productions of *The Tempest* present the play in a dreamlike atmosphere, and many critics of our day take for granted the organic unity of the drama. Coleridge was probably the first commentator to characterize *The Tempest* as structured organically. Distinguishing between "mechanic and organic regularity," he explains that "in the latter there is a law which all parts obey, conforming themselves to the outward symbols and manifestations of the essential principle."[9] Conceiving of the drama in these terms entails seeing the events and characters in relation to one another, not as referring outside the dreamworld of the play.

Coleridge explains that this realm is to be distinguished from reality or a version of reality: "It is laxly said that during sleep we take our dreams for realities, but this is irreconcilable with the nature of sleep, which consists in suspension of the voluntary and, therefore, of the comparative power. The fact is that we pass no judgement either way: we simply do not judge them to be unreal, in consequence of which the images that act on our minds, as far as they act at all, by their own force as images. Our state while we are dreaming differs from that in which we are in the perusal of a deeply interesting novel in the degree rather than in the kind. . . . [In the latter case,] we *choose* to be deceived." [10] Coleridge uses the opening scene of *The Tempest* to illustrate how Shakespeare directs his audience to select the appropriate form of deception. This "busy scene" provides the "keynote to the whole harmony" of the drama. "It prepares and initiates the excitement required for the entire piece, and yet does not demand anything from the spectators, which their previous habits had not fitted them to understand." Lulled into a tempest dream, the spectators find that the real horrors of the storm have been excluded; in this respect the tempest is "poetical" because it is "restrained from concentering the interest on itself, but [is] used as an induction or tuning for what is to follow." [11]

Johnson's understanding of this scene, however, is somewhat different. Part of the headnote, already cited from Warburton, prepares for his reading: "The *Tempest* . . . soars above the Bounds of Nature without forsaking Sense: or, more properly, carries Nature along with him beyond her established Limits" (1:3). The last phrase is the most important for Johnson. Instead of perceiving an immersion into a dreamlike state, Johnson points to the manner in which natural or waking elements are appropriated and transformed by the storm. Johnson explains that this scene contains perhaps the first example of sailors' language on the stage: we are informed that "the Courses are the Mainsail and Fore-sail" (1:5; 7:117). When the ship starts to break up and Gonzalo cries, "Brother, farewell," Johnson points out that the speaker has no brother and that the line should be given to Alonso. The point here is not that Johnson is being literal-minded; he recognizes the figurative import of Gonzalo's words in this scene, remarking of the speaker that "being the only good Man . . . he . . . preserves his Cheerfulness in the Wreck, and his Hope on the Island" (1:4; 7:117). Rather, Johnson is eliminating minor inconsistencies that might prevent our seeing how "Nature" has been carried beyond its limits. But the limitations of nature are left behind only for a short time, and Johnson reminds us early on that the drama ends by returning to nature. The first entrance of Ariel occasions the longest note in this play, on magic as practiced by Prospero and Ariel. During the Renaissance, we are told, this "System of Enchantment" was widely credited, a practice disapproved of by Johnson. "This Art . . . I am afraid, was believed very seriously," but "which in reality was surely never practised," he comments, adding, "of these Trifles enough." Moreover, the note includes reference to Prospero's final abjuration of his art in strong, moral terms: "Prospero repents of his Art in the last Scene" (1:17; 7:123). In his *Dictionary*, Johnson defines repent as follows: "1) To remember with sorrow 2) to remember with pious sorrow." The previous interjections suggest the relevance of the second definition, since magic is regarded as potentially sacrilegious. But in spite of the fact that Prospero's art is responsible for almost the entire play, Johnson does not disapprove of *The Tempest*. On the contrary, the stricture gives it high praise: "In a single drama are here exhibited princes, courtiers, and sailors, all speaking in their real characters. There is the agency of airy spirits, and of an earthly goblin. The operations of magick, the tumults of a storm, the adventures of a desert island, the native effusion of untaught affection, the punishment of guilt, and the final happiness of the pair for whom our passions and reason are equally interested" (7:135).[12]

Johnson tolerates what he calls the superstitious trifles involved in Prospero's art and Ariel's practice because they serve a worthwhile goal, the love of Ferdinand and Miranda, which constitutes for him a return to "reality." Initiated by magical means, their relationship develops into natural love. Indeed, it is precisely the lack of a similar return to actuality in the two other Shakespearean romances that accounts for Johnson's unsympathetic attitude to them. *Cymbeline* is roundly condemned for "much incongruity": "To remark the folly of the fiction," Johnson concludes, "the absurdity of the conduct, the confusion of the names and manners of different times, and the impossibility of events in any system of life, were to waste criticism upon unresisting imbecillity, upon faults too evident for detection, and too gross for aggravation" (7:403; 8:908). And, *The Winter's Tale*, although entertaining, is full of "absurdities" (2:349; 7:310). Yet it should not be assumed that Johnson was unable to appreciate the entertaining element of magic and fantasy upon the stage. The final paragraph of his stricture on *Midsummer Night's Dream* is sufficient evidence against that misconception: "Of this play, wild and fantastical as it is, all the parts in their various modes are well written, and give the kind of pleasure which the authour designed. Fairies in his time were much in fashion; common tradition had made them familiar, and Spenser's poem had made them great" (7:160).

Nevertheless, I shall demonstrate that *The Tempest* is the only one of Shakespeare's "wild and fantastical" plays that Johnson believed related to the issue of the function of magic in art. The reference to "the punishment of guilt" and to "reason" suggests that for Johnson *The Tempest* raises more serious issues than the other dramas of its kind. The ensuing analysis will show that the end of this romance—the renunciation of magic and the marriage of

Ferdinand and Miranda—provides for Johnson a unique element, the source of the significance of *The Tempest*. Johnson's emphasis on Prospero's laying aside of his wand is not surprising in view of his deep religious convictions and his wariness of superstition. But the significance of the love relationship is more difficult to understand, particularly when one recalls the following section in the *Preface*.

> Upon every other stage the universal agent is love, by whose power all good and evil is distributed, and every action quickened or retarded. To bring a lover, a lady and rival into the fable; to entangle them in contradictory obligations, perplex them with oppositions of interest, and harrass them with violence of desires inconsistent with each other . . . is the business of a modern dramatist. . . . But love is only one of many passions, and as it has no real influence upon the sum of life, it has little operation in the dramas of a poet, who caught his ideas from the living world, and exhibited only what he saw before him. He knew, that any other passion, as it was regular or exorbitant, was a cause of happiness or calamity. (7:63–64)

In view of this passage, Johnson's stipulation that the happiness of the "pair" engages not only our "passions" but also our "reason" takes on new significance. The famous scene in the last act that reveals the lovers playing chess does not for Johnson represent merely the triumph of romantic love. This scene represents how the imaginative passions have reference to what Johnson calls reason, reality, or nature.

THE LIMITS OF NATURE

Johnson's attitude to Ariel in act 1 contrasts with that of Coleridge, who again founds the modern position. The former emphasizes that the bounds of nature are exceeded, while the latter focuses on the freedom beyond those limits. Coleridge clearly associates his own view of *The Tempest* with the character of Ariel: "The very first words uttered by this being introduce the spirit, not as an angel, above man; not a gnome, or a fiend, below man; but while the poet gives him the faculties and the advantages of reason, he divests him of all mortal character, not positively, it is true, but negatively. In air he lives, from air he derives his being, in air he acts; and all his colours and properties seem to have been obtained from the rainbow and the skies." [13]

Johnson saw this airy aspect of Ariel but regarded it as somewhat whimsical. Consider, for example, his remarks on Ariel's well-known song, "Full fathom five thy father lies": "*Ariel's* lays, however seasonable and efficacious, must be allowed to be of no supernatural dignity or elegance, they express nothing great, nor reveal any thing above mortal discovery" (1:25–26; 7:124). This remark relates to Warburton, who defends Ariel against Gildon's attack on this "senseless trifling" by asserting that the lyrics have the following plot function: by informing Ferdinand of his father's death, Ariel, according to Warburton, allows the young man to pursue Miranda whom he could not otherwise court without the permission of his father (1:25–27; 7:124). As will soon become clear, Johnson, like most modern editors, finds this explanation farfetched; he believes that the famous sea-change song must be understood on the figurative level as an early rendering of the theme of repentance, redemption, and rebirth. Johnson is wary because the purveyor of these sacred Christian notions is a figure derived from superstition. Johnson's attitude toward superstition was always skeptical but seldom scornful. After investigating in the highlands of Scotland the belief in "second sight," for example, he came away uncertain but willing to believe.[14] There can be no such uncertainty concerning Ariel, and one cannot escape his spiritual significance by attempting, like Warburton, to explain it in literal terms of the plot.

But Johnson, unlike his predecessors, would not disagree with Coleridge's concept of Ariel as symbolizing the creative imagination. The difference is that for the former Ariel is a means toward an end, while the latter sees him as the embodiment of the most important idea in the drama, or what Coleridge, in *Biographia Literaria*, calls the "esemplastic" power of the imagination.

In fact, in his characterization of Caliban, Coleridge employs a concept of nature in a way similar to that of Johnson: "After we have heard Caliban's voice he does not enter, until Ariel has entered like a water-nymph. All the strength of contrast is thus acquired without any of the shock of abruptness, or of that unpleasant sensation, which we experience when the object presented is in any way hateful to our vision. . . . Still, Caliban is in some respects a noble being: the poet has raised him far above contempt: he is a man in the sense of the imagination: all the images he uses are drawn from nature, and are highly poetical; they fit in with the images of Ariel."[15] Here the continuity in discontinuity between these two critics suggests something more subtle than a radical dissociation of sensibility. Coleridge recognizes that nature, as represented by Caliban, cannot be divorced from the imagination. Prospero employs both Ariel and Caliban, the one providing the material that the other, when properly supervised, imaginatively transforms. This concept continues in the tradition of Johnson's view that nature is stretched beyond its limits.

The difference reappears in the ethical dimension. Coleridge takes no moral position concerning Caliban. Johnson condemns Caliban, but not, as we might expect, for vulgarity, stupidity, and boorishness. Johnson makes his case against the "monster" for ingratitude. First, he establishes his agreement with Warburton on the question of Caliban's language.

> Whence these criticks derived the notion of a new language appropriated to *Caliban* I cannot find: They certainly mistook brutality of sentiment for uncouthness of words. *Caliban* had learned to speak of *Prospero* and his daughter, he had no names for the sun and moon before their arrival, and could not have invented a language of his own without more understanding than *Shakespear* has thought it proper to bestow upon him. His diction is indeed somewhat clouded by the gloominess of his temper and the malignity of his purposes; but let any other being entertain the same thoughts, and he will find them easily issue in the same expressions. (1:21; 7:123)

Having established that Caliban inhabits a world no different in kind from our own and is by nature brutal and uncouth, Johnson allows Warburton to explain, on the next page, the manifestation of his malignity: "The benefit which *Prospero* here upbraids *Caliban* with having bestowed, was teaching him language. He shews the greatness of this benefit by marking the inconvenience *Caliban* lay under for want of it" (1:22). Ingratitude, Caliban's sin, relates the subplot to the spiritual concerns of the main plot: repentance, forgiveness, and redemption. Caliban cannot be held responsible for his malignity in these terms unless he is located on earth, where traditional moral strictures can be applied. Indeed, Johnson's belief that *The Tempest* is to be seen in religious and ethical terms entails demonstrating how the island of the drama makes continuous reference to actuality.

Accordingly, most of Johnson's notes to the middle acts establish the terms of this reference. For instance, concerning Antonio's comment on Gonzalo's utopian commonwealth speech (2:1, 143–52)—"The latter end of his commonwealth forgets the beginning"—Johnson agrees with Warburton's remark, "All this Dialogue is a fine Satire on the *Utopian* Treatises of Government, and the impracticable inconsistent Schemes therein recommended" (1:35). Gonzalo has been inspired to his idealistic thoughts by this enchanted island as revealed to him by Ariel; the eighteenth-century reader is reminded of the factual basis for Antonio's ironical aside lest he, like Gonzalo, forget that Prospero's commonwealth is marked not only by freedom, forgiveness, and love but also by slavery, malice, and hate. Moreover, we are shown that the visitors to this charmed place bring with them psychological attitudes from their past. Urging Sebastian to join the conspiracy against Alonso, Antonio makes reference to destiny, causing Johnson to remark, "It being a common plea of wickedness to call temptation destiny" (1:39; 7:127).

In the next scene, one from the subplot, Johnson reproduces a similar note by Warburton to emphasize the serious aspect of a comic scene: "'TRIN-CULO. I afraid of him? a very shallow monster': It is to be observed that *Trinculo* the speaker is not charged with being afraid: but it was his consciousness that he was so that drew this brag from him. This is Nature" (1:47). Most modern productions encourage the audience to applaud Ariel for ingeniously bringing together these grotesque figures for our amusement. We are thus distanced from and, to some extent, distracted from Trinculo's cowardice. But Johnson's characteristic attitude toward Shakespeare's romances is to bring his reader down from the clouds to mundane, often unpleasant, earthly concerns. In *The Winter's Tale*, Leontes' sudden and unexpected change of heart articulated in his confession (3.2.154–72) is not seen as in any sense miraculous: "This vehement retraction of *Leontes*, accompanied with the confession of more crimes than he was suspected of, is agreeable to our daily experience of the vicissitudes of violent tempers, and the eruptions of minds oppressed with guilt" (2:280; 7:298). Similarly, a scene in *Cymbeline* that often defies credibility is naturalized. At the climactic moment in act 4, with the well-known stage direction "Enter Guiderius (with Cloten's head)," Johnson remarks on Belarius's discovery of the disguised Cloten's voice:

> BELARIUS. the snatches in his voice.
>   And burst of speaking, were as his:
>
> This is one of our authour's strokes of observation. An abrupt and tumultuous utterance very frequently accompanies a confused and cloudy understanding. (7:349; 8:897)

Such observations in the context of *Cymbeline* and *The Winter's Tale* are of little critical interest. In *The Tempest*, however, I believe that they lead Johnson to an important and innovative interpretation. His high estimate of *The Tempest* helps him locate an important insight concerning the spiritual element in earthly love.

REASON AND PASSION

In the last two acts, Johnson spiritualizes Warburton's moral view, thus pointing to a religious dimension in *The Tempest*. After the presentation of the masque to Ferdinand and Miranda, Prospero suddenly remembers the plot of

Caliban and announces that he is "vext." Johnson cites Warburton's question about why Prospero would be vexed by "the Plot of a contemptible *Savage* and two drunken Sailors, all of whom he had absolutely in his power" and explains that the answer is the "*Sense of Ingratitude.*" "But these reflections on *Caliban's* Ingratitude would naturally recal to mind his brother's: And then these two working together were very capable of producing all the disorder of passion here represented" (1:68). In order to understand the difference between Warburton and Johnson, one must be aware of another Warburton note to this same speech, which Johnson omitted. Troubled by the phrase "baseless Fabric of this vision," Warburton altered it to "baseless Fabric of th'air-visions," explaining at great length that Prospero alludes only to the masque and its stage accoutrements, not to the remainder of the play *The Tempest* (*W* 1:67–69). Johnson omits this comment, leading us to assume what most spectators, readers, and editors have assumed, then and now: that Prospero's remarks refer to the entire drama. The "*Sense of Ingratitude,*" which for Warburton linked the subplot to the masque, is applied by Johnson to the entire play.

Johnson can now go on to clarify how ingratitude in the subplot is related to repentance and forgiveness in the main plot. The resolution of *The Tempest*, the love of Ferdinand and Miranda, engages both our "passions" and our "reason" because it has a moral and religious dimension, which, in Johnson's text, begins to emerge more clearly in preparation for the chess scene. For instance, when Prospero informs Ariel that they must now "prepare to meet with Caliban," Johnson illustrates the meaning of "meet" with a quotation from Herbert's *Country Parson: "The Parson knows the temper of every one in his house, and accordingly either meets with their vices, or advances their virtues"* (1:68; 7:132). Ferdinand and Miranda are here witnesses to Prospero's linking the sin of Caliban to that of Antonio and Sebastian. In outwitting both sets of plotters, Prospero promises to explain his means of dealing with the worst of these schemers, a promise paraphrased by Johnson in terms that reinforce the moral dimension: "I will resolve you by yourself, which method, when you hear the story, (of *Anthonio's* and *Sebastian's* plot) *shall seem probable,* that is, *shall deserve your approbation*" (1:82; 7:134). On the page opposite to this note, moral disapprobation is again highlighted by the explanation of the term "true," which, significantly, is in reference to Caliban's plot: "That is, *honest. A true man* is, in the language of that time, opposed to a Thief" (1:83; 7:134). We are to approve of Prospero's gulling and outmaneuvering of the various plotters, from Trinculo to Sebastian, because Johnson believes that his goal is to reform the criminal, to redeem the best in man.

But since the means to this end is, for Johnson, questionable because it involves usurping the part of God, or, in the terms of Shakespeare's day, practicing the black arts, we are being prepared for the replacement of Prospero's magic by Miranda and Ferdinand's spiritual love. Johnson therefore has no difficulty with Prospero's final abjuration of his art and makes use of a note of Warburton's to emphasize the danger of black magic. In the epilogue, Prospero's request for our prayer is explained by Warburton: "This alludes to the old Stories told of the despair of Necromancers in their last moments; and of the efficacy of the prayers of their friends for them" (*W* 1:89). Again, the difference between Warburton and Johnson involves the strategy of omission. In his edition, Warburton comments on Prospero's speech and distinguishes the magical charms used by Prospero from those resorted to by Ariel. Warburton believes that Ariel's brief moments of necromancy are instances of license not sanctioned by his master. In omitting this note, Johnson encourages us to assume, as most of us still do, that Prospero is responsible for the actions of Ariel. In the chess scene, Johnson distinguishes between questionable means and good ends.

> MIRANDA. Sweet lord, you play me false.
> FERDINAND. No, my dear love, I would not for the world.
> MIRANDA. Yes, for a score of kingdoms. You should wrangle, And I would call it fair play.

> I take the sense to be only this: *Ferdinand* would not, he says, play her false for the *world;* yes, answers she, I would allow you to do it for something less than the world, for *twenty kingdoms,* and I wish you well enough to allow you, after a little *wrangle,* that your play was fair. So likewise Dr. *Gray.* (1:79; 7:134).

For modern editors, this passage presents problems because, as the Arden editor explains, "the general idea is obvious enough, but the passage is not easy to understand in detail." Specifically, the difficulty is that in this scene of "high-born and romantic love" the above conversation would be clear "if only *wrangle* could mean 'play unfairly, cheat.'" The Oxford editor who, on the other hand, accepts this definition of the term recognizes that he is in the minority: "Miranda in this exchange (most commentators to the contrary notwithstanding) is certainly accusing Ferdinand of cheating, and is declaring her perfect complicity in the act."[16] Johnson, however, has no difficulty with the ordinary meaning of "wrangle": under its definition in the *Dictionary,* "to dispute peevishly; to quarrel perversely; to altercate; to squabble," the above passage from *The Tempest* is cited as an illustration. Johnson is able to admit this reference to perverse squabbling that, for moderns, breaks the illusion of highborn and romantic love because he sees both reason and passion operating in this final scene. Miranda's prediction of what she would do out of love for Ferdinand is at once a manifestation of passion and a rational reflection on her passion, a commitment to the irrational element of love and an understanding of the perversity of lovers. What Johnson isolates in this passage is that in giving herself to the realm of passionate and peevish love, Miranda does so knowingly.

It seems to me that Johnson valued this love scene above all others in Shakespearean romance because reason and passion have application to the readers of or spectators at *The Tempest.* We tolerate Prospero's magic, knowing it is not always fair play, because we trust that the questionable means will be justified by the goal of human redemption. The audience of *The Tempest* is not willingly deluded but consciously permissive of the trifling of magic, both black and white, because we anticipate its final replacement.

It now becomes clear that in his view of *The Tempest,* Johnson is closer to Coleridge than to Warburton. Unlike Warburton, who separates Ariel's flights of fancy from Prospero's art and the love of Ferdinand and Miranda, Coleridge and Johnson recognize that all three are functions of the human imagination and are intertwined in the dramatic unfolding of *The Tempest.* And now the difference between Johnson and Coleridge can be reformulated: the sacrilegious possibility inherent in the creative imagination that worries Johnson is not a problem for Coleridge—at least, not until later in his career, well after he had formulated his concept of the imagination.[17]

Johnson's attitude toward the magic of *The Tempest* is aptly illustrated by his use of Warburton's next-to-last comment on the play. Alonso asks about the liquid source of Trinculo's "reeling": "Where should they Find this grand liquor that hath gilded them." Warburton points out that "grand liquor" and "gilded" are alchemical terms being used humorously: "The joke here is to insinuate that, notwithstanding all the boasts of the Chymists, Sack was the only restorer of youth, and bestower of immortality" (1:84). But Warburton does not explain how the magic which throughout the body of the play was taken seriously by the main characters and served important dramatic purposes is now relegated to the superstitions of the low characters. Johnson demonstrates that in its conclusion *The Tempest* can treat such matters ironically because it has reference to a higher level where magic is seen as a means of disposing of magic. Prospero, we have been informed since the first act of Johnson's edition, "repents of his Art in the last scene."

Repentance involves the breaking of the magic wand and the recognition that the "fabric" of this vision was "baseless." Hence Johnson sees Caliban's language not as a new creation but as a part of that temporary vision. The "mooncalf" cannot speak a separate language because that element of the vision might persist after the dissolving of this "insubstantial pageant." Similarly, character criticism is avoided by Johnson so that the cast of characters serves as part of the fabric of the vision but does not have an independent existence. The people of the play are seen as subordinate to the last "event," Prospero's abjuration of magic and presentation of the lovers at the chess board.

For Johnson, *The Tempest* is to be distinguished from the other Shakespearean romances and other fanciful plays, such as *Midsummer Night's Dream*, in that it concludes by reflecting upon the limitations of the conventions of romance and fantasy. Reasoning on her passion, Miranda internalizes Prospero's magic, the play itself. In this respect, we should keep in mind that Johnson, at the beginning of the play, cited a comment that placed *The Tempest* in the genre of Milton's *Comus* (1:3).

CRITICISM AND THE HISTORY OF IDEAS

In the end, Johnson comes to isolate the same element of the imagination that interests Coleridge; the difference between them is a matter of perspective. Johnson stresses the limitations of the creative imagination that unbridled could trespass on religion; Coleridge emphasizes how the creative imagination frees man from the bonds of nature. The former sees the matter from the perspective of Miranda; the latter, from that of Ariel.

However, the belief that a radical dichotomy exists between Johnson and Coleridge persists among historians of ideas. Most recently, a scholar studying the history of the imagination has asserted that Johnson's attitude toward the imagination is generally negative: "Though Johnson conceives the omnipresence and power of the imagination as vividly as the high Romantics forty years later, he differs from them in being much less able to trust the imagination. He does not see it, by itself, as 'constructive' in a healthful and optimistic sense." [18] On the other hand, Coleridge, we are informed, sees the imagination as central to all forms of art and, for most of his career, views the power of the imagination in positive terms as "the highest, ineffable truths as they animate the mind." [19] Given the persistence of this polarity, it is not surprising that modern critics of *The Tempest* turn to Coleridge, not Johnson.

It should now be clear, however, that in his notes to *The Tempest* Johnson is keenly aware of the artistic function of the imagination, which is viewed, not in predominantly negative terms, but as possessing a capacity for good as well as evil. The problem is compounded by Coleridge's assertion that Johnson lacks any concept of artistic illusion. Before demonstrating, in chapter 8, that Coleridge is mistaken in this regard, I should stress that Johnson is the first to understand the function of the creative imagination in *The Tempest*. In this sense Coleridge's position is a continuation of Johnson's. But that discovery need not obscure the difference between them; Coleridge soars above with Ariel, and Johnson insists that we, like Miranda, keep our feet firmly planted on earth. This reassessment of the history of the idea of the imagination can, however, assist our understanding of the conclusion of *The Tempest* and of the transition of this idea from the eighteenth century to romanticism.

Although Coleridge's notion of the play as a sort of dream is widely accepted, modern critics of *The Tempest* are divided along lines suggestive of the difference between Coleridge and Johnson: some emphasize the freedom of the dream vision, while others focus upon its ultimate limitations. The difficulties concern the conclusion, Prospero's abjuration of magic and the chess scene. A number of critics argue that this abrupt end serves to fix the limitations of art, to demarcate literary structure. But then the question becomes, How can a dream set the limits of a dream?[20] Others suggest that it is the awakening from the dream that functions to place the dream in the waking world of reality. But then we are left to wonder, How can a dreamworld place itself in the waking world? We have seen in chapter 5, where a similar question arose, that these problems cannot be resolved by mimetic or formalist methods in isolation from one another.

Again, I propose a combination of both, only here the solution will point beyond the concerns of literary theory. If we recognize that Coleridge's concept of the dream is only one aspect of the creative imagination, a polemical position taken in opposition to a "neoclassical" stereotype, we can accommodate both the Coleridgean and the Johnsonian aspects of the imagination in *The Tempest*. The play's conclusion can then suggest that the power of the creative imagination resides in the ability of art to call attention to its own limitations. Prospero, circling his own magic, inscribes himself in the circle; in breaking his wand, refusing to commit sacrilege, the artist soars above nature in order to refer us back to it. But whether or not one accepts this reading of *The Tempest*, my point is that Johnson does not merely distrust the imagination as irrational and that the terms of the transition from the eighteenth century to romanticism—reason versus the imagination—may need to be modified. Here I defer to the historian of ideas, who is better able to assess whether Johnson's innovation is an anomaly or symptomatic of his age.

In referring the imagination back to nature, Johnson reminds us that literature is related to topics that pertain to other humanistic disciplines. In particular, the literary critic helps sensitize the historian of ideas to the literary anomaly, and the historian aids the critic in understanding how the innovative idea fits into the larger picture. My conclusion is that literary criticism can only come into its own as a discipline by joining with other humanistic endeavors to understand man's place in the cosmos. Our innovations can be successfully expropriated to other fields only if we accept our need for the expertise of other disciplines. The commitment to this joint effort involves special new problems. If literature refers us to the extraliterary not by imitative but by interpretive means, then we must consider what constitutes the object of interpretation and where the literary work begins and ends, two questions that hermeneutics teaches us are a function of one another. The next chapter, therefore, analyzes closure, or the decision about what constitutes a significant conclusion.

CHAPTER SEVEN

Evaluation of Closure in *Hamlet*

One of the "qualities that constitutes genius," judgment is defined by Johnson as that "which selects from life or nature what the present purpose requires, and, by separating the essence of things from its concomitants, often makes the representation more powerful than the reality" (*Lives* 3:247). The ability to isolate from Shakespearean drama what the present purpose requires is the mark of the evaluative aspect of Johnson's criticism.[1] But because it is couched in moral terminology, especially in the strictures, these statements are largely ignored by modern critics. In fact, these judgments constitute an assessment of Shakespeare's artistic goal. Here Johnson manifests in practice an important principle for criticism: literary interpretation involves an evaluation of the aim of the work of art. Recognizing that evaluation is involved in decisions about critical teleology advances our understanding of the problem of *Hamlet*. My contention is that we must follow the example of Johnson and make our interpretive value judgments explicit so that they too can be subject to critical analysis. Specifically, in *Hamlet* humor provides the foundation for a decision about the critical goal.

Since T. S. Eliot, in 1919, declared that *Hamlet* was "an artistic failure" because it lacked an "objective correlative" for the prince's emotions, most moderns have attempted to demonstrate that Hamlet's problems are in fact resolved in *Hamlet*.[2] Present-day editors, accordingly, suggest various ways in which the problems, questions, and issues raised in the prince's soliloquies are resolved by the conclusion of the play. Indeed, the project of modern critical editions of *Hamlet* is to find formalist or postformalist kinds of closure. Samuel Johnson, on the other hand, declares that *Hamlet* is a success in spite of its structural flaws. Closure in *Hamlet* is, in Johnson's view, achieved by accretive satire, not by formal means. Specifically, the comedy of the grave-yard scene (act 5, scene 1) resolves more issues of *Hamlet* than does the end of the play. But Johnson's alternative kind of closure has been ignored because modern criticism values only totalizing kinds of closure. Since this tacit judgment has impeded understanding of the alternative approach to *Hamlet* inherent in Johnson's *Notes*, we need to isolate and scrutinize the evaluative element of literary criticism.

THE VIRTUE OF AN INCONVENIENCE

For Johnson, the problem of *Hamlet*—the difficulty of locating the overall principle of the play—constitutes its achievement. In his stricture, Johnson declares that the "particular excellence" of *Hamlet* is its "variety."

> The scenes are interchangeably diversified with merriment and solemnity; with merriment that includes judicious and instructive observations, and solemnity, not strained by poetical violence above the natural sentiments of man. New characters appear from time to time in continual succession, exhibiting various forms of life and particular modes of conversation. The pretended madness of *Hamlet* causes much mirth, the mournful distraction of *Ophelia* fills the heart with tenderness, and every personage produces the effect intended, from the apparition that in the first act chills the blood with horrour, to the fop in the last, that exposes affectation to just contempt (8:311; 8:1011).

Hamlet is applauded for its range of characters, ideas, and sorts of audience reactions. Why do these features constitute "excellence"? For Johnson variety is a literary value, but precisely what he means by this term can be clarified only by examining his notes to the drama.

Before turning to the notes, we should complete our summary of the stricture. The "conduct" or action of the play is seen by Johnson as flawed in four respects: (1) Hamlet's "feigned madness" lacks "adequate cause," "for he does nothing which he might not have done with the reputation of sanity"; (2) Hamlet is not the agent but the instrument in the death of Claudius; (3) the exchange of rapiers in act 5 is not very "happily produced," since a "scheme" might have been devised for killing "Hamlet with the dagger, and Laertes with the bowl"; (4) Shakespeare has neglected "poetic probability" because the ghost appears to little purpose: "The revenge which he demands is not obtained but by the death of him that was required to take it; and the gratification which would arise from the destruction of an usurper and a murderer, is abated by the untimely death of *Ophelia,* the young, the beautiful, the harmless, and the pious." Johnson thus concludes his remarks on *Hamlet.* This summary indicates that for Johnson the structure of the tragedy is too defective and incomplete to resolve the difficulties. At the same time, it is precisely this range of materials and issues that is the source of variety.

HISTORY VERSUS PSYCHOLOGY

Because modern criticism on and editions of *Hamlet* are so numerous, I shall restrict myself to commentary on the great soliloquies and to four present-day editions that contain copious notes and are readily available. As we shall see, Johnson distinguishes himself from his own contemporaries as well as ours by giving more emphasis to the graveyard scene than to the last scene of the drama. While moderns search for a psychological principle at the end of the tragedy, Johnson finds an ironical resolution for Hamlet's situation in the graveyard scene. However, this kind of resolution is of little interest to the moderns because it does not help to explain the end of the play.

Indicating that Hamlet's remarks are often double-edged, Johnson's comments on the first soliloquy differ from Warburton's. Believing that the final phrase of the prince's reply to Claudius—"A little more than kin and less than kind"—is incomprehensible, Warburton offers an emendation. Johnson, however, explains the original words: "*Kind* is the Teutonick word for *Child. Hamlet* therefore answers with propriety, to the titles of *cousin* and *son,* which the King had given him, that he was somewhat more than *Cousin,* and less than *son*" (8:141; 8:961). Taking "kind" as a term related to kindliness, Warburton sees no occasion for a reflection on kindness; Johnson finds that the prince is playing upon the term "kind" with reference to the marriage to Gertrude. Modern editors agree with Johnson, as they do with his explanation of Hamlet's other cryptic remark prior to this first soliloquy. In reply to the king's question "How is it that the clouds still hang on you?" (1.2.66), Hamlet explains, "Not so, my lord, I am too much in the sun." Warburton has no note here; Johnson explains that the prince "perhaps alludes to the proverb, *Out of heaven's blessing into the warm sun*" (8:141; 8:962).

While accepting Johnson's explanation, modern editors disagree with his estimate of Hamlet's frame of mind. For example, the editor of the new Arden *Hamlet* (1982) accepts the above explanation but adds the following: "The obvious meaning of the metaphor (in the sun) is that Hamlet, with the mel-

ancholiac's characteristic preference for the shade, objects to the brightness
into which he is brought."[3] The mention of the prince's melancholy at this
early point in the play makes plain that the term is used to denote, not a response to outward circumstances, but a personality trait, a predisposition.
The nature of the difference here is crucial, a critical crossroad. Johnson
leaves the reader to infer that the prince's attitude is in response to his situation; the modern editor sees Hamlet as revealing a constant of his personality,
the tendency to see the dark side of life. The matter is complicated because
no one can deny that Hamlet is, at times, melancholy, since he himself refers
to "my melancholy" at the end of act 2. The question is whether the melancholy, when not feigned, is due to the outward circumstances, the state of
Denmark, or to the inner man, the personality of the prince.

Our four modern editors believe that Hamlet is predisposed to melancholy.
This so-called romantic view of Hamlet, which was most probably begun
in 1771 by George Steevens,[4] continues to dominate in our day, as is made
plain by the present status of the famous textual crux in the first line of the
soliloquy: "O that this too too solid/sullied flesh would melt" (1.2.129). Like
his predecessors, Johnson followed the folio in printing "solid." John Dover
Wilson was the first to establish textual authority for "sullied," a conjecture
from the nineteenth century. Arguing that "sullied" was a variant spelling of
"sallied" in Q 2, he explains that " 'sullied flesh' is the key to the soliloquy
and tells us that Ham. is thinking of the kindless incestuous marriage as a
personal defilement." Dover Wilson goes on to point out that "Ham. obviously has in mind here . . . snow, symbolical of the nature he shares with
his mother, once pure but now befouled."[5] Hamlet's sense of personal defilement, his feeling sullied by his mother's crime of incest, is the sort of response to be expected of one predisposed toward melancholy. Harold Jenkins
follows Dover Wilson in asserting that "sullied" gives at once the clue to the
emotion which the soliloquy will express . . . the suggestion of contamination
and self-disgust."[6] Similarly, T. J. B. Spencer asserts, " 'Sullied' fits well
into the feeling of contamination expressed by Hamlet," and he adds, "The
importance of this soliloquy lies in its establishing Hamlet's personality and
revealing his mental condition."[7] Only the Kittredge and Ribner text prints
"solid," but the editors feel obliged to remark that "critics who favour 'sullied' or 'sallied' argue that it is to the impurity of his flesh rather than its
solidity that Hamlet is referring."[8]

Johnson differs from our contemporaries in emphasizing the outward
situation rather than the personal predisposition of the speaker, a fact made
plain in two other notes to this speech. When Hamlet compares his father

to Hyperion and Claudius to a satyr, Johnson reproduces Warburton's comment: "This similitude at first sight seems to be a little far-fetch'd; but it has an exquisite beauty. By the *Satyr* is meant *Pan*, as by *Hyperion, Apollo. Pan* and *Apollo* were brothers, and the allusion is to the contention between those two Gods for the preference in musick" (8:144–45). While the moderns explain that Hyperion was the sun-god and the satyr was half-human, half-beast, Johnson employs Warburton's note to remind us of the mythological contest between Pan and Apollo. It will be recalled that all of the Muses voted for Apollo and that Midas, who alone sided with Pan, was rewarded with the ears of an ass. Johnson emphasizes that Hamlet's point is that only an ass could fail to see the difference between his father and Claudius.

Johnson reinforces this point by disagreeing with Warburton's assessment of the phrase "discourse of reason." Warburton finds that "this is finely expressed, and with a philosophical exactness," but Johnson explains it in more mundane terms: "*Discourse of reason*, as the *logicians* name the third operation of the mind, is indeed a philosophical term, but it is *fine* no other wise than as it is proper; it cost the authour nothing, being the common language of his time. Of finding such beauties in any poet there is no end" (8:145; 8:963). Johnson expresses impatience here because the prince's point is that mourning for the king, like seeing the difference between him and Claudius, requires simple reason, not "philosophical exactness." The terms of Warburton's compliment detract from the flagrancy of the queen's sin. For Johnson, this first soliloquy is concerned less with Hamlet's personality than with Denmark, a state so "rotten" that, as we shall see, its dilemmas can be resolved only in the graveyard.

POLONIUS AND THE DANISH COURT

Since Johnson makes no comment on the next soliloquy, we can move on to act 2, where it becomes clear that, although Johnson regards Hamlet's context as most important, he does not neglect Hamlet's character. In fact, Johnson prepares his reader for the soliloquy in act 2 which begins, "O what a rogue and peasant slave am I," by suggesting how Polonius, Rosencrantz, and Guildenstern serve as foils to Hamlet. For instance, Polonius's lecture to the king and queen about Hamlet occasions Johnson's use of Warburton's remarks to the effect that Polonius's "declamation" represents a "satire on the impertinent oratory then in vogue, which placed reason in the formality of method, and wit in the gingle and play of words" (8:181; 8:973). Attempting to account for how Polonius can speak "excellent *precepts*" while being the subject of "ridicule," Warburton explains that Polonius's manner of presentation is meant to be halting so that the audience will realize that his words were "got by heart" but not fully understood by the speaker. Not satisfied with this explanation, which "makes the character of *Polonius*, a character only of manners, discriminated by properties superficial, accidental, and acquired," Johnson sees him as a combination "of manners and of nature." "Polonius," Johnson continues, "is a man bred in court, exercised in business, stored with observations, confident of his knowledge, proud of his eloquence, and declining into dotage" (8:182–83; 8:974). The ridicule concerns, not Polonius's manner of speaking, but his inappropriate application of the general principles. "This idea," Johnson concludes, "of dotage encroaching upon wisdom, will solve all the phaenomena of the character of *Polonius*" (8:183; 8:974).

Instead of supporting Warburton's speculations about the lord chamberlain's misunderstanding of what he has read, Johnson suggests that Polonius fully understands his laudable precepts but misapplies them. Approaching dotage, this well-meaning adviser is unable to see the most important function of his own advice in specific situations. Few modern editors, however, distinguish between the matter and manner of Polonius's speeches. For instance, Jenkins reprints Johnson's criticism of Polonius's "mode of oratory" but neglects to include the passage from the same note praising the content of these orations. Refusing to dismiss Polonius as merely a pompous courtier, Johnson dwells on a passage in which Polonius questions his own judgment, a moment not accounted for by moderns.

POLONIUS. That hath made him mad.
  I'm sorry that with better speed and judgment
  I had not quoted him. I fear'd he trifled
  And meant to wreck thee; but beshrew my jealousy;
  It seems, it is as proper to our age
  To cast beyond ourselves in our opinions,
  As it is common for the younger sort
  To lack discretion. Come, go we to the King.
  This must be known, which, being kept close, might move
  More grief to hide, than hate to utter, love.
                  (8:177–78)

Although Warburton and the modern editors pass over this passage with brief glosses on a few obscure words, Johnson calls our attention to Polonius's intelligence: "This is not the remark of a weak man. The vice of age is too much suspicion. Men long accustomed to the wiles of life *cast* commonly *beyond themselves*, let their cunning go further than reason can attend it. This is always the fault of a little mind, made artful by long commerce with the world" (8:177; 8:973). Typically evenhanded with Polonius, Johnson implies that although Polonius is probably not fully aware of the applicability of this speech to himself, the thought did originate with him. Similarly, Johnson gives some credence to Polonius's criticism of Hamlet's letter to Ophelia. In Hamlet's exhortation "to the celestial, and my soul's idol, the most beautified Ophelia," Polonius objects to the word "beautified." Warburton, following Theobald, emended "beautified" to "beatified," asserting, with reference to the latter, that Polonius "as a *Roman* Catholick, [might] call it a *vile* phrase, i.e. savouring of profanation" (8:184). But Johnson finds this emendation unnecessary: "Both Sir *T. Hanmer* and Dr. *Warburton* have followed *Theobald*, but I am in doubt whether *beautified*, though, as *Polonius* calls it, a *vile phrase*, be not the proper word. *Beautified* seems to be a *vile phrase*, for the ambiguity of its meaning" (8:184; 8:974).

Modern editors reject Theobald's emendation, but they justify their decision in terms that give less credit to Polonius. Dover Wilson explains that "the jest is that Pol. who himself uses such far-fetched vocabulary should boggle at an innocent word."[9] And Spencer believes that "presumably Polonius objects to the word as being a past participle of the verb 'to beautify' and therefore an incorrect usage for 'beautiful.' "[10] Johnson, however, suggests that Polonius is right about the vileness of the term but unaware that its ambiguity reflects on the affectation that he has encouraged in his daughter. Johnson's attitude to Polonius, as we shall see shortly, is related to his reading of the next soliloquy, which involves distinguishing Hamlet's attitude toward Polonius from his attitude toward Rosencrantz and Guildenstern. The older courtier assumes that others, like himself, are what they appear to be: the younger men fail to realize that what they suspect of Hamlet he may suspect of them.

But before turning to this scene, we should recognize that Johnson was aware of the limitations of Polonius. When the latter offers his "declension" of Hamlet's state of mind—"a short tale to make, fell to a sadness, then into a fast"—Johnson cites Warburton's note without comment: "The ridicule of this character is here admirably sustained. He would not only be thought to have discovered this intrigue by his own sagacity, but to have remarked all the stages of *Hamlet's* disorder, from his sadness to raving, as regularly as his physician could have done; when all the while the madness was only feigned. The humour of this is exquisite from a man who tells us, with a confidence peculiar to small politicians, that he could find *where truth was hid, though it were hid indeed within the centre*" (8:186). Polonius is the butt of the satire because Johnson, like the other editors of his age, assumed that Hamlet's madness is always feigned. This speech is a satirical instance of "dotage encroaching upon Wisdom," for the aged counselor, in applying accurate and learned descriptions of dementia, remains totally unaware that the patient is feigning the role of the "classic case." Like the "players" who are introduced in this act and with whom he feels a natural kinship, the young prince is able to anticipate what role is expected of him and assume it. Refining our view of Polonius, Johnson helps us understand Hamlet's situation, for this courtier typifies, in many respects, the Danish court, the setting for the tragedy.

HAMLET AND THE COURTIERS

Johnson uses Warburton's comment to make plain that it is important to keep in mind Hamlet's capacity for role-playing, especially in the scene with Rosencrantz and Guildenstern where the prince explains that he has "lost all [my] mirth": "This is an admirable description of a rooted melancholy sprung from thickness of blood, and artfully imagined to hide the true cause of his disorder from the penetration of these two friends, who were set over him as spies[.] Warburton" (8:193). Modern editors are less certain that Hamlet is feigning madness here; they cite Elizabethan sources on melancholy—especially Timothy Bright's *Treatise of Melancholy*—to suggest that the melancholiac may waver between real and assumed madness. Johnson, on the other hand, believes that Hamlet remains in control of the situation, outmaneuvering Rosencrantz and Guildenstern.

> ROSENCRANTZ. Truly, and I hold ambition of so airy and light a quality, that it is but a shadow's shadow.
> HAMLET. Then are our beggars, bodies; and our monarchs and outstretch'd heroes, the beggar's shadows.
>
> *Shakespeare* seems here to design a ridicule of these declamations against wealth and greatness, that seem to make happiness consist in poverty. (8:192; 8:975)

Not only does Rosencrantz, according to Johnson, misapply his advice, in a way reminiscent of Polonius, but he also willfully deceives his friend. Rosencrantz and Guildenstern are spies that offer glib, misleading advice. Unlike Polonius, they are able to feign a role, but the prince immediately sees through them. As foil figures, they further refine the distinction already apparent with Polonius. Hamlet differs from the older courtier in his ability to discern what role is expected of him and to adapt himself to that mask; he differs from the younger courtiers in being aware that others may be capable of and wary of such a practice. Johnson brings his reader to see that by the end of act 2 we have evidence that the tragic protagonist is a very acute analyst of people, able to understand the different personality types at the Danish court. In place of the Johnsonian Hamlet in complete control of himself, skillfully manipulating those around him, the modern Hamlet is at times deranged, having lost control of the situation.

Not surprisingly, the result is two different editorial views of the speech beginning, "O what a rogue and peasant slave am I." Johnson's Hamlet progresses inexorably from meditative outrage to a clear plan of action. The modern editors' Hamlet wavers between self-disgust and a project for overcoming his inertia. Reinforcing the active element of Hamlet, Johnson repeatedly replaces Warburton's passive terminology with words of action. When Warburton renders the prince's phrase "unpregnant of my cause" as "having not due sense of," Johnson declares, "rather, *not quickened with a new desire of vengeance; not seeming with revenge.*" And Warburton's explanation of "defeat," in the phrase "a damn'd defeat was made," "destruction," is modified to "dispossession," making the action more specific (8:203; 8:979).

The modern editors, as we would expect, show little interest in these references to action; indeed, Jenkins remarks of Hamlet's "Oh vengeance" that this phrase "has all the marks of an actor's addition." Instead, they focus upon the instances of the prince's psychological state. "The devil," Jenkins explains, "not only exploits but is able to intensify the melancholy which predisposes Hamlet to be deluded," and the "spirits" are seen as "the vapours out of which melancholy is engendered." [11] Similarly, at Hamlet's mention of his "weakness" and "melancholy," Dover Wilson points out that these terms are "an important testimony to Ham.'s true state of mind." [12] Spencer explains the same passage: "According to Elizabethan physiology, persons suffering from an excess of black bile (*melancholy*) were prone to exercising strong imaginations, and were therefore subject to mental instability and hallucinations. So they were an easy prey to the devil." [13]

At this point Johnson makes no comment on melancholy, presumably because he feels that the circumstances of the play are sufficient to explain the attitude of the protagonist. We begin to see that each position has its advantages and disadvantages. Johnson is able to explain in a straightforward manner the idea of the mousetrap that arises at the end of the speech. Seeking evidence that the ghost is telling the truth and having himself already employed role-playing with Polonius, Hamlet understandably devises a dramatic kind of test. But why does this active prince, after confirming Claudius's guilt, delay taking his revenge? The modern editors can explain the delay but not an action such as the mousetrap. Their position is designed to clarify the prince's psychological state. Johnson, on the other hand, focuses on what Hamlet plans to do to resolve the issues raised by his soliloquies.

CRITICAL ACCRETION

Despite all the difficulties and differences about the organizing principle of the drama, Johnson and one modern editor agree about the purport of the most famous soliloquy in the play. Act 3 brings us almost immediately to the "to be or not to be" speech, which Jenkins believes to be the most frequently discussed passage in all of Shakespeare. Johnson explains the reason for the speech: "*Hamlet*, knowing himself injured in the enormous and atrocious degree, and seeing no means of redress, but such as must expose him to the extremity of hazard, meditates on his situation" (8:207; 8:981). Instead of stressing the external injuries of the prince, modern editors focus on his state of mind. Ribner asserts, "Hamlet is thinking of suicide."[14] Spencer agrees, as does Dover Wilson, who points out, "Johnson, Dowden and others contend that Ham. is meditating upon his task, the fulfilment of which will prob. involve his own death; but I think ll. 75–6 rule this out, and show that he is thinking of suicide."[15] Jenkins, while not sharing the view that the soliloquy is about suicide, nevertheless agrees that Hamlet is severely dejected. Hamlet's predicament, he concludes, is that of one who sees through the spectacles of melancholy, not, as in Johnson, of one who is melancholy because of how he has been treated by his family and friends.[16]

Surprisingly, Jenkins's and Johnson's paraphrases of the content of this speech are strikingly similar: this agreement indicates some consensus on the development of ideas in the body of the play despite differences concerning the personality of the protagonist and the conclusion of the tragedy. Johnson explains the famous opening phrase: "*Before I can form any rational scheme of action under this pressure of distress*, it is necessary to decide, whether, *after our present state, we are* to be or not to be" (8:207; 8:981). Jenkins concurs, because "we come to the end of life's 'troubles' not when we put an end to them but when they put an end to us." Suicide, he continues, is introduced only as a rhetorical question which is then "dismissed." Moreover, the question is decided in terms larger than those of this existence: "The alternative we choose is 'to be,' 'to suffer,' 'to bear' because of our fear of the 'afterlife.'"[17] This paraphrase is reminiscent of Johnson: the "question," Johnson explains, is whether "*tis nobler . . . to suffer the outrages of fortune* patiently, or to take arms

against them and by opposing end them, *though perhaps* with the loss of life."
For both editors, the question is not whether to commit suicide but whether
to risk opposition that may result in death. Johnson, like Jenkins, notes that
we bear the vexations of life because of fear of "unknown futurity" that gives
"efficacy to conscience."

In spite of this congruence, Jenkins takes issue with Johnson, objecting to
the phrase "before I can form any rational scheme of action." Hamlet is not
contemplating a scheme of action, Jenkins retorts; he is debating a question,
"whether, in the light of what *being* comprises, it is preferable to have it or
not." [18] But, as we have already noted, Johnson would not disagree with this
statement. Put off by the phrase "rational scheme of action," Jenkins neglects
to notice that the operative term in Johnson's sentence is the word "before,"
which indicates that the speech is perceived, not as a rational scheme of
action, but as the meditation that precedes such a scheme. This pseudodiffer-
ence between Jenkins and Johnson is an important indicator of the power of
this great soliloquy. In a sense, two Hamlets, the eighteenth-century active
prince and the twentieth-century melancholy one, face the same problem:
how the meditation that precedes action is related to action.

The modern editor does not recognize congruence because his eighteenth-
century counterpart uses a term of his era, rationality, instead of a psychological term of the kind favored in our time. Having objected to Johnson's
"rational" explanation, Jenkins concludes his remarks on the speech by defending Hamlet's logic: "I do not know why it should be made an objection
to this speech that it lacks *logical* connection when the progress of its ideas is
so supremely natural and lucid." [19] Our metacritical perspective shows that
Hamlet communicates profound notions despite leaving unresolved crucial
matters concerning Hamlet. At this point, Johnson's advice in his stricture
seems appropriate: instead of becoming overly concerned about consistency
of personality and action, savor the variety of *Hamlet*.

INTELLIGENCE AS A VICE

Insofar as this justly celebrated soliloquy brings together two critical traditions it highlights the profundity of the speaker's intelligence: the two major
critical approaches to Hamlet's dilemma are to be found in the prince's own
thoughts. However, this virtue occasions a vice. Because of his appreciation
for Hamlet's profound mind, Johnson is the first editor to comment on an
inconsistency in the prince that still troubles some modern editors. Hamlet's
response to Claudius at prayer Johnson finds shocking. "This speech," he

exclaims, "in which *Hamlet,* represented as a virtuous character, is not content with taking blood for blood, but contrives damnation for the man that
he would punish, is too horrible to be read or to be uttered" (8:236; 8:990).
Hamlet's desire for revenge is understandable, but it is difficult to believe
that a virtuous, intelligent man would require, in addition to death, eternal
damnation. However, Dover Wilson disagrees, taking exception in the following terms: "Johnson and others have found these lines 'too horrible to be
read or to be uttered.' They would not have shocked an ordinary Elizabethan; the quiet Kentish gentleman, Iden, expresses very similar sentiments
in *2 Hen. VI*, 4.10.84–86, while they are scarcely more barbarous than Ham.'s
own words at 2.2.582–83, or than what the K. and Laer. say at 4.7.123–
27."[20] Jenkins supports Dover Wilson's position, while Kittredge, Sisson,
and Alexander side with Johnson, who does not dwell on this point because
the value of the "to be or not to be" soliloquy, like that of previous ones,
can be appreciated in spite of the inconsistency in Hamlet.[21] For the moderns consistency of character is desirable, not because the interest is solely
in Hamlet as a character but because it enables one to find closure at the
conclusion of *Hamlet.*

However, before the end is discussed in detail, we need to consider some
representative editorial attitudes toward the last soliloquy, which begins,
"Oh, how occasions do inform against me" (4.4.32–66). One particular
passage, Jenkins explains, has caused difficulties since the early eighteenth
century.

> Rightly to be great
> Is not to stir without great argument,
> But greatly to find quarrel in a straw
> When honour's at the stake.
>
> (4.4.53–56)

According to Jenkins, the question contested since the time of Pope concerns
whether one considers the predicate in line 54 to be "is" or "is not." A long
line of critics from Malone to Kittredge concludes that it is great, at times,
not to stir. Another long distinguished line "running from Furness through
Dowden, Verity and Dover Wilson, find that it *is not* great to stir."[22]

For Johnson, however, Hamlet first contemplates two opposing views of
the matter, a "philosophical" consideration of the "argument" and a "roman-
tick" idea that sweeps aside consideration of the "argument." The prince
then goes on to say that because matters of honor are seldom substantial
enough to warrant "great argument," he must seek a less substantial justifi-

cation, "find cause of quarrel in a straw." Modern editors neglect the event taking place on stage—the "straw" of this soliloquy refers us back to the battle between Poland and Norway, "the question of this straw"—since their concern is with Hamlet's attitude toward the revenge motif. On the same page, however, Johnson has two notes emphasizing man's consideration of his place in history.

chief good and market—] If his highest, good, and *that for which he sells his time,* be to sleep and feed (8:255; 8:994).

large discourse,] Such latitude of comprehension, such power of reviewing the past, and anticipating the future.

In fact, one modern editor uses Johnson to explain the term "discourse" in this same speech. Hamlet muses:

> What is a man
> If his chief good and market of his time
> Be but to sleep and feed? A beast, no more.
> Sure he that made us with such large discourse,
> Looking before and after, gave us not
> That capability and god-like reason
> To fust in us unus'd.
>
> (4.4.33–39)

Ironically, Jenkins's note here makes use, not of Johnson's commentary on this passage, but of his *Dictionary* definition: "discourse, power of reasoning. 'The act of the understanding, by which it passes from premises to consequences.'"[23] Jenkins believes that Hamlet is here referring to the traditional belief that man differs from beasts in his capacity to reason. Kittredge also glosses "discourse" as "power of thought, rational faculty."[24] Neither notices, however, that Johnson does not use his own dictionary definition, preferring to emphasize, not merely logic, but also comprehension of the past and future, precisely the capacity Hamlet evidences in his conversation with the captain. Moreover, Johnson's final note to this soliloquy further emphasizes that more than "reason" is at stake. The lines, "How stand I then / That have a father kill'd, a mother stain'd, / Excitements of my reason and my blood," is paraphrased by Johnson as "provocations which excite both my reason and my passions to vengeance" (8:256; 8:995). The overall effect of Johnson's commentary on this soliloquy highlights, not the question of to "stir" or not to "stir," but the event that provokes that decision. Johnson leads us to consider that Hamlet may be motivated to revenge by events beyond his control, such as those that embroil the Norwegian and Danish armies.

Accordingly, Johnson explains the end of the soliloquy as referring to both passion and reason: "How stand I then, / That have a father kill'd, a mother stain'd, / Excitements of my reason and my blood." This sentence refers to both reason and passion because, for Johnson, Hamlet is not merely, as some moderns believe, reconciling himself to the chore imposed upon him by the ghost, but also recognizing that no one can evade the constraints of historical "occasions." (Note that here, as with Miranda's love in *The Tempest*, reason and passion are terms Johnson employs to establish how abstract and imaginative ideas relate to the earth or the realm of history.) This point is not of interest to modern editors because, while explaining the profundity of this particular soliloquy, it does not advance us toward the conclusion. Hamlet's consideration of his place in history does not help us understand what personality traits prevent him from resolving his dilemma.

MIMETIC HUMOR IN THE GRAVEYARD

If we are to appreciate fully the innovative nature of Johnson's reading of *Hamlet*, we must turn to the graveyard scene, where Johnson departs most markedly from his contemporaries as well as from ours and reveals what for him is the value of *Hamlet*.[25] Unlike his predecessors who were put off by what they regarded as language inappropriate for tragedy, Johnson recognized the interpretive significance of the humor. Here we see that what we value as closure is a function of our interpretation. The humorous element of the graveyard scene was generally disapproved of in the eighteenth century. In 1710, Charles Gildon explained his objections: "The Discourse betwixt *Hamlet* and the Grave-Maker is full of moral Reflections, and worthy minding—tho' that Discourse itself has nothing to do where it is, nor of any use to the Design, and may be as well left out; and whatever can be left out has no Business in a Play, but this being low Comedy has still less to do here. The Character *Hamlet* gives of *Osrick* is very satirical, and wou'd be good any where else" (*SCH* 2:258).[26] In 1736, George Stubbes indicated his agreement with Gildon: "The Scene of the Grave-Diggers I know is much applauded, but in my humble Opinion is very unbecoming such a Piece as this and is only pardonable as it gives Rise to *Hamlet's* fine moral Reflections upon the infirmity of human Nature" (*SCH* 3:61).[27] In 1752, an anonymous reviewer condemned the opening scene of act 5 in no uncertain terms: "Though this Scene is full of Humour, and had not been amiss in low Comedy, it has not the least Business here. To debase his sublime Compositions with wretched Farce, commonplace Jokes, and unmeaning Quibbles seems to have been the Delight of the laurelled, the immortal *Shakespeare*" (*SCH* 3:461). This

negative opinion of the "low" comedy, however, was not shared by everyone
in this period; for instance, George Colman remarked, in 1761, that "the
Grave-diggers in Hamlet . . . are not only endured, but applauded" (*SCH*
4:442).[28]

Nonetheless, by the time Johnson was editing *Hamlet,* most critics had reg-
istered their disapproval of the "buffoonery" in the final act of the drama.
In fact, David Garrick and George Steevens even proposed removing the
entire scene from the play. Although Garrick's production of *Hamlet* omitting the comedy of the last act was not staged until 1772, George Winchester
Stone, Jr., explains that "Garrick had been planning this alteration for a
long time and, moreover, had been encouraged in the attempt by Dr. Hoadly
and George Steevens. He realized that it was a bold undertaking, and that
it would evoke unfavorable criticism, yet he persisted and was proud, in a
way, of the result. He wrote to Sir William Young: 'It was the most impru-
dent thing I ever did in my life; but I had sworn I would not leave the stage
till I had rescued that noble play from all the rubbish of the fifth act. . . .
The alteration was received with general approbation, beyond my most warm
expectations.' "[29]

It seems highly unlikely that Johnson knew nothing of Garrick's plans
for the alteration of *Hamlet,* particularly as Steevens, who collaborated with
Johnson in the revision of the Shakespeare edition, was writing to Garrick in
1771, in the following terms.

> I expect great pleasure from the perusal of your altered *Hamlet.* It is a cir-
> cumstance in favour of the poet which I have long been wishing for. Dr. Johnson
> allots to this tragedy the praise of variety; but in my humble opinion, that variety
> is often impertinent, and always languishing on the stage. In spite of all he has
> said on the subject, I shall never be thoroughly reconciled to tragi-comedy; for if
> the farce of theatrical deceptions is but short-lived at best, their slightest success
> ought not to be interrupted. This play of Shakespeare, in particular, resembles
> a looking-glass exposed for sale, which reflects alternately the funeral and the
> puppet-show, the venerable beggar soliciting charity, and the blackguard rascal
> picking a pocket. (*SCH* 5:456)

We note here the probable beginning of the modern position: the variety of
Hamlet, particularly the low humor, detracts from a coherent resolution of
Hamlet's dilemma. Steevens goes on to suggest to Garrick that what he has
cut from the play, "the loppings and excrescences," could be compiled in a
separate play entitled *The Grave-diggers; with the Pleasant Humours of Osrick,
the Danish Macaroni.*

Johnson was surrounded by friends and critics who disapproved of the

comic elements of the last act of *Hamlet*. Indeed, Johnson's famous characterization of Garrick in Boswell's *Life* may well have resulted from earlier
plans for this alteration of *Hamlet:* "I [Boswell] complained that he had not
mentioned Garrick in his Preface to Shakespeare. . . . Johnson. 'My dear
Sir, had I mentioned him, I must have mentioned many more: Mr. Pritchard,
Mrs. Cibber,—nay, and Mr. Cibber too; he too altered Shakespeare.' " [30]
The alterers of Shakespeare would have been encouraged to change or omit
the graveyard scene by the eighteenth-century editors of *Hamlet* who preceded Johnson. Most simply neglected to explain the indecorous words of
the clowns, as the gravediggers were then called, implying that their "buffoonery" was beneath our interest. Warburton is exemplary of the first half of
the eighteenth century; since Johnson includes all of his comments, they will
be attended to shortly. The overall impression of Warburton's notes on this
scene, however, is radically different from that created by Johnson. Warburton comments briefly and only at four points, either to clarify the "ridicule"
in the clown's speech or to extract from a comical situation a didactic point
that may have gone unnoticed by the unwary reader. In place of this conde-
scending attitude toward the scene, Johnson's analysis suggests his respect,
especially for the "low-comical" parts.

This particular scene, in fact, provides a vivid instance of one of Johnson's
variorum techniques. Warburton registers two examples of "ridicule" in the
scene. The first concerns the clown's speech on suicide.

> 1 CLOWN. It must be *se offendendo*, it cannot be else. For here lies the point; If
> I drown myself wittingly, it argues an act; and an act hath three branches; it
> is to act, to do, to perform; *Argal*, she drowned herself wittingly.

Warburton points out that the three branches of action constitute a "ridicule
on scholastic divisions without distinction; and of distinctions without difference" (8:278). To explain the other instance of ridicule, Warburton offers an
anecdote on Hamlet's reflection upon the skull, which, the prince speculates,
"might be the pate of a politician": "This character is finely touched. Our
great historian has explained it in an example, where speaking of the death of
Cardinal *Mazarine*, at the time of the Restoration, he says, *The Cardinal was
probably struck with wonder, if not the agony of the undream'd of prosperity of our
King's affairs; as if he had taken ill, and laid it to heart that God Almighty would
bring such a work to pass in Europe without his concurrence, and even against all his
machinations. Hist of the Rebellion*, Book 16" (8:281). For Warburton the satire
is directed against the mighty, the noted scholars and cardinals who are made
powerless by death, their empty skulls being bandied about by a mere clown.

While he includes all of Warburton's notes, Johnson expands upon them and adds others in order to suggest that the ridicule is not directed solely at those in high positions. Unlike his predecessor, Johnson attends carefully to the clown's song, citing as authorities for the source of the first stanza Theobald and Percy, who discovered that the lyrics derive, not from a popular source, but from a poem entitled "The Aged Lover Renounceth Love," written by either Henry Howard, earl of Surrey, or Lord Vaux. With regard to the second stanza, Johnson suggests an emendation in order to provide "an alternate rhyme" that is missing. We see that the sexton's song is based upon a ballad worthy of our attention, not merely the ingenious product of a bumbling rustic.

Yet Johnson recognizes that the clown's words suggest notions beyond his own intentions. When Hamlet refers to the skull as possibly that of a politician "which this ass o'er offices; one that would circumvent God," Johnson first cites Warburton's note and then adds his own comment. Warburton explains how "this ass" can refer to the sexton: "People in office, at that time, were so over-bearing, that *Shakespeare* speaking of insolence at the height, calls it *Insolence in office*. . . . Alluding to this character of ministers and politicians, the speaker observes, that this insolent officer is now *o'er officer'd* by the Sexton, who, knocking his scull about with his spade, appears to be as insolent in his office as they were in theirs. This is said with much humour." However, Johnson does not accept this reading: "In the quarto, for *over-offices* is, *over-reaches*, which agrees better with the sentence: It is a strong exaggeration to remark, that an *Ass* can *over-reach* him who would once have tried to *circumvent.*—I believe both words were *Shakespeare's*. An authour in revising his work, when his original ideas have faded from his mind, and new observations have produced new sentiments, easily introduces images which have been more newly impressed upon him, without observing their want of congruity to the general texture of his original design" (8:281–82; 8:1002). Johnson prefers "over-reaches" but leaves "o'er officer'd" in the text because his interest is in contesting Warburton's reading of this passage. For Warburton, the point concerns how those in low offices, like the sexton, are disrespectful to the remains of their social betters, those in higher offices. "Over-reaches," on the other hand, does not restrict the irony to social class or "office" alone, especially not to those in lower positions. Johnson sees the matter in more spiritual terms: from a religious viewpoint, anyone—minister, prince, or sexton—who is disrespectful to human remains, "over-reaches" the place of God. Indeed, the overall force of Johnson's notes on this scene is to extend the range of the satire to include those in high offices, like Hamlet himself.

Johnson uses a similar technique to implicate the speaker in another famous comic moment in Shakespearean tragedy, the porter's scene in *Macbeth*. Again, Johnson reproduces his predecessor's note, then adds his own comment, which transforms and extends the sphere of reference. Warburton explains that by the term "equivocator" the porter means the Jesuits, who were "the inventors of the execrable doctrine of *equivocation.*" Later in this scene, Johnson adds a note pointing to an "equivocation" in the porter's own speech, thus involving the porter in the sin Warburton attributed solely to the Jesuits (6:411–12; 8:772).

In *Hamlet*, Johnson also broadens the range of the satire by glossing words that are not commented upon by Warburton. When the prince takes the skull from the gravedigger, remarking, "And now my lady worm's," Johnson explains that "the scull that was my *Lord such a one's, is now my lady Worm's*"— extending the referent from ambitious politicians to vain ladies. Another example of Johnson extending the range of the irony is seen in his comment on the following conversation between the prince and the sexton.

> HAMLET. Who is to be buried in't?
> CLOWN. One, that was a woman, Sir; but, rest her soul, she's dead.
> HAMLET. How absolute the knave is? We must speak by the card, or equivocation will undo us. By the Lord, *Horatio,* these three years I have taken note of it, the age is grown so picked, that the toe of the peasant comes so near of our courtier, he galls his kibe.
>
> *the age is grown so picked*] So *smart,* so *sharp;* says *Hanmer,* very properly; but there was, I think, about that time, a *picked* shoe, that is, *a shoe, with a long pointed toe,* in fashion, to which the allusion seems likewise to be made. *Every man now is smart; and every man now is a man of fashion.* (8:283–84; 8:1002)

Most editors point out that "picked" means "fastidious." Johnson extends this meaning by suggesting that this word relates to a mode of fashion, enriching our understanding in two respects: the sexton's fastidiousness is seen as a petty vanity analogous to the "paint" of she "who was a woman"; the prince, undoubtedly more fashionably dressed than the gravedigger, is implicated in the vanity he characterizes as "so picked."

For Johnson, death ridicules all of man's worldly ambitions, from the greatest political aspirations to the petty foibles of dress. But the skull of Yorick undermines more than a court jester's "gibes" and a lady's "paint." The most important point is that the sexton, in his playful quips, and Hamlet, in his reflections upon the circumvention of God, both raise the skull with a fleshly arm that at any moment may become the next relic of the charnel house. Johnson helps to make clear that the profundity of the humor in this scene derives from the fact that death is indiscriminate, striking at random and cutting off in their prime both those who neglect and those who comprehend the meaning of death.

The black humor of the graveyard scene, the grim irony of death, is all-inclusive and thus epitomizes the "variety" of *Hamlet*, which is the source of the "particular excellence" of the tragedy. Indeed, in his *Preface* Johnson makes use of his conception of variety to defend Shakespeare's intermingling of comedy and tragedy, of which the graveyard scene is the most famous example.

> That this is a practice [uniting seriousness and levity] contrary to the rules of criticism will be readily allowed; but there is always an appeal open from criticism to nature. The end of writing is to instruct; the end of poetry is to instruct by pleasing. That the mingled drama may convey all the instruction of tragedy or comedy cannot be denied, because it includes both in its alternations of exhibition, and approaches nearer than either to the appearance of life, by shewing how great machinations and slender designs may promote or obviate one another, and the high and the low co-operate in the general system by unavoidable concatenation. (7:67)

Since life combines comedy and tragedy, Johnson reasons, art that imitates life may admit of the same combination. Few would now accept an argument based on *Hamlet* as an imitation of reality: in fact, the end of this tragedy is so unnaturally strewn with corpses that the director must guard against the audience being distracted by the sound of falling bodies. But this passage from the *Preface* reveals a subtler point when seen in conjunction with the notes to the graveyard scene. So pervasive in *Hamlet*, death becomes on the sad occasion of Ophelia's burial the subject matter. At the same time, it is death that gives prominence to the variety of human life. The grim reaper interrupts people, ideas, and events, cutting a swath through a cross section of existence. The humor in the graveyard enables us to recognize that death is the most vivid way to show the variety of life.

In my view, Johnson's insight, if extended, suggests that the tragedy concludes, not merely with variety, but with the principle of variety. We fully appreciate the complexity and depth of man's ideas, of his history, of man himself, only when we witness the saddest of all spectacles: the progress of all aspects of humanity interrupted by death. In this sense, death can be understood as the subversion of traditional closure. This insight provides the basis for an innovative idea about the conclusion of *Hamlet*. Johnson can forgive Shakespeare's unresolved plot, with its ghost who "left the regions of the dead to little purpose," because the interruptive nature of death introduces the more valuable principle of the variety of human existence.

Heedless of Johnson's warning, modern commentators still seek a structural principle of closure. A recent schoolbook on *Hamlet* indicates how deeply embedded in our culture is the belief that *Hamlet* must be understood as arriving at a totalizing conclusion. This particular text begins by asserting that Dover Wilson's question—"What is the play about?"—is the appropriate beginning. Four possible answers to this question are proposed: it is a revenge play; it is a play concerned with the nature of evil; it is a play about death; it is a play about "not knowing for sure." Not perceived as related to what the play is about, Johnson's concept of variety is relegated to another section of the book, entitled "Dramatic Style."[31] The four possible answers to the initial question provide unifying themes or ideas; because it is not all-encompassing but accretive, Johnson's is not placed in this category.

The extent of the modern quest for a totalizing concept in *Hamlet* leads scholarly editors to adopt toward the humor of the gravediggers attitudes reminiscent of those of Johnson's contemporaries. The song, for instance, which, as we have seen, Johnson believed to be important, is characterized as "blundering" by Dover Wilson, as "garbled" by Spencer and Ridler, and as "corrupt" by Jenkins.[32] But the contrast between modern editors and Johnson is most clear in their comments upon Hamlet's reference to the sexton as "this ass." While Johnson, as we know, implicates the prince in what he observes in the gravedigger, four modern editors point to an alternative reading, one that is dependent on a previous sentence in the speech. Hamlet muses, "That skull had a tongue in it, and could sing once. How the knave jowls it to th' ground, as if 'twere Cain's jawbone, that did the first murder. This might be the pate of a politician which this ass now o'er offices, one that would circumvent God, might it not?" (5:1, 74–79). Dover Wilson comments on the phrase "Cain's jawbone": "Cain 'did the first murder' with the jaw-bone of an ass. Ham. implies that it is now this ass's turn to 'o'er-reach' Cain." Turning to the phrase "circumvent God," Dover Wilson notes that "Cain was the first politician: he denied that he was his brother's keeper, and when God asked him where Abel was he quibbled."[33] By suggesting how this "ass" is related to Cain, Dover Wilson leads us to believe that Hamlet associates the gravedigger's disrespect for the skull with Claudius's usurpation of the throne. Kittredge reinforces this reading of the passage, pointing out that the antecedent of "that" is "Cain," who, unlike the politician, "was clever enough, while he lived, to disregard God's law and apparently to escape unscathed."[34] Ribner reproduces this note in his edition, and Spencer makes the same point in even stronger terms: "According to legend [Cain] used an ass's jawbone to murder his brother Abel. Hamlet's mind reverts to fratricide, as does the King's."[35] Finally, the Arden edition of 1982 reasserts the position that Dover Wilson had presented in 1934: "Cain's crime, not merely murder but fratricide, is the prototype of Claudius's, as we are reminded at III,iii,37."[36] Apart from the question of the validity or plausibility of this reading of the passage, it is striking how far these analyses are from the humor of the scene. None of these modern editors attempts to bridge the gap between the literal and the figurative. Neither a murderer nor a politician, the gravedigger adopts a matter-of-fact attitude toward his work that hardly qualifies him to be included in either category. Although it is, in principle, possible that the legend of Cain's jawbone leads the prince to associate this "ass" with his uncle, such a reading requires considerably more explanation than is offered. On a literal level, Hamlet refers to Cain's jawbone to illustrate the sexton's disrespect for the skull: that is, he throws it either with the sort of contempt that should be reserved for Cain's jawbone or with the sort of contempt displayed by Cain himself in killing his brother. But aside from the prince's cerebral view of the matter, what about the clown—how is his playful attitude to Yorick's skull to be related to fratricide?

Why do these modern editors insist on pursuing this high road, that of the melancholy Hamlet, the prince who can only see around him prototypes of evil at the Danish court, and neglect the low road, the humor of a prince who understands the gravedigger in the same physical and empirical terms that the gravedigger himself understands the skulls? Surely, the reason is that the low humor of this scene cannot be accounted for within any unifying principle. Indeed, Spencer goes so far as to characterize the entire graveyard scene as an "afterthought."[37] The best hope for those pursuing totalizing kinds of closure is to demonstrate that the prince associates aspects of this scene with the revenge plot, thereby moving the reader beyond this remarkable digression.

Two centuries earlier Johnson pointed toward an important new kind of concluding principle inherent in the "low" humor of the graveyard. When understood as something more than a joke, when taken, so to speak, seriously, comedy can point to contingent aspects in history that are not wholly compatible with our expectations, ranging from the literary to the philosophical, from the thematic to the ideological. The critic's sense of humor, his or her ability to be moved by the comedy of the graveyard scene, is one of the means by which literary criticism exposes our values and stretches us beyond our most cherished presuppositions. However, the full significance of this procedure of questioning one's own values requires more than a sense of humor; the comedy must be seen as having significance, not merely with regard to the literary question of closure but also with regard to history. It is important to remember that Johnson defended the mingling of comedy with tragedy on the basis that it occurs in life. Furthermore, Johnson includes a judgmental aspect in his stricture because he recognizes that by this means the critic relates literature to the extraliterary. Morality is, for Johnson, the basis of the decision about how literature applies to the human predicament, and humor helps to determine precisely where it touches the earth. The comedy of the graveyard has to be seen as pertinent not only to Hamlet's situation but also to ours. The next chapter considers the question of aesthetic empathy, the procedure enabling us to relate the tragic dilemma to our situation. Remaining implicit, modern critical values have precluded consideration of this issue. We need to recognize that our values have a profound effect on what we seek as a valid and satisfactory conclusion. These ethical assumptions, as we shall see, are related to how we respond to literature.

CHAPTER EIGHT

Aesthetic Empathy in *Macbeth*

As we have seen, Coleridge asserted that Johnson did not have a concept of dramatic "delusion." Here I will demonstrate that the *Notes* to *Macbeth*, in conjunction with a portion of the *Preface*, contain the outline of a theory of aesthetic empathy alternate to that of the romantics, one that helps to resolve a modern critical dilemma in *Macbeth*. In fact, Johnson's concept of aesthetic empathy further clarifies how interpretation enables the literary critic to locate the extraliterary referent.

The entire matter of aesthetic empathy has ceased to be a major concern because many present-day critics deny or ignore the importance of the referential aspect of language.[1] Recently, some critics have recognized the import of ideological references in literature, a problem attended to in chapter 4. But because ideological differences, although possibly modified and influenced by literary criticism, are unlikely to be resolved by literary critical means, we found, in chapter 7, that a mediating factor between literature and ideology was humor. For Johnson, comedy brings us down to the earth, to the distinctly human, where Falstaff quibbles, Pandarus jests, Viola schemes, Sly sets off to tame his wife, Miranda wrangles with Ferdinand, and the grave-digger toys with a skull. But humor alone cannot establish contact between the literary and the extraliterary; the audience must decide that the comedy has significance, an issue that for Johnson involves the concept of aesthetic empathy. Focusing on our response to *Macbeth*, I shall argue in this chapter that as a part of the larger enterprise of comprehending man in the cosmos, literary criticism needs to relate tragedy to the human dilemma. In establishing this link, Johnson's position requires a spectator who, unlike the romantic audience in its dreamlike state, actively engages in interpretation that becomes the basis of aesthetic empathy.

Johnson's first published work on Shakespeare was *Miscellaneous Observations on Macbeth*, which appeared in 1745. It was presented as a "specimen" or sample of the forthcoming edition of Shakespeare's plays, a project that was postponed for another decade possibly because Thomas Hanmer's edition appeared in 1744 and William Warburton's was soon expected. I believe that Johnson selected certain of his comments on *Macbeth* as samples of his forthcoming edition of Shakespeare's dramas because his extensive research on the demonology suggested an alternative to the prevalent view of the tragedy, one that points to a new concept of aesthetic empathy.

SOLEMN FICTION VERSUS PERSONAL AMBITION

The belief that *Macbeth* is about personal ambition relates to the stage tradition of the tragedy that goes back to the seventeenth century. However, Johnson discovered in his research on the printed text a shadow of enchantment that blurred character distinction and rendered moot the question of personal responsibility. During the Restoration and the first half of the eighteenth century, William D'Avenant's operatic version of *Macbeth* was the only form of the play that was performed.[2] In 1744, Garrick presented his *Macbeth*, which involved some reversion from D'Avenant's to Shakespeare's language. But Garrick did not change the Restoration witches, who remained faery creatures, dancing, singing, miraculously appearing and vanishing by means of a "machine."[3] Throughout the Restoration and eighteenth century, the witches were presented not as evil demons but as somewhat comical, naughty "milk-curdlers." Garrick's reason for employing D'Avenant's operatic witches is made clear in the final speech, an addition of Garrick's that makes explicit what for him is the message of the play: "MACBETH. 'Tis done! the scene of life will quickly close. Ambition's vain, delusive dreams are fled, And now I wake to darkness, guilt and horror. I cannot bear it! Let me shake it off.—Twa' not be; my soul is clogged with blood I cannot rise! I dare not ask for mercy. It is too late, hell drags me down, I sink, I sink—Oh!—my soul is lost forever! Oh! (Dies)."[4] Since Garrick concludes with Macbeth's descent to hell, evil witches would detract from the responsibility of the protagonist, who in the end accepts the justness of his own condemnation.

Although over a century has passed since the witches were presented on the stage as comic, operatic figures, modern commentators, while recognizing the weird sisters as sinister, stress that both Banquo and Macbeth are tempted but only the latter succumbs. The witches are seen as serving to make manifest the latent criminal ambition of Macbeth. Moreover, while twentieth-century scholars have unearthed a great deal of material that further validates Johnson's view of the witches, this research has had little effect upon modern critical positions on *Macbeth*. In fact, Garrick's view of the tragedy as the defeat of criminal ambition is still maintained in our time.

The difficulty involves integrating the tragic, heroic dimension of Macbeth with his repugnant, criminal acts. The nature of the problem is revealed in a controversy that began in 1947 and remains unresolved. In that year, Cleanth Brooks wrote an essay, entitled "The Naked Babe and the Cloak of Manliness," which provoked responses from Oscar James Campbell in 1948 and Helen Gardner in 1949 representative of two kinds of objections. The naked babe in Brooks's title refers to Macbeth's comparison of pity for Duncan to "a naked new-born babe, / Striding the blast, or heaven's cherubim, hors'd / Upon the sightless couriers of the air." Brooks pointed out that the babe is here characterized in two opposite ways—as a helpless newborn babe who can barely toddle, let alone "stride the blast," and as an "infant Hercules," capable of striding upon the wind itself.

Brooks related this paradoxical image to the imagery of the cloak of manliness: the clothing tropes throughout the drama suggest that Macbeth as usurper and murderer has assumed stolen garments inappropriate to his being. The babe image was therefore seen to provide a unifying principle: "the babe signifies not only the future; it symbolizes all those enlarging purposes which make life meaningful, and it symbolizes, furthermore, all those emotional and—to Lady Macbeth—irrational times which make man more than a machine—which render him human. It signifies pre-eminently the pity which Macbeth, under Lady Macbeth's tutelage, would wean himself of as something 'unmanly.' "[5] Brooks concluded that the imagery of clothing and that of the babe unite in the following terms: "What will it avail Macbeth to cover the deed with the blanket of the dark if the elemental forces that ride the winds will blow the horrid deed in every eye? And what will it avail Macbeth to clothe himself in 'manliness'—to become bloody, bold and resolute—if he is to find himself again and again viewing his bloody work through the 'eye of childhood / That fears a painted devil'?"[6]

Oscar James Campbell asserted that Brooks mistakenly assumed that Macbeth's primary fear concerns the future, specifically the chance that the succeeding kings of Scotland will be of Banquo's lineage. On the contrary,

Campbell insisted, Macbeth is concerned, not about the future, but about the present: "The expectation of inevitable revenge is the reason why his fear of Banquo sticks deep."[7] Helen Gardner, on the other hand, called attention to the way that the image of the babe concludes: "The final image of the wind dropping as the rain begins is the termination of the sequence of ideas and images. . . . The final condemnation of the deed is not that it will meet with punishment, not even that the doer of it will stand condemned; but that even indignation at the murder will be swallowed up in universal pity for the victim. The babe, naked and new-born, the most helpless of all things, the cherubim, innocent and beautiful, call out the pity and the love by which Macbeth is judged."[8]

This humane element led Gardner to conclude that Macbeth fears, not the external vengeance that is appropriate to melodrama, as Brooks maintained, but inner corruption, the stuff of tragedy. Thus Brooks was attacked on two opposing fronts: Campbell felt that he neglected Macbeth's immediate concerns that account for his violent, bloody actions, while Gardner faulted him for making too little of the spiritual and heroic dimension of Macbeth. This polarity between Macbeth as uncaring butcher or as conscience-stricken criminal has persisted. In a 1982 volume of critical essays entitled *Focus on Macbeth*, R. A. Foakes asserted that in the end Macbeth ceases to care, while M. Goldman, writing in the same volume, concluded that Macbeth finally sees the evil as his own.[9] Still more recently, this moral dichotomy has been converted to one involving gender. Robert Kimbrough argued that Macbeth as butcher succumbs to the male stereotype that is complemented by a female counterpart in the gentle, reflective, hesitant Macbeth aware of his own evil.[10]

Modern critics leave unresolved a fundamental issue raised by their own analyses. However this binary opposition within the protagonist is defined and whether it is seen to conclude with the predominance of one of the two or with an equilibrium between them, a question remains: how do Macbeth's inner thoughts relate to his actions, how does he reconcile his conscience to the murder of innocents? In short, the inner being of Macbeth remains as mysterious and unfathomable as the witches. Johnson's research on the demonology of the witches led him to recognize that enchanted and, in that sense, possessed by these demons, Macbeth is partially covered by their blanket of blackness, which prevents our full comprehension of him. Understood in these terms, Johnson's stricture on *Macbeth* is as startling and revolutionary in our time as it was in his own day.

THIS play is deservedly celebrated for the propriety of its fictions, and solemnity, grandeur, and variety of its action; but it has no nice discriminations of character, the events are too great to admit the influence of particular dispositions, and the course of the action necessarily determines the conduct of the agents.

The danger of ambition is well described; and I know not whether it may not be said in defence of some parts which now seem improbable, that, in *Shakespeare's* time, it was necessary to warn credulity against vain and illusive predictions.

The passions are directed to their true end. Lady *Macbeth* is merely detested; and though the courage of *Macbeth* preserves some esteem, yet every reader rejoices at his fall. (6:484; 8:795)

The first paragraph above radically calls into question most readings of *Macbeth* for the past two and a half centuries. The tragedy is not about Macbeth or anyone else in the cast because the characters are neither sufficiently distinguished from one another nor free agents. Equally surprising is the lack of prominence given by "the great moralist" to the matter of ambition. The deep distinction drawn between the somewhat estimable Macbeth and his detestable wife reinforces our impression that the ambition shared by the main characters is of secondary concern for Johnson. In order to understand the primary concern, we need to turn the *Notes*, paying particular attention to what Johnson values most highly in *Macbeth*, "the propriety of its fictions, and solemnity, grandeur, and variety of its action." My contention is that what Johnson locates as "deservedly celebrated" in *Macbeth* points to a resolution to the modern dilemma.

AN ESTIMABLE CHARACTER ENCHANTED

The first issue a modern audience confronts is the relation between Macbeth and the evil of the witches. Grasping this problem as a result of his research, Johnson faces the question posed by any performance of *Macbeth*, which, unlike those of the Restoration and eighteenth century, presents the witches as they were originally staged. While Shakespearean ghosts can be staged as disembodied voices or imaginative projections of diseased or haunted minds, the witches are present on the stage, visible to Macbeth, Banquo, and the audience. Johnson is the earliest commentator to attempt to account for that dramaturgical fact.

Johnson's first note is devoted to the "supernatural agents" of the drama. The opening stage direction, "Enter three Witches," prompts one of his longest comments, four columns of small print. First, he explains why the remarks are necessary: "In order to make a true estimate of the abilities and merit of a writer, it is always necessary to examine the genius of his age, and the opinions of his contemporaries" (6:308; 8:752–55). In his *Preface,* Johnson explains himself in more specific terms: "Nations, like individuals, have their infancy. A people newly awakened to literary curiosity, being yet unacquainted with the true state of things, knows not how to judge of that which is proposed as its resemblance. Whatever is remote from common appearances is always welcome to vulgar, as to childish credulity; and of a country unenlightened by learning, the whole people is the vulgar. The study of those who then aspired to plebeian learning was laid out upon adventures, giants, dragons, and enchantments. *The Death of Arthur* was the favourite volume" (7:82).

The specific "opinion of Shakespeare's contemporaries" that Johnson refers to in *Macbeth* is the widespread Elizabethan and Jacobean belief in witchcraft. With a thoroughness that has only been surpassed in our own day, Johnson documents the nature and extent of the concern with witches, showing that people of all social degrees and intellectual levels took this matter very seriously. The grandeur and solemnity of this fiction derives from the fact that the witches are not simply riddlers or prognosticators but have power to do evil. Johnson's note on the first words of the play exemplifies his now familiar variorum technique.

> [Three Witches] Fair is foul, and foul is fair. ie. We make these sudden changes of the weather. And *Macbeth,* speaking of this day, soon after says. *So foul and fair a day I have not seen.*
>
> Warburton
>
> I believe the meaning is, that to us, perverse and malignant as we are, *fair is foul, and foul is fair.* (6:372; 8:755)

Typical of Restoration and early eighteenth-century editors, Warburton limits the witches' powers to the weather or atmosphere in keeping, one imagines, with D'Avenant's "spectacle" of batlike creatures flying across the stage on a "machine." Johnson extends their powers considerably. The entire situation, both the human context and the natural setting, can be totally transformed by the weird sisters, and, unlike Warburton, Johnson stresses that their influence is often of a malignant and perverse kind.

As we have come to understand, Johnson often achieves his aim in the *Notes* incrementally. For instance, in another early scene, the witches' curse, "He shall live a man forbid," occasions the use of Theobald's comment—"i.e. as one under a Curse, an *Interdiction*" (6:379; 8:758). Johnson remarks: "Mr. *Theobald* has very justly explained *forbid* by *accursed,* but without giving any reason of his interpretation. To *bid* is originally *to pray*, as in this Saxon fragment," which is appended to illustrate this use of the term (6:379; 8:758). While Theobald asserts what he believed to be the meaning of "forbid" and Warburton makes no comment, Johnson provides historical evidence for Theobald, giving this view more prominence and authority. The 1765 edition establishes what neither Theobald nor Warburton had elucidated: the witches serve to create an atmosphere of doom and gloom and are implicated in the murder of Duncan and the other victims.

This point is clarified in one of Johnson's subtlest instances of a variorum technique. For the phrase "weyward sisters" in 1.3, Johnson reproduces both Theobald's and Warburton's comments, which comprise over four columns of small print.[11] Theobald points out that as the term "weyward" means "perverse and obstinate," it is unlikely that the witches would so describe themselves. Rather, he believes that the original word was "weird," meaning "Fates or Destinies," a more appropriate term for the sisters' description of themselves. Warburton mentions Theobald's difficulties with "wayward," agreeing with him that the original word was "weird," but for a different reason: "Weyward had anciently the very same sense, as *weird;* and was, indeed, the very same word differently spelt" that was used to refer to the "*Fates* of the northern nations" (6:380–81). Combining the notes of two of his predecessors, Johnson implies that "weyward" means both "fates or Destinies" and "perverse and obstinate." The 1765 edition conveys something different from the previous editions: the witches have a fatal effect that is perverse.

But, not surprisingly, Johnson's originality is most obvious when he articulates his differences with critics of the past. In this same scene, Banquo asks the witches, "Are ye Fantastical?" Warburton explained, "By fantastical is not meant, according to the common signification, creatures of his own brain; For he could not be so extravagant to ask such a question; but it is used for supernatural, spiritual." Johnson retorts, "By fantastical, he means creatures of fantasy or imagination; the question is, Are these real beings before us, or are we deceived by illusions of fancy?" (6:382; 8:758–59). The difference between Warburton and Johnson constitutes a turning point. Warburton eliminates a possibility that Johnson insists must remain: the witches may be figments of the imagination. Kenneth Muir explains, in his Arden edition of 1951, "The word [fantastical] is used by Holinshed in the context ('some vaine fantasticall illusion') and Craig quotes Scot, *Discoverie of Witchcraft,* 'these prestigious things which are wrought by witches are fantasticall.'"[12] In contrast to Warburton and the modern editor, who both take

Banquo's question to be about the nature of the image of the witches, John-son believes that the question concerns the relationship between the image and its perceiver, that is, "Is what I see before me actually present or is it a projection of my mind and/or that of my companion?"

This last question refers to the psyches of the witnesses of the witches, not a consideration for Warburton or his modern counterpart. Johnson insists on the possibility that Banquo wonders if the appearance of the witches is related to the deep psychological drives and desires of himself and Macbeth. The strange creatures, in their solemn, grand manner, employ various actions to incite different kinds of evil. A similar point is made later on in this same scene.

> MACBETH. This supernatural Solliciting
> Cannot be ill; cannot be good
> *This supernatural* Solliciting] *Solliciting*, for information.
> Warburton
>
> *Solliciting* is rather in my opinion, *incitement* than *information*. (6:385; 8:759)

Johnson again feels that Warburton underestimates the potency of the witches, who go beyond mere inquiry to play upon the deepest and most secret wishes of the protagonist. At the same time, Johnson stresses Mac-beth's understanding of the seriousness of the crime being contemplated. In the speech cited above, Macbeth asserts that "present fears are less than horrible imaginings." Warburton understood this phrase to mean that "to execute this murder, I shall find it much less dreadful than my frighted imagi-nation now presents it to me." Johnson, however, takes a different view: "*Present fears* are *fears of things present*, which *Macbeth* declares, and every man has found, to be less than the *imagination* presents them while the objects are yet distant" (6:386; 8:759). Warburton believes that Macbeth expects the execution of the murder will be less frightening than the anticipation of it. Johnson feels that Macbeth knows that the opposite is, in fact, the case; the deed itself will exceed his worst expectations. The tragic protagonist, John-son implies, realizes that the horror of the criminal deed is beyond imagina-tion and that, as he approaches it, the horror will increase; Macbeth always faces the consequences of his contemplated crimes. Courage now takes the form of conscience.

For instance, concerning Macbeth's famous soliloquy at the beginning of act 1, "If it were done," Johnson is the first editor to recognize the difficulties involved in understanding the term "here."

MACBETH. If it were *done*, when 'tis done, then 'twere well
It were done quickly;

. . . .

We'd jump the life to come.—But, in these cases,
We still have judgment *here*, that we but teach
Bloody Instructions, which, being taught, return
To plague th'inventor; this even-handed justice
Commends th'ingredients of our poison'd chalice
To our own lips.

(6:398; 8:765–66)

Johnson paraphrases the end of this speech as follows: "If the murder could
terminate in itself . . . if this could be my condition; even *here in this world*,
in this contracted period of temporal existence, on the narrow *bank* in the
ocean of eternity, *I would jump the life to come*, I would venture upon the deed
without care of a future state. But this is one of *these cases* in which judgment is pronounced and vengeance is inflicted upon us *here* in the present
life. We teach others to do as we have done, and are punished by our own
example" (8:766). We might have expected Johnson to have been offended
by the heretical notion of avoiding consideration of the afterlife. But, on the
contrary, he recognizes that, focusing upon this life, Macbeth refers only par-
enthetically to the hereafter. The point is that he would risk the problems of
the next world if the mortal obstacles could be removed. Since they cannot,
Macbeth concludes that as the overreacher he will eventually be overreached.
Killing Duncan initiates the process of his own throne being usurped. For
Johnson, it is important to understand that Macbeth's passionate desire for
the kingship never blinds him to the self-defeating nature of his own desire.
If the witches are to win their way, they must manipulate a man who refuses
at this stage to deceive himself or evade moral responsibility.

REPRESSION AS DETESTABLE

Hence Johnson is particularly interested in the psychological strategy used
by Lady Macbeth for the purpose of convincing Macbeth to commit regicide. Admiring the means that Lady Macbeth uses on her husband, Johnson
is contemptuous of her attitude toward herself because it involves the repression of her conscience. And although Macbeth, not his wife, commits the
crimes, for which Johnson holds him responsible and justly punished, that
entire matter is rendered somewhat moot by the spell of the witches. So John-

son focuses on the manner in which Macbeth is manipulated toward crime. Lady Macbeth is of interest at this point because she, like the witches, plays upon the virtuous and honorable aspect of the protagonist, the very aspect she represses in herself.

She employs, according to Johnson, the most effective argument that can be used with a soldier—the reproach of cowardice. Macbeth replies, "I dare do all that may become a man, Who dares do more is none," and these words are deemed by Johnson sufficient to have immortalized Shakespeare: "[Lady Macbeth] then urges the oaths by which he had bound himself to murder *Duncan,* another art of sophistry by which men have sometimes deluded their own consciences, and pursuaded themselves that what would be criminal in others is virtuous in them; this argument *Shakespeare,* whose plan obliged him to make *Macbeth* yield, has not confuted, though he might easily have shown that a former obligation could not be vacated by a latter: that obligations laid on us by a higher power, could not be over-ruled by obligations which we lay upon ourselves" (6:399; 8:767–68). No previous editor has any equivalent of this comment. Shakespeare's plan, we are again reminded, takes precedence over interest in the further development of Macbeth as a character. For the most part, the plan involves inciting Macbeth to do evil by playing upon his virtues. In particular, Lady Macbeth appeals to the rational and ethical faculties of a soldier; it is "just and reasonable" to expect a soldier to keep his word and to regard such a principle as honorable. Instead of merely appealing to the negative characteristic of her husband, his overweening ambition, Lady Macbeth plays upon the best of his principles: she "deludes his conscience" by making him believe "that what would be criminal in others is," in him, "virtuous." Paradoxically, we here see the "courage" that serves to preserve "some esteem" on our part for Macbeth.

Yet Macbeth's inner being remains mysterious because the same method used here by Lady Macbeth is employed by Macbeth in the next scene, leaving us to wonder whether he was willingly deluded or actually deceived. At this point, Johnson adopts one of his significant revisions. In 1765, Warburton's explanation of Macbeth's veiled promise to Banquo immediately prior to the murder of Duncan is considered adequate.

> MACBETH. If you shall cleave to my consent, when 'tis,
>   It shall make honour for you

> *Consent,* for will. So that the sense of the line is, if you shall go into my measures when I have determined of them, or when the time comes that I want your assistance. Warburton (6:403)

By 1773, Johnson replaced this note with one of his own: "Macbeth expresses his thought with affected obscurity; he does not mention the royalty, though he apparently has it in his mind, 'If you shall cleave to my consent,' if you shall concur with me when I determine to accept the crown, 'when 'tis, "when that happens which prediction promises," it shall make honour for you' " (8:769). Warburton makes it seem that Macbeth has not yet decided or is unwilling to tell Banquo what he will do; by 1773, Johnson decides that this "obscurity" is "affected," a ploy on Macbeth's part enabling him to speak to Banquo in terms of "honour" when he is, in fact, referring to regicide. Macbeth now uses the same means Lady Macbeth had used on him; he tries to delude Banquo's conscience by suggesting that what would be criminal for others is for him honorable.

Macbeth's skillful use of his wife's technique reinforces our sense of his deeply held belief that regicide is a wrong and dishonorable act. The question then becomes, how does Macbeth bring himself to kill Duncan? Here Johnson emphasizes that Macbeth, while rational, remains under the spell of the witches. Instead of attempting to resolve these questions about the protagonist, Johnson calls our attention to the murky atmosphere; in a long note that is clearly designed to make the reader stop and dwell upon the mood of this section of the play, he compares Shakespeare to Dryden.

In the famous "is this a dagger which I see before me" soliloquy, Macbeth looks out into the moonless night:

> Now o'er one half the world
> Nature seems dead, and wicked dreams abuse
> The curtain'd sleep; now witchcraft celebrates
> Pale *Hecat's* offerings.

Characterizing the opening image of this passage as "perhaps the most striking that poetry can produce," Johnson cites a similar passage from Dryden's *Conquest of Mexico* and compares them in the following terms: "He that reads Dryden, finds himself lull'd with serenity, and disposed to solitude and contemplation. He that peruses Shakespeare, looks round alarmed, and starts to find himself alone. One is the night of a lover, the other of a murderer" (6:404–5; 8:769–70). The atmosphere here applies to both the speaker and the reader, the "peruser" who, as Johnson points out, starts and looks round, sharing in the mental procedure of the tragic protagonist. This moment is, however, fleeting, for Macbeth soon "discovers the absurdity of his suspicion" that the earth might hear and report his footsteps. Johnson paraphrases this final section of the soliloquy as follows.

Macbeth has . . . disturbed his imagination by enumerating all the terrors of the night; at length he is wrought up to a degree of frenzy, that makes him afraid of some supernatural discovery of his design, and calls out to the stones not to betray him, not to declare where he walks, nor *to talk.*—As he is going to say of what, he discovers the absurdity of his suspicion, and pauses, but is again overwhelmed by his guilt, and concludes, that such are the horrors of the present night, that the stones may be expected to cry out against him. . . . It is now a very just and strong picture of a man about to commit a deliberate murder under the strongest conviction of the wickedness of his design. (6:406; 8:771–72)

Macbeth whips himself up to such a frenzy that he is awakened by the absurdity of his excessive fears to a moment of self-reflection that is followed by a deeper sense of guilt. Nevertheless, he proceeds with his plans for murder, as if the recognition of the excess of his imagination enables him to shoulder the real guilt and get on with the monstrous deed. Johnson is interested in the fact that the protagonist proceeds, however hesitantly, in his determination to act while never ceasing to be convinced of the "wickedness of his design." Indeed, this conviction almost seems to provide the means, as it were, for the murders. The manner in which Macbeth's virtue serves him in his evil purposes is a topic of continual interest to Johnson. We are never led to understand how Macbeth reconciles himself to these horrid deeds, but we see how the weird sisters drag him toward them by keeping his conscience intact. In a sense, they tempt him by leaving an aspect of his innocence untainted.

For instance, after the murder of Duncan, Macbeth describes the gory scene to Macduff, Banquo, and the others: "Here, lay Duncan; / His silver skin lac'd with his golden blood." Pope had felt it necessary to change "golden blood" to "goary blood," but Johnson understands that these "forced and unnatural" metaphors are deliberate: "It is not improbable, that *Shakespeare* put these forced and unnatural metaphors into the mouth of *Macbeth* as a mark of artifice and dissimulation, to show the difference between the studied language of hypocrisy, and the natural outcries of sudden passion" (6:417; 8:774). Macbeth's real guilt aids in his expression of hypocritical concern about the death of Duncan, a fact that is revealed to us but not to those addressed on stage by the excessive rhetoric of the phrase "golden blood." Johnson, by the way, is the first to explain the pun on "gilt/guilt." Macbeth wades forward into further crime, his own guilt aiding in the service of crime. In that respect, he is, for Johnson, to be distinguished from Lady Macbeth.

Here Johnson adapts a traditional position to a new purpose. When Lady Macbeth returns from the sleeping king and asserts, "Had he not resembled /

My father as he slept, I had don't," Johnson reproduces Warburton's note: "This is very artful. For, as the poet has drawn the lady and husband, it would be thought the act should have been done by her. It is likewise highly just, for tho' ambition had subdued in her all the sentiments of nature toward *present* objects, yet the likeness of one *past*, which she had been accustomed to regard with reverence, made her unnatural passions, for a moment, give way to the sentiments of instinct and humanity" (6:407–8).

Warburton reminds us that Lady Macbeth's compassion has been temporarily repressed but not eliminated, for, as many nineteenth- and twentieth-century commentators have pointed out, she unsexes herself in order to prevent her natural feelings from surfacing. In order to help commit the murder, Lady Macbeth stifles her conscience, which, as Freud would have predicted, subsequently erupts, leading to her suicide. Johnson finds her "merely" (defined in the *Dictionary* as "only," "simply") detestable because, unlike her husband, she is incapable of reminding herself of the evil of the act. In comparison to her husband, Lady Macbeth is, for Johnson, an ordinary criminal, and as these two clear paths emerge, we are directed to focus upon that of Macbeth, who never represses his "strongest conviction of the wickedness of his design." The witches center on Macbeth, not Lady Macbeth, because he alone has the strength of conscience necessary to sustain him in their realm of murky evil.

CONSCIENCE RECOGNIZES HELL

In fact, Macbeth's active conscience seems to prevent him from considering that he has been enchanted by the riddling sisters. Act 3 begins with a reminder that although he is rational and ever able to face his conscience, Macbeth is nonetheless bewitched. In soliloquy, Banquo reflects on the witches' prophecy: "If there come truth from them, / As upon thee, Macbeth, their speeches shine." Warburton defines "shine" as "prosper," but Johnson proposes an alternative: "*Shine*, for appear with all the *lustre* of *conspicuous* truth" (6:422; 8:775). Banquo, according to Johnson, is referring to a "truth" that may only appear to be prosperous for Macbeth: unlike Warburton, Johnson reminds us that the witches' outward appearance is always deceptive and that Banquo differs from Macbeth in suspecting that these fates may be riddlers.

In the next scene, Macbeth reveals that he knows his path leads directly to the devil: "and mine eternal jewel / Given to the common enemy of man" (6:424). In a long note, Johnson demonstrates that Shakespeare refers to the belief that the common enemy of man was synonymous in the Renaissance with the devil, for he wants us to pause and contemplate the fact that the tragic protagonist knows full well that his actions will bring him to hell.

One of Johnson's revisions in 1773 is instructive in this regard. When Macbeth is preparing to have Banquo murdered, he reflects in a soliloquy on his rival and companion.

> There is none but he,
> Whose Being I do fear: and, under him,
> My Genius is rebuk'd; as, it is said,
> *Anthony*'s was by *Caesar.*

In 1765, Johnson dismissed this allusion to *Antony and Cleopatra* as "an insertion of some player, that having so much learning as to discover to what Shakespeare alluded, was not willing that his audience should be less knowing than himself" (6:424; 8:775). By 1773, however, he changed his mind: "This note was written before I was fully acquainted with Shakespeare's manner, and I do not now think it of much weight; for though the words, which I was once willing to eject, seem interpolated, I believe they may still be genuine and added by the authour in his revision" (8:776). Macbeth's allusion to *Antony and Cleopatra*, his comparison of his rivalry with Banquo to that of Antony and Caesar, reinforces the perverse courage of Macbeth, his dignity in damnation. For he knows that, like Antony, he is doomed to final defeat; furthermore, he recognizes that Banquo's lineage will succeed to the throne. Macbeth is the most extraordinary of murderers. He exalts his intended victim to a place above himself, knowing that the attempt to displace Banquo's future regal line will fail. Such a perverse progress aided by the knowledge of its futility can be credited only in the black, eerie realm of Hecate.

EVIL AND THE AUDIENCE

Since the ultimate nature of Macbeth's crimes remains unexplained, by the second half of the tragedy the audience itself begins to feel transported to the realm of Hecate. Nowhere is the function of Johnson's awareness of the atmosphere of enchantment more clearly set forth than at the beginning of act 4. The long note on the witches, unchanged from *Miscellaneous Observations,* is without equivalent in any previous edition: "As this is the chief scene of inchantment in the play, it is proper in this place to observe, with how much judgment *Shakespeare* has selected all the circumstances of his infernal ceremonies, and how exactly he has conformed to common opinions and traditions" (6:444; 8:783–84). This introductory remark is followed by four columns of small print in which Johnson demonstrates that even the most unlikely details—"Fillet of fenny snake" or "Finger of a birth-strangled child"—are derived from sources available to Shakespeare and his contemporaries.

Yet the point is not that the playwright simply extracted sections from demonologies; rather, "it is observable that *Shakespeare*, on this great occasion, which involves the fate of a king, multiplies all the circumstances of horror. The babe, whose finger is used, must be strangled in its birth" (6:446; 8:785). Shakespeare appropriates from this source, creating variations upon or slight exaggerations of standard aspects of witchcraft. In this way, he does not strain the credulity of the audience while nonetheless adding some special significance to the evil prophecy concerning a king. Johnson interrupts his reader at this black moment preceding the most hideous crime of the play, the killing of Macduff's wife and children, to remind us that Shakespeare is manipulating the Renaissance tradition of witchcraft in order to point to moments of mysterious evil on earth.

The implication is that we cannot completely fathom why Macbeth orders the slaughter of this family; his pointless murder of innocents is ultimately as inexplicable and mysterious as the effects of the witches' brew. We can, however, try to follow the mental progress of the tragic protagonist as he trudges along on his path of increasing crime and increasing remorse. At this point it is helpful to know that Johnson was aware of another connection between James I and Macbeth, in addition to Shakespeare's direct references to the king's research on demonology. A reference to the reigning monarch is indicated by reproducing Warburton's note on the line "That twofold balls and treble scepters carry." Warburton pointed out that "this was intended as a compliment to King *James* the first, who first united the two islands and the three kingdoms under one head; whose house was said to be descended from *Banquo*" (6:451). In the context of Johnson's edition, this note suggests a second level of historical reference, for the allusion to the belief that James I descended from Banquo's line gives added authority to the witches' prophecy and further encourages the audience to share in the atmosphere of enchantment. For Johnson, the witches have entered Renaissance history.

THE HUMANITY OF MACBETH

Johnson begins to establish Macbeth's humanity by placing him firmly in history, making the fictive protagonist a predecessor of James I. Turning now to the denouement, we can best understand Johnson's contribution to our understanding of the final section of the drama by examining the historical reference in his remarks on the scene where Malcolm tests the loyalty of Macduff.

> MALCOLM. That which you are, my thoughts cannot transpose;
> Angels are bright still, though the brightest fell,
> Though all things foul would bear the brows of Grace,
> Yet Grace must look still so.

In addition to citing Pope's note that this conversation was taken from the "chronicles of Scotland," Johnson comments upon the language of the above passage: "This is not very clear. The meaning perhaps is this: '*My suspicions cannot injure you, if you be virtuous, by supposing that a traitor may put on your virtuous appearance. I do not say that your virtuous appearance proves you a traitor; for virtue must wear its proper form, though that form be often counterfeited by villany*'" (6:458–59; 8:789). This scene depicting a historical occurrence enables Johnson to point out that the "fair" appearance does not always hide the "foul" behind it. Macduff is, in fact, as fair as he appears to be. In this way, Johnson prepares us to accept the fair side of Macbeth and not to dismiss it as a disguise for the foul. When Macduff is told of the massacre of his family, Malcolm austerely advises him to be comforted by the thought of revenge. Macduff replies, "He has no children," which occasions Johnson to remark: "It has been observed by an anonymous critick that this is not said of Macbeth, who had children, but of Malcolm, who having none, supposes a father can be so easily comforted" (6:466; 8:790–91). Macbeth, the villain, and Macduff, the victim of his villainy, share an essential humanity, and it is because of these shared elements of what Johnson calls "human nature" that we are able to understand and care about the man who cruelly and pointlessly murdered Macduff's wife and children.

Indeed, keeping in mind the essential similarities as well as the differences between Macduff and Macbeth may help throw new light on a famous passage from the *Preface*.

> Shakespeare is above all writers, at least above all modern writers, the poet of nature; the poet that holds up to his readers a faithful mirrour of manners and of life. His characters are not modified by the customs of particular places, unpractised by the rest of the world; by the peculiarities of studies or professions, which can operate but upon small numbers; or by the accidents of transient fashions or temporary opinions: they are the genuine progeny of common humanity, such as the world will always supply, and observation will always find. His persons act and speak by the influence of those general passions and principles by which

all minds are agitated, and the whole system of life is continued in motion. In the writings of other poets a character is too often an individual; in those of Shakespeare it is commonly a species. (7:62)

This section is usually cited as evidence that Johnson admired Shakespeare for his "grand generalizations." But when understood in relation to Macbeth and Macduff, it is clear that neither the general nor the particular predominates. Although different in so many specific respects, these two characters share an essential humanity. Johnson's point is that only if criminal and victim are of the same species can *Macbeth* be viewed as a human tragedy.

Emphasizing that Macbeth should be seen as within our species, Johnson clearly distinguishes himself from Warburton. When Seward refers to Macbeth as the "confident tyrant," Warburton suggests that "the editors have here spoil'd the measure in order to give a tyrant an epithet that does not belong to him; (namely *confidence*, or reposing himself securely in any thing or person) while they rejected the true one, expressive of a tyrant's jealousy and suspicion, and one declarative of the fact. We must surely read, the confin'd *tyrant*" (6:474–75). Warburton is certain that the purpose of *Macbeth* is to demonstrate that improper ambition does not finally succeed; Macbeth, at the end, must surely therefore be a confined, not a confident, tyrant. Johnson, however, finds no need to change the text: "He was *confident* of success; so *confident* that he would not fly, but endure their *setting down* before his castle" (6:475; 8:792).

Johnson refuses to dismiss Macbeth as of the reprobate; a tyrant he certainly is, but not one without any redeeming qualities. On the contrary, for Johnson, Macbeth here reveals a peculiar sort of courage: Macbeth will stand his ground against his enemies, in part because he still hopes against hope that the witches' prophecy will be realized and in part because he wants to face the matter out. Understanding this kind of courage leads Johnson to establish the terms that distinguish the denouement of tragic tyranny from that of the tyrant suitable for a melodrama. Even Macbeth's enemies recognize that he is not a "hardened criminal" in the traditional sense of that term. Menteith remarks of Macbeth that "all that is within him does condemn itself, for being there," and Johnson paraphrases this line in order to be certain that the reader understands: "That is, when all the faculties of the mind are employed in self-condemnation" (6:471; 8:791).

But for Johnson the clearest illustration that Macbeth "preserves" our "esteem" through the end of the drama occurs at his response to the news of the death of Lady Macbeth. Johnson comments at length upon this famous "tomorrow" speech, which Warburton passes over without remark. And although Johnson grew less confident about an emendation he suggested in 1745, he continued to believe that Macbeth retained his affection and respect for Lady Macbeth.

> MACBETH. She should have dy'd hereafter;
> There would have been a time for such a word.

In 1745, Johnson thought that "word" should have been changed to "world"; by 1765, he realized that "word" was understandable in this context. Nevertheless, he reprinted his original paraphrase of the speech: "*Her death should have been deferred to some more peaceful hour; had she lived longer,* there would at length have been a time for *the honours due to her as a Queen, and that respect which I owe her for her fidelity and her love*" (6:476–77; 8:793). Johnson's tyrant is still capable of deep respect and sympathy for his wife.

Finally, we arrive at Johnson's most important and justly famous textual suggestion. Upon being told that Birnam Wood is moving toward Dunsinane, Macbeth, in stunned agony, remarks,

> I pull in Resolution, and begin
> To doubt the equivocation of the fiend,
> That lies like truth.

Although leaving "pull" in the text, Johnson remarked that "it is surely better to read, *I pall in Resolution—I languish in my constancy, my confidence begins to forsake me*" (6:478; 8:794). Johnson prefers "pall" to "pull" because the latter suggests that Macbeth pulls back from his fate; "pall," on the other hand, a psychological term, suggests the inward anguish of a man who stands up to his fate and who, in Macbeth's words, is "tyd to a stake . . . but, bear-like . . . must fight the course." Again, we find Johnson pointing up the dignity, the humanity of Macbeth, that element of the protagonist that lends him a tragic dimension.

Having proceeded through the text, we can now assess Johnson's contribution. Macbeth is able to remain human and thereby to merit the esteem of the audience, in spite of his appalling crimes, because, according to Johnson, his conscience is "fair" while nonetheless serving as a means of sustaining him in evil. Johnson thus points us beyond the modern dualism of Macbeth—the confident, butchering, male stereotype versus the hesitant, conscience-stricken, female stereotype. Johnson suggests a transformation of this dualism into a dialectical notion: in the realm of the witches, Macbeth's conscience does not, as in the unenchanted world, militate against but forwards crime, enabling him to wade on through evil that finally destroys his wife, who tried to evade reflection upon the consequences of his acts. We cannot expect to understand him completely as a character because he is, in some sense, in the thrall of the witches. For Johnson, *Macbeth* is the tragedy of a man who, in succumbing to the temptations of sorcery, has entered a realm where conscience is no longer a guide to virtue. For Elizabethans, this realm is literally that of Hecate; for post-Elizabethans, it is an interior landscape, a psychological witches' brew made up of superstition and conscience.

THE ORGANIC PSYCHE AND AESTHETIC EMPATHY

It is startling to find Johnson taking a psychological position on *Macbeth* while we adopt a moral one, a role reversal worthy of the witches themselves. Johnson's interpretation would seem to be more in keeping with our psychological age than with the eighteenth century, yet his view of *Macbeth* is neglected in our time. The explanation, I believe, resides in the fact that Johnson's reading limits itself to an aspect of Macbeth and does not encompass the character as a whole.

Here we must consider the present-day theoretical presuppositions concerning dramatic empathy. In our time, the prevalent view of the nature of the involvement of the spectators of *Macbeth* derives from Thomas De Quincey's "On the Knocking at the Gate." De Quincey, it will be recalled, focuses upon the porter's scene, which occurs immediately after the murder of Duncan. The porter, according to De Quincey, awakens the audience to the fact that during the murder it had empathized with Macbeth: "Hence it is, that when the deed is done, . . . the knocking at the gate is heard; and it makes known audibly that the reaction has commenced; . . . the pulses of life are beginning to beat again; and the re-establishment of the goings-on of the world in which we live, first makes us profoundly sensible of the useful parenthesis that had suspended them." [13] De Quincey believes that during the murder the audience suspends its belief in reality, that is, suspends its disbelief in the witches, and becomes one with Macbeth; then, the knocking at the gate reawakens us to reality, to the horror of the crime and to sympathy for the victim. This concept of empathy can apply only to characters with complete personal identities: first we are at one with Macbeth against the king, and then we join with Duncan against his host. Johnson, however, suggests, in his *Preface*, an entirely different view of audience involvement.

In the course of discussing the unity of place, Johnson refers to a general notion of the audience's state of mind. Having asserted that the movement between Rome and Egypt in *Antony and Cleopatra* is not a problem because the audience realizes that they are in neither Rome nor Egypt but the theater, he considers the question of the spectators' beliefs, or what is now called empathy.

> It will be asked, how the drama moves, if it is not credited. It is credited with all the credit due to a drama. It is credited whenever it moves, as a just picture of a real original: as representing to the auditor what he himself would feel, if he were to do or suffer what is there feigned to be suffered or to be done. The reflection that strikes the heart is not, that the evils before us are real evils, but that they are evils to which we ourselves may be exposed. If there be any fallacy, it is not that we fancy the players, but that we fancy ourselves unhappy for a moment; but we rather lament the possibility than suppose the presence of misery, as a mother weeps over her babe when she remembers that death may take it from her. The delight of tragedy proceeds from our consciousness of fiction; if we thought murders and treasons real, they would please no more. (7:78)

Johnson believes that the audience of a drama never completely suspends its disbelief; "completely" is the word to be emphasized here. We never forget that we are in a theater; in *Macbeth*, the audience is never completely at one with Macbeth or with Duncan. We identify with an aspect of a character or with an element of an action by relating it to our own life. Selection of the appropriate aspect or element not only entails the recognition that what is on stage is a fiction but also requires—and here I go beyond Johnson—the act of interpretation.

Within this view the witches pose a special problem because we no longer believe that such creatures have the capacity to do evil. In place of the witches, Johnson believes that we have to imagine ourselves under the spell of a force that can condemn us to do evil against our own conscience. And, as Johnson makes clear earlier in his *Notes*, the audience is enchanted, though like Banquo rather than Macbeth. We partially succumb to the witches' sorcery but remain mindful of their place in the action of the play, aware that they are the means by which Macbeth is manipulated. We also know from the notes to *Lear* that delusion is not neglected by Johnson, for his objection to the blinding of Gloucester is that it compels the audience "to relieve its distress by incredulity." Johnson's concept of dramatic empathy entails selectivity, a function of interpretation.

The modern problem with *Macbeth* results from a holistic concept of aesthetic empathy that is divorced from interpretation. Assuming that in the end we empathize with the protagonist, modern critics make a tragic hero of a criminal, a criminal of a tragic hero, or relegate the two forces to a field of free play. The alternative to holistic empathy allows us to admit that we are moved not by the fall of illicit ambition or by the failure to reconcile the male stereotype with its female counterpart. These are themes suitable for a morality play or a melodrama. We are moved, I submit, by the manner in which Macbeth's sincere horror at his own evil aids him in his crimes.

This truly tragic element of Macbeth is accessible only if we are willing to forsake knowledge of Macbeth as a complete character. In *Macbeth*, sorcerers can turn an estimable man's conscience to their purposes because he believes in them. But how Macbeth reconciles his conscience with his belief in witches or how Banquo resists such a temptation is beyond the scope of the tragedy; *Macbeth*, Johnson tells us, does not have such "nice discrimination of character." My claim that the spectator selects an aspect of the protagonist by way of interpretation leads to literary theory.

Aesthetic empathy is, in our time, treated in terms of psychology, as distinct from those of interpretation. The result is a neglected aesthetic premise based upon an outmoded psychological assumption.[14] The organic psyche is now but one view of the ego; alternatives are available. Here we see the converse of the issue in chapter 6. There I suggested expropriation of an innovative literary critical insight; here a newer model of the psyche is appropriated from critics with expertise in psychology. The separation of this psychological issue from the literary one has prevented our understanding Johnson's innovative reading of *Macbeth*. An example from another play may further illustrate the utility of considering aesthetic empathy within the hermeneutic circle.

How the concept of empathy is generally related to interpretation may be further clarified by a brief look at Johnson's notes to *Richard III*. Another drama concerning an evil protagonist, *Richard III*, Johnson feels, is overrated by the critics of his day. "This is one of the most celebrated of our author's performances, yet I know not whether it has not happened to him as to others, to be praised most when praise is not most deserved" (5:362; 8:632). Although Johnson admits that the play has some "noble" scenes, he asserts that "some parts are trifling, others shocking, and some improbable."

One need only glance at the two most famous scenes of the drama to understand that Johnson's objections stem from a misunderstanding of the basis of Richard's appeal to women. But first it should be understood that Johnson in his final stricture asserts that Shakespeare holds Richard responsible for his evil: "Shakespeare very diligently inculcates, that the wickedness of Richard proceeded from his deformity, from the envy that rose at the comparison of his own person with others, and which incited him to disturb the pleasures that he could not partake" (5:230; 8:613). This play contains no equivalent of the witches, no external evil agents, for its topic is the wickedness of Richard III. What clearly disturbs Johnson is the portrayal of Richard's ability to sway the women. The comment on act 1, scene 2, is illustrative.

> GLOUCESTER. Nay, do not pause; for I did kill King *Henry;*
> But 'twas thy beauty that provoked me.
>
> *Shakespeare* countenances the observation, that no woman can ever be offended with the mention of her beauty. (5:241; 8:616)

Johnson finds this scene shocking and improbable; he responds in a similar fashion to one in which Richard proposes that Queen Elizabeth offer her daughter as his wife (4.4). "On this dialogue," Johnson remarks, "'tis not necessary to bestow much criticism: part of it is ridiculous, and the whole improbable" (5:329; 8:627). Although the immorality of the proposal is consistent with what one expects of Richard, it seems improbable to Johnson that the proposals will be accepted, because they are based upon the unwarranted assumption that women, if flattered, will succumb to anything.

The problem here derives from the fact that Johnson places Richard III in the tradition of the medieval devil. Appended to his final stricture on *Richard III* are two dissertations on the "Vice-Devil" of medieval miracle and morality plays that, Johnson explains, provide the source for Richard. Seen in the tradition of the farcical devil, Richard could hardly be taken seriously by Anne and Elizabeth. But it seems to me that here Johnson has selected an inappropriate aspect of Richard to evoke our empathy. Although at times reminiscent of the vice-devil, Richard III also acts like a precursor of *Paradise Lost*'s Satan, that subtle and insidious fallen angel who responds to and mesmerizes Eve when he appears as the serpent of fascinating, horrible beauty. This Renaissance tradition of the devil enables us to "credit" the combined attraction and repulsion experienced by Anne and Elizabeth.

Johnson's interpretation of *Richard III* directly affects his assessment of what is credible in the play, of what elicits our empathy. The alternative here proposed is no less selective than that of Johnson, for all interpretation entails selection. Once we recognize that dramatic empathy is a function of interpretation, we must decide what aspect of the human world is the significant referent of the tragedy.

One way in which literature refers beyond itself is by means of humor. The key moments involve, for Johnson, the most earthy characters—Falstaff, Pandarus, Sir Toby Belch, Sly, Miranda, the gravedigger, and the porter. While for De Quincey the last-mentioned signals a return to reality, Johnson makes clear that the porter is subsumed by the descent he initiates, for, like his counterparts in *Hamlet*, the porter does not reflect on the meaning of his jokes and thereby also becomes a butt of the comedy. Interpretation enables us to understand what subsumes us. The porter's scene and the scene in the graveyard show us how our serious, tragic dimension—our deepest agonies and most cherished theories or ideologies—can become the subject of comedy, bringing them down to a level where other interpreters will make of them new comic quips, new theories, and modified ideologies. If we are to empathize with the tragic protagonist, then we must laugh along with Falstaff at the breaking down of theories and ideologies, for the most profound moments of Shakespearean tragedy are those that encompass comedy.

Toward a New Humanism

As early as 1903, David Nichol Smith defended Johnson's edition of Shakespeare against the attack by Thomas Macaulay, who asserted, "It would be difficult to find a more slovenly, a more worthless edition of any great classic." In a volume that contained the *Preface* without any of the *Notes,* Nichol Smith replied, "Other editions are distinguished by accuracy, ingenuity, or learning; the supreme distinction of [Johnson's] is sagacity."[1] In 1956, Arthur Sherbo wisely pointed out that the general observations "must be read not alone, but in conjunction with everything else Johnson wrote on the plays, particularly the notes in his commentary."[2] But as recently as 1986, Bertrand Bronson continued to separate the *Notes* from the remainder of the Shakespeare commentary.

> Despite the fluctuations of opinion in the years since the appearance of Johnson's edition of the works in 1765, and despite all legitimate subtractions, his notes still rest on solid ground. Raleigh's prediction at the beginning of our century, that Johnson's critical reputation would be redeemed from the disparagement of the nineteenth century, has been more than amply sustained and verified. Nothing since the appearance of his noble *Preface* has dislodged or replaced it. As was said years ago, its best passages subsume and supersede earlier statements and compel later ones into their own channel. Measured by the terms of human survival it will endure.[3]

The unmistakable implication is that although the *Notes* contain much solid common sense, the *Preface* constitutes Johnson's claim to fame as a Shakespearean. On the contrary, we have seen that the *Notes* contain original criticism that is, at times, obscured by the orthodox terminology of the *Preface*. In fact, I claim that Johnson's edition of Shakespeare is the first critical edition because he is the first to make explicit his interpretation of the plays in the *Notes*. This discovery resulted from treating the *Preface* and the strictures, the general observations, as assessments of Shakespeare's artistic ends that were then seen as the goals of the *Notes*. The teleological nature of Johnson's Shakespeare commentary became apparent, a principle that was then forwarded by me as an axiom of literary criticism.

In fact, understanding how the *Preface* and *Notes* are related to each other entailed a new methodogy. Accordingly, each chapter exemplified in its own unfolding a critical principle that was uncovered in Johnson's critical practice. What remained on the referential level for Johnson was transformed by my method to the symbolic register.

My first chapter developed what I believe to be the most basic principle of literary criticism: the foundation of our discipline is what Johnson called "naked criticism," judgmental interpretations of particular works of literature. The moral, judgmental aspect of interpretation requires that the critic measure literature in relation to the human dilemma. Ethical teleology is fundamental to literary criticism. When, as is often the case, the critic does not make his position overt, we should attempt, detective-style, to discover his interpretive goal. Such a procedure will often be speculative, but the price paid for avoiding it is the loss of the most valuable aspect of literary criticism: new insights about and new ways of approaching literature.

If finding the best in criticism involves the search for interpretation, interpretation would seem to be a key term. Yet it is only vaguely defined, in the Introduction, as an explanation of closure that is itself defined as not merely an end but a judgment about a significant conclusion. And significance is a function of interpretation. No attempt is made at further definitional clarity because interpretation is not exclusive to criticism. Applied in nearly all disciplines as well as in our daily lives, interpretation takes on a special significance, becomes literary criticism, when applied to literature.

Instead of attempting to define literature, which, as Johnson pointed out, "will only show the narrowness of the definer," I examined how Shakespeare editors determine what constitutes the text of the play, since these scholars decide what is the subject matter for the literary critic. Similarly, instead of defining interpretation, I turned to examples of the art, Johnson's strictures. But literary analysis cannot be confined to literary matters. Even bibliography, the most scholarly element of our discipline, refers beyond itself to ideology. While it is important to understand how criticism and ideology can affect and modify one another, major ideological differences are unlikely to be resolved by means of criticism.

Consequently, I turned from ideology to theory in the belief, as Clifford Siskin put it, that the former cannot escape the discourse of the latter.[4] Insofar as criticism is a discipline, it is defined and even constrained. Yet, like many other disciplines, it functions in the fluidity of human life, comprehending and becoming a part of history. That fluidity has provided various antithetical critical theories, from mimeticism to poststructuralism, with the opportunity for a dialogic and/or dialectic relationship that can create new theories. Because innovation arises from the recombining and revising of old theories, it is clear that willful neglect of past methods can lead only to paucity of new ones. Literary criticism, not an end in itself, should be committed to the larger endeavor of understanding the human situation, what it means to be human and to live in a civilization.

Humor, if not a distinctly human characteristic, has surely been most highly developed by humans. Johnson is seldom associated with humor, especially in his Shakespeare criticism. Yet comedy has proved crucial in this study. Falstaff's kind of humor led to a distinction between didacticism and morality, and comedy helped isolate a Pandarus/Thersites point of view. Malvolio's lack of a sense of humor was, in large part, the reason for his final isolation from the other characters, and satire located the extraliterary reference in *The Taming of the Shrew*. *King Lear* was a turning point in this regard. The loss of "my poor fool," understood as an allusion both to the fool and Cordelia, manifested a critical crisis that shattered Johnson's concept of reality. What, in effect, he asks, is the point of life without the down-to-earth humor and love of the fool and Cordelia? This question took us to the higher register of theory: Johnson's terms, life and reality, were transformed into symbolic ones, functions of interpretation that delineate the extraliterary referent.

Comedy, even at this level, continued to be a touchstone. Miranda's "wrangle" with Ferdinand helped to explain the nature of Prospero's decision to give up magic, and the gravedigger's irreverent jokes pointed toward a new kind of closure, as the drunken porter's allusion to equivocating conscience highlighted a tragic dimension of *Macbeth*.

For Johnson, humor is the means by which literature returns to earth. Its absence at the end of *Lear* makes him feel the loss of the firm ground of what he believes is reality.[5] But the joke or idle humor is not what interests him: the two plays Johnson leaves without a stricture are comedies, presumably those that he regards as serving merely to entertain. The kinds of humor that catch his attention, that he insists require the justice of criticism—the sort of critical justice he demands for Falstaff—are key moments where the dramas gesture beyond their bounds: to ethics in *Henry IV,* history in *Troilus and Cressida,* sociology in *Twelfth Night,* ideology in *The Taming of the Shrew,* literary theory in *King Lear,* theology in *The Tempest,* philosophy in *Hamlet,* and psychology in *Macbeth.* Perhaps it is for this reason that Johnson prefers Shakespeare's comedies to his tragedies.

> In tragedy he often writes with great appearance of toil and study, what is written at last with little felicity; but in his comick scenes he seems to produce without labour, what no labour can improve. In tragedy he is always struggling after some occasion to be comick, but in comedy he seems to repose, or to luxuriate, as in a mode of thinking congenial to his nature. In his tragick scenes there is always something wanting, but his comedy often surpasses expectation or desire. His comedy pleases by the thoughts and the language, and his tragedy for the greater part by incident and action. His tragedy seems to be skill, his comedy to be instinct. (7:69)[6]

But only perhaps. It is equally possible that Johnson preferred comedy because it is less often concerned with those magisterial, regal matters that Johnson felt seldom moved the common reader. Always on less sure ground when we extract Johnson's generalizations from their practical context, we confront the extraliterary critical morass of Johnson's sensibility, derivative and brilliant ideas, eccentric and original tastes, inconsistent and incisive opinions, outmoded and innovative ideologies. These are the essential ingredients of Johnson's edition of Shakespeare, a great document of literary criticism because it exemplifies the kinds of achievements that result from channeling our drives, beliefs, insights, and theories into a discipline.

For Johnson, the task of criticism only begins with the deconstructive possibility inherent in functional humor. The critic has a moral obligation that in this study has been transformed into the need to interpret judgmentally. We are obliged, according to Johnson, to do justice to Falstaff—the brilliant deconstructor of ideologies—and to avoid a "lame and impotent conclusion." The task of articulating what constitutes a significant conclusion, closure, and explaining the assessment of that significance, interpretation, involves recognizing the limitations of Falstaff, his refusal to mend his ways, to seek an alternative to the venial and all too pleasurable sin of exposing the limitations of himself and other people. Criticism entails not merely description but also value judgments. When Johnson feels that there is nothing that he can say about a play that points beyond its role as entertainment, he leaves it without a stricture. Explicit evaluative interpretation in turn leads the critic to analyze his view in relation to his predecessors' views. The theoretical differences that emerge between critics need to be distinguished; extraliterary or ideological differences should be separated from distinctions of literary method. The last and most important task of the critic is to justify his interpretation by explaining how it applies to the human dilemma, by taking risks, such as asserting that *Hamlet* is most moving at the seriocomic point when death becomes a principle of closure or that *Macbeth* is most significant when conscience is a tragic equivocator.

Johnson believes that interpretation is a moral imperative. At the moment, it seems to me, literary criticism is in a poststructuralist or Falstaffian stage, content to expose the fissures in theories and ideologies. My contention is that the deconstructive and new historicist strategies are important initial steps, but they move in separate orbits, the former playfully ambling in discourse and the latter austerely restricting itself to the realm of ideology. A point of contact between them, closure seeks to fuse fissures with ideological sealants. Closure involves a decision about the human comedy, how the irony of tragedy and the laughter of comedy touch our lives. The resulting interpretation can open the way to alternatives to outmoded orthodoxies by explaining which fissures are important and by articulating their ideological innovative purport. Literary criticism will come into its own as a discipline only when it demonstrates that the singularity of literature resides in the way it contributes to the humanities, to the discovery and articulation of procedures that enable us to better endure and understand the human condition.

NOTES

Introduction

1. I first heard this term when it was used by Ralph Cohen at the conference, "Theory and Tradition in Eighteenth-Century Studies," held at Georgetown University in 1987.

2. Jean Hagstrum, *Samuel Johnson's Literary Criticism* (Chicago: Univ. of Chicago Press, 1967), p. 176. This edition also contains the 1967 preface.

3. William R. Keast, "The Theoretical Foundations of Johnson's Criticism," in *Critics and Criticism: Ancient and Modern*, ed. Ronald S. Crane (Chicago: Univ. of Chicago Press, 1952), pp. 402, 407.

4. William K. Wimsatt, Jr., and Cleanth Brooks, *Literary Criticism: A Short History* (New York: Alfred A. Knopf, 1957), p. 318. Subsequent quotations from this chapter give the page number in the text. Arthur Friedman responded to Wimsatt, in a review of *The Prose Style of Samuel Johnson, Philological Quarterly* 21 (1942): 211–13, and Wimsatt responded in *Philological Quarterly* 22 (1943): 71–76. For my discussion of this matter in the context of *Rasselas*, see *Johnson, "Rasselas," and the Choice of Criticism* (Lexington: Univ. Press of Kentucky, 1989), pp. 62–72.

5. Hagstrum, *Johnson's Literary Criticism*, p. ix.

6. Robert Voitle, *Samuel Johnson the Moralist* (Cambridge, Mass.: Harvard Univ. Press, 1961), and Paul Alkon, *Samuel Johnson and Moral Discipline* (Evanston, Ill.: Northwestern Univ. Press, 1967).

7. Leopold Damrosch, Jr., *The Uses of Johnson's Criticism* (Charlottesville: Univ. Press of Virginia, 1976).

8. William Edinger, *Samuel Johnson and Poetic Style* (Chicago: Univ. of Chicago Press, 1977), p. xiii.

9. R. D. Stock, *Samuel Johnson and Neoclassical Dramatic Theory* (Lincoln: Univ. of Nebraska Press, 1973), pp. ix–xi.

10. John Needham, "Complexity and the Doctrine of Propriety in Johnson's Shakespeare Criticism," in *The Completest Mode: I. A. Richards and the Continuity of English Literary Criticism* (Edinburgh: Edinburgh Univ. Press, 1983), pp. 120–34.

11. G. F. Parker, *Johnson's Shakespeare* (Oxford: Clarendon Press, 1989).

12. Arthur Sherbo, *Samuel Johnson, Editor of Shakespeare, with an Essay on "The Adventurer"* (Urbana: Univ. of Illinois Press, 1956), p. 62. Sherbo edited the *Notes* for the edition published by the Augustan Reprint Society in 1951 as well as the edition published by the Yale University Press in 1968. Donald D. Eddy offers some modifications of Sherbo's bibliographic position in "Samuel Johnson's Editions of Shakespeare (1765)," *Papers of the Bibliographical Society of America* 56 (1962): 428–44.

13. For a traditional theoretical approach to the *Preface* apart from the *Notes*, see Murray Krieger, "Fiction, Nature, and Literary Kinds in Johnson's Criticism of Shakespeare," *Eighteenth-Century Studies* 4 (1970): 184–98. For a satirical reading of the *Preface*, see Donald T. Siebert, Jr., "The Scholar as Satirist: Johnson's Edition of Shakespeare," *Studies in English Literature* 15 (1975): 483–503. For a stylistic approach, see James Black, "Johnson, Shakespeare, and the Dyer's Hand," *Transactions of the Samuel Johnson Society of the Northwest* 8 (1975): 5–28.

14. On Johnson's eminent "common sense," see Bertrand Bronson's introduction to the Yale edition of Johnson's *Notes to Shakespeare* and Charles T. Harrison, "Common Sense as Approved," *Sewanee Review* 79 (1971): 1–10.

15. Sherbo discusses the relationship between the *Notes* and the *Dictionary* in *Samuel Johnson*, pp. 15–27, and that between the *Notes* and the *Lives of the Poets* in "Johnson's Shakespeare and the Dramatic Criticism in the *Lives of the English Poets*," in *Shakespeare: Aspects of Influence*, ed. G. B. Evans, Harvard English Studies, no. 7 (Cambridge, Mass.: Harvard Univ. Press, 1976), pp. 55–69.

16. J. Hillis Miller, "Presidential Address, 1986: The Triumph of Theory, the Resistance to Reading, and the Question of the Material Base," *PMLA* 102 (1987): 281–91; see also the essays by Edward Pechter and Tania Modleski in the same issue of *PMLA*. More recently, Hillis Miller has again expressed his view in "The Function of Literary Theory at the Present Time," in *The Future of Literary Theory*, ed. Ralph Cohen (London: Routledge, 1989), pp. 102–11. In a cryptic way, Hillis Miller displays some disillusionment with ideological studies when he concludes his essay with reference to "that disastrous confusion of linguistic with material reality, one name for which is 'ideology'" (p. 111).

17. Ernesto Laclau and Chantal Mouffe, *Hegemony and Socialist Strategy: Towards a Radical Democratic Politics* (London: Verso, 1985). Morality is first seen as a turning point in the work of Gramsci (pp. 65–75).

CHAPTER ONE
Morality in *Henry IV*

1. See Sherbo, *Samuel Johnson*, pp. 46–60. For a more recent consideration of the *Preface*, see R. D. Stock, *Johnson and Neoclassical Dramatic Theory*. For an updated version of Sherbo's position, see Arthur Sherbo, *The Birth of Shakespeare Studies: Commentators from Rowe to Boswell-Malone* (East Lansing, Mich.: Colleagues Press, 1988), especially pp. 18–26. For another recent view of Johnson and his predeces-

sors, see Peter Seary, "The Early Editions of Shakespeare and the Judgments of Johnson," in *Johnson after Two Hundred Years,* ed. Paul Korshin (Princeton: Princeton Univ. Press, 1986), pp. 175–86. The latest book on this topic is G. F. Parker's *Johnson's Shakespeare.* Parker implies that Johnson's conception of general nature is original or at least used by Johnson in a special way (see pp. 2–8). Unfortunately, Parker does not explain how Johnson's concept is to be distinguished from those of the contemporaries and predecessors discussed by Sherbo and Stock. His claim is therefore implicit and unsubstantiated. For an assessment of Johnson's analysis of Shakespeare's use of his sources, see Karl Young, "Samuel Johnson: One Aspect," *University of Wisconsin Studies in Language and Literature* 18 (1923): 146–226. For an account of why Johnson's contribution as editor of "accidentals" has not been sufficiently appreciated, see Arthur M. Eastman, "Johnson's Shakespeare and the Laity in Textual Study," *PMLA* 65 (1950): 1112–21.

2. Jeremy Collier, *A Short View of the Immorality, and Profaneness of the English Stage* (London, 1698), p. 154.

3. Maurice Morgann, *An Essay on the Dramatic Character of Sir John Falstaff* (London, 1777), p. 410.

4. Nicholas Rowe, *The Works of Mr. William Shakespeare* (London, 1709), 1:xviii.

5. Charles Gildon, *The Works of Mr. William Shakespeare, Volume the Seventh* (London, 1725), p. 376.

6. John Nichols, ed., *Illustrations of the Literary History of the Eighteenth Century* (London, 1733), 3:379.

7. Corbyn Morris, *An Essay Towards Fixing the True Standards of Wit, Humour, Raillery, Satire, and Ridicule* (London, 1744), pp. 28–29, and edited by James L. Clifford for the Augustan Reprint Society (Los Angeles: Univ. of California Press, 1947).

8. John Upton, *Critical Observations on Shakespeare* (London, 1756), pp. 70–71. For other evidence of Johnson's awareness of the continuity of the history plays, see *Henry V* (4:383; 8:536) and *Richard III* (5:319; 8:625).

9. Arthur Sherbo finds some evidence to suggest that Samuel Johnson began work on the edition before 1745. See Sherbo, " 'Sanguine Expectations': Dr. Johnson's Shakespeare," *Shakespeare Quarterly* 9 (1958): 426–28.

10. Lewis Theobald, ed., *The Works of Shakespeare* (London, 1733), 1:xviii. For the attribution to Warburton, see *SCH* 2:18.

11. E. M. W. Tillyard, "*Henry IV* and the Tudor Epic," in *Shakespeare: Henry IV Parts I and II, a Casebook,* ed. G. K. Hunter (London: Macmillan Press, 1970), p. 107. For further evidence of Johnson's understanding of the political import of these plays, see *Henry V* (4:414; 8:547; 4:444; 8:555; 4:461; 8:560; 4:479; 8:565) and *Henry VIII* (5:490; 8:657).

12. Clifford Leech, "The Unity of *2 Henry IV*," in *Twentieth-Century Interpretations of Henry IV, Part 2,* ed. David P. Young (Englewood Cliffs, N.J.: Prentice-Hall, 1968), p. 41.

13. Harold Toliver, "Workable Fictions in the *Henry IV* Plays," *University of Toronto*

Quarterly 53 (1983): 53–71, and Harry Levin, "Falstaff's Encore," *Shakespeare Quarterly* 32 (1981): 5–17.

14. In spite of his disapproval of the quibble, Johnson takes time elsewhere to explain Falstaff's puns, as in *Merry Wives* (2:484; 7:332), and even notes his own reliance on Falstaff's puns, in *Timon of Athens* (6:192; 8:716) and *Coriolanus* (6:499; 8:798).

15. For references in other plays to Hal's character, see *Henry V* (4:379; 7:534) and *Richard II* (4:92; 8:450).

16. William Shakespeare, *The First Part of Henry IV*, ed. A. R. Humphreys (London: Methuen, 1960), p. 78.

17. Boswell, in his *Life of Johnson*, records that Johnson, in 1783, commented on this essay: " 'Why, Sir, we shall have the man come forth again; and as he has proved Falstaff to be no coward, he may prove Iago to be a very good character' " (*Life of Johnson* 4:192). Probably no character is more often referred to in Johnson's *Notes* than Falstaff. On his personality, see the stricture to *The Merry Wives of Windsor*, where Johnson discusses Queen Elizabeth's delight with Falstaff and the difficulty of showing him in love (7:341). In *All's Well That Ends Well*, Johnson compares him as a coward to Parolles (3:384; 7:399). At the last appearance of Falstaff in *Henry V*, Johnson discusses the difficulty of finding future adventures that would be as entertaining as those before (4:397; 8:441–42). Later in the same play, Johnson registers his sorrow at the last of the comic scenes of *Henry IV* and *Henry V* (4:474; 8:563). While recognizing the comic genius of Falstaff, Johnson continually reminds his audience that in moral terms he was below Hal (4:379; 8:534). For further evidence that Johnson stands out from his contemporaries in his concern for the theatrical spectacle of the characters, see S. P. Zitner, "Staging the Occult in *1 Henry IV*," in *Mirror Up to Shakespeare; Essays in Honour of G. R. Hibbard*, ed. J. C. Gray (Toronto: Univ. of Toronto Press, 1984), pp. 138–48.

18. See above, n. 3.

19. A. R. Humphreys, ed., *The Second Part of Henry IV*, by William Shakespeare (London: Methuen, 1966), p. 34.

20. Leech, "Unity of *2 Henry IV*," p. 38.

21. Humphreys, *Second Part of Henry IV*, p. 184.

22. Stephen Greenblatt, *Shakespearian Negotiations: The Circulation of Social Energy in Renaissance England* (Oxford: Clarendon Press, 1988), p. 38. For a British equivalent of Greenblatt's position, see Jonathan Dollimore and Alan Sinfield, "History and Ideology: The Instance of *Henry V*," in *Alternative Shakespeares*, ed. John Drakakis (London: Methuen, 1985), pp. 206–27. Like Greenblatt, Dollimore and Sinfield conclude with ambiguity: "We might conclude from this that Shakespeare was indeed wonderfully impartial on the question of politics. . . . Alternatively, we might conclude that the ideology which saturates his texts, and their location in history, are the most interesting things about them" (p. 227).

23. Greenblatt, *Shakespearian Negotiations*, pp. 55–57.

24. Ibid., pp. 63–65. For an example of how the new historicist position evades the constrictions of literary structure and genre, see Leonard Tennenhouse, "Strategies of State and Political Plays: *A Midsummer Night's Dream, Henry IV, Henry V, Henry VIII,*" in *Political Shakespeare: New Essays in Cultural Materialism,* ed. Jonathan Dollimore and Alan Sinfield (Manchester: Manchester Univ. Press, 1985), pp. 109–28. Alternatively, Marjorie Garber stresses the importance of genre within a reader-response framework, in "'What's Past Is Prologue': Temporality and Prophecy in Shakespeare's History Plays," in *Renaissance Genres: Essays on Theory, History, and Interpretation,* ed. Barbara Kiefer Lewalski (Cambridge, Mass.: Harvard Univ. Press, 1986), pp. 301–31.

25. For some examples of Johnson's didactic notes, see *Measure for Measure* (1:377; 7:213), *The Merchant of Venice* (1:456; 7:227), and *Othello* (8:397; 8:1032–33).

26. Laclau and Mouffe, *Hegemony and Socialist Strategy,* pp. 65–75.

CHAPTER TWO
Critical Editing of *Troilus and Cressida*

1. See above, chap. 1, n. 1. Sherbo, in *Samuel Johnson,* p. 87, asserts that Charles Gildon set a precedent in his "Remarks" (see above, chap. 1, n. 7) for the stricture. In fact, Gildon's remarks differ from Johnson's strictures in a number of respects. Gildon begins with a plot summary and continues by citing particularly beautiful or useful passages. Johnson has this practice in mind when he terms his stricture a departure from the practice of marking passages for blame and praise. Furthermore, Gildon's remarks are attached to texts edited by others; Johnson's stricture provides the interpretive principles that form the foundation for his edition of the drama.

2. See above, Introduction, n. 12. For an assessment of Johnson's revisions of the Shakespeare edition, see T. J. Monaghan, "Johnson's Additions to His Shakespeare for the Edition of 1773," *Review of English Studies* n.s. 4 (1953): 234–47, and Arthur Sherbo's review of this essay in *Philological Quarterly* 33 (1954): 283–84, and "1773: The Year of Revision," *Eighteenth-Century Studies* 7 (1973): 18–39.

3. The term "double hermeneutic" is from Fredric Jameson, *Marxism and Form: Twentieth-Century Dialectical Theories of Literature* (Princeton: Princeton Univ. Press, 1971), pp. 99–118. For my previous use of this idea, see "The Art of Politics in James McClure's *The Artful Egg,*" *Human Rights Quarterly* 4 (1982): 230–39.

4. Arthur H. Scouten, ed., *The London Stage: 1660–1800* (Carbondale, Ill.: Southern Illinois Univ. Press, 1961), pp. 3–99.

5. For instances where Johnson records an emendation in the *Notes* that is not reproduced in the text, see *Measure for Measure* (2:87; 7:200); *The Merchant of Venice* (3:167; 7:225); *Love's Labour's Lost* (2:130; 7:270); *Richard II* (4:37; 7:435); *3 Henry VI* (5:176; 7:605). As Johnson moved into the second half of the project, he began to formulate himself more overtly. In *Henry VIII,* after rejecting an emendation of Warburton's, he concludes: "I wish every commentator, before he suffers his confidence

to kindle, would repeat, 'We are all men / In our own natures frail, and capable / Of frailty; few are angels'" (5:479; 8:654). In *Coriolanus*, under similar circumstances, he asserts: "But when a word is to be admitted, the first question should be, by whom was it ever received? in what book can it be shewn? If it cannot be proved to have been in use, the reasons which can justify its reception must be stronger than any critick will often have to bring" (6:609; 8:820).

6. Kenneth Palmer, ed., *The Arden Edition of "Troilus and Cressida,"* by William Shakespeare (London: Methuen, 1982), p. 227.

CHAPTER THREE
History of Criticism in *Twelfth Night*

1. This note is omitted from Sherbo's Yale edition (7:319).

2. M. M. Lothian and T. W. Craik, eds., *The Arden Edition of the Works of William Shakespeare: "Twelfth Night,"* by William Shakespeare (London: Methuen, 1975), p. 143. On the other hand, Richard Levin, in "Viola: Dr. Johnson's 'Excellent Schemer,'" *Durham University Journal* 71 (1979): 213–22, uses Johnson's notes to undermine the romantic reading of *Twelfth Night* by suggesting that "the intricate web of deception is the norm" (p. 222). My own position goes further, attempting to explain why deception is the norm and how this affects the end of the drama.

3. See Lothian and Craik, *Arden Edition: "Twelfth Night,"* p. lvii. For an interesting modern alternative, see Geoffrey Hartman, "Shakespeare's Poetical Character in *Twelfth Night,*" in *The Question of Theory*, ed. Geoffrey Hartman and Patricia Parker (New York: Methuen, 1985), pp. 37–53. Because Hartman focuses on language and exposes similar games to those seen by Johnson, we are left without a conclusion as to how this deconstructive analysis applies to the action of the drama. Clifford Siskin, in *The Historicity of Romantic Discourse* (Oxford: Oxford Univ. Press, 1988), pp. 50–51, makes some penetrating comments about this aspect of Hartman's criticism.

4. Johnson records a similar difficulty with the end of *As You Like It*, where he remarks, "I know not how the ladies will approve the facility with which both Rosalind and Celia give away their hearts" (2:108; 7:264).

5. Shirley White Johnston, "From Preface to Practice: Samuel Johnson's Editorship of Shakespeare," in *Greene Centennial Studies: Essays Presented to Donald Greene,* ed. Paul Korshin and Robert R. Allen (Charlottesville: Univ. Press of Virginia, 1984), pp. 250–70, demonstrates that Johnson was more fair and judicious to his predecessors than they were to one another. In my view, Johnson was thus not only being decent to his colleagues but engaging in the art of the history of criticism. For instances of Johnson's forbearance with his predecessors, see *As You Like It* (2:107; 7:164); *The Winter's Tale* (2:248; 7:291); *Othello* (8:405; 8:1035).

CHAPTER FOUR
Feminist Satire and Bibliographic Ideology in
The Taming of the Shrew

1. Walter J. Bate, "Johnson and Satirist Manqué," in *Eighteenth-Century Studies in Honor of Donald F. Hyde*, ed. W. H. Bond (New York: Grolier Club, 1970), pp. 145–60. For a healthy antidote to this position, see Siebert, "Scholar as Satirist," 483–503. While Siebert focuses on the *Preface*, I am interested in this chapter in how the concept of satire informs the *Notes* to *The Taming of the Shrew* and in subsequent chapters in how the more general idea of humor informs the *Notes* to *Lear, Hamlet,* and *Macbeth.*

2. Jonathan Swift, "The Preface to the Author" (of *The Battle of the Books*), in *The Prose Writings of Jonathan Swift*, ed. Herbert Davis (London, 1938), 1:138. John H. Middendorf describes Johnson's descent to earthly matters in "Ideas vs. Words: Johnson, Locke, and the Edition of Shakespeare," in *English Writers of the Eighteenth Century*, ed. John H. Middendorf (New York: Columbia Univ. Press, 1971), pp. 149–71.

3. Robert Weimann, "Towards a Literary Theory of Ideology: Mimesis, Representation, Authority," in *Shakespeare Reproduced*, ed. Jean E. Howard and Marian R. O'Connor (New York: Methuen, 1987), p. 265.

4. Richard Hosley, in "Was There a Dramatic Epilogue to the *The Taming of the Shrew?*" *Studies in English Literature* 1 (1961): 17–34, makes the negative case. Karl P. Wentersdorf, in "The Original Ending of *The Taming of the Shrew:* A Reconsideration," *Studies in English Literature* 18 (1978): 201–15, argues for including this material and demonstrates how the epilogue resolves the problem, near the end, concerning the "law of reentry."

5. For two typical modern editors' views on this issue, see H. J. Oliver, ed., *The Taming of the Shrew*, by William Shakespeare (Oxford: Clarendon Press, 1982), pp. 233–35, and Brian Morris, ed., *The Arden Edition of "The Taming of the Shrew,"* by William Shakespeare (London: Methuen, 1981), pp. 303–5. All future references to Morris's edition will provide the page numbers in the text. In his review of Morris's edition, William Proctor Williams, in "Three New Arden Editions," *Shakespeare Quarterly* 33 (1982): 502, points out that the bad quarto theory is by no means universally accepted. Specifically, Williams points to evidence cited in T. H. Howard-Hill, "The Compositors of Shakespeare's Comedies," *Studies in Bibliography* 26 (1973): 61–106. Fortunately, the question of copy-text is unlikely to arise here, since most editors are willing to grant that the folio, the usual copy-text, accommodates the material Pope found in the quarto. However, it is well to keep in mind that recent bibliographic theorists have called into question Greg and Bowers's assumption of a single authorial, eclectic copy-text. Jerome J. McGann, *A Critique of Modern Textual Criticism* (Chicago: Univ. of Chicago Press, 1983) analyzes the implicit ideological assumptions embodied in this concept (see pp. 37–49) and exposes its flaws with regard to post-Shakespearean texts such as that of Byron D. F. McKenzie, *Bibliography*

and the Sociology of Texts (London: British Library, 1986), argues that different historical ages produce different texts and that they must be understood in relative, not absolute, terms (pp. 7–11). My own position is that an authorized text is grounded in an interpretation and that alternatives are recognized as authoritative by way of new interpretations. We need to make overt the literary critical criteria for our textual decisions so that they can be examined, refined, and better understood.

6. For a history of the staging of *The Taming of the Shrew*, see Tori Haring-Smith, *From Farce to Metadrama: A Stage History of "The Taming of the Shrew,"* (Westport, Conn.: Greenwood Press, 1985), especially pp. 7–22, on the eighteenth century.

7. See Garrick, 3:220, and Morris, *Taming of the Shrew*, p. 109.

8. Richard Hurd, *Horatii Flacci Epistola ad Augustum* (London, 1753), 2:84.

9. Ibid., 2:90.

10. See above, chap. 4, n. 5, and the appendix of Ann Thompson, ed., *The Taming of the Shrew*, by William Shakespeare (Cambridge: Cambridge Univ. Press, 1984).

11. See Oliver, *Taming of the Shrew*, p. 62, and Thompson, *Taming of the Shrew*, p. 41.

12. See Oliver, *Taming of the Shrew*, p. 52, and Thompson, *Taming of the Shrew*, pp. 40–41.

13. For Johnson's use of the satirical mirror elsewhere in the *Notes*, see *Merry Wives of Windsor* (2:530; 7:337); *Timon of Athens* (6:171; 8:709); *Coriolanus* (6:534; 8:804, and 6:552; 8:807); *Cymbeline* (7:260; 8:875). For another instance of a female character who, like Katherina, expresses her personality by playing many roles, see the stricture on Cleopatra, *Antony and Cleopatra* (7:254; 8:873).

14. Robert B. Heilman, "The Taming Untamed; or, The Return of the Shrew," *Modern Language Quarterly* 27 (1966): 151, 160. For a convenient reprint of Heilman's introduction to his edition, see "Introduction to *The Taming of the Shrew*," in Sylvan Barnet, ed., *The Complete Signet Classic Shakespeare* (New York: Harcourt Brace Jovanovich, 1966), pp. 321–29.

15. Coppelia Kahn, *"The Taming of the Shrew:* Shakespeare's Mirror of Marriage," in *The Authority of Experience: Essays in Feminist Criticism*, ed. Arlyn Diamond and Lee R. Edward (Amherst: Univ. of Massachusetts Press, 1977), pp. 85, 92, 91, 99.

16. For an example of an essay favoring Heilman's position, see Marion D. Perret, "Petruchio: The Model Wife," *Studies in English Literature* 23 (1983): 223–35. For an essay forwarding the opposite position, see Jeanne Addison Roberts, "Horses and Hermaphrodites: Metamorphoses in *The Taming of the Shrew*," *Shakespeare Quarterly* 34 (1983): 159–70.

17. Joel Fineman, "The Turn of the Screw," in *Shakespeare and the Question of Theory*, ed. Patricia Parker and Geoffrey Hartman (New York: Methuen, 1985), pp. 141, 155, 157. Siskin's remark about McGann's position is also applicable to Fineman's argument: "Presenting ideology as an alternative to theory . . . belies the fact that the former is now a feature of the discourse of the latter" (*Romantic Discourse*, p. 52).

CHAPTER FIVE
Mimetic Theory in *King Lear*

1. Scouten, *London Stage*, I, 3–99.

2. Nahum Tate, *The History of "King Lear,"* ed. James Black (Lincoln: Univ. of Nebraska Press, 1975).

3. Ibid., p. 7. For a recent essay that assumes that Johnson agrees with Tate, see Norman N. Holland, "How Can Dr. Johnson's Remarks on Cordelia's Death Add to My Response?" in *Psychoanalysis and the Question of the Text* (Baltimore: Johns Hopkins Univ. Press, 1978), pp. 18–44.

4. Gildon, *Works of Mr. William Shakespeare*, p. 406.

5. Joseph Addison, *The Spectator*, no. 40, 1711.

6. Lewis Theobald, *The Censor* (London, 1715).

7. Thomas Cooke, *Considerations on the Stage* (London, 1731), p. 55.

8. Dionysius Longinus, *On the Sublime*, trans. William Smith (London, 1740), p. 110.

9. Samuel Foote, *A Treatise on the Passions* (London, 1747), p. 18.

10. Peter Whalley, *An Enquiry into the Learning of Shakespeare* (London, 1748), p. 60.

11. John Upton, *Critical Observations on Shakespeare* (London, 1748), p. 284.

12. Thomas Edwards, *The Canons of Criticism* (London, 1750), p. 40. See Sherbo, *Samuel Johnson*, pp. 39–41, on Johnson and Edwards. For another reference to the difficulty of "rash oaths," see *Love's Labour's Lost* (2:133; 7:269).

13. Joseph Warton, *The Adventurer*, no. 132, 1754.

14. Arthur Murphy, *Gray's-Inn Journal*, no. 16, 1754. For other instances in the *Notes* where Johnson points to the importance of the domestic and private for public and regal characters, see *3 Henry VI* (5:156; 8:602) and *Antony and Cleopatra* (7:245; 8:871).

15. George Colman, *The History of "King Lear"* (London, 1768), p. ii.

16. See above, chap. 5, n. 12.

17. Sherbo, in the Yale edition (8:665), points out that Johnson omitted this note in his revised edition, but Sherbo does not explain why. Johnson is often concerned in the *Notes* about the death of innocence, particularly if the victim is female and pious: see *Henry VIII* (5:462; 8:653); *Hamlet* (8:311; 8:1011); *Othello* (8:391; 8:1030); (8:446; 8:1043); (8:470; 8:1047). However, Johnson's distress at the fate of Catherine, Ophelia, and Desdemona is not the same as his attitude toward that of Cordelia. Catherine's demise is sad and touching, Ophelia's is disturbingly unnecessary, and Desdemona's is shocking because of its religious, sacrificial nature. But only Cordelia's death merits altering the play, because her end seems to Johnson to undermine the meaning of *Lear*.

18. Kenneth Muir, ed., *The Arden Edition of the Works of William Shakespeare: "King Lear"* (Cambridge, Mass.: 1952), p. 82. Sherbo, in *Samuel Johnson* (p. 35), notes a

similarity in wording here between Johnson and Benjamin Heath. I have not become concerned with verbal similarities with Heath or Edwards, because their remarks were miscellaneous and did not form notes to an edition. Johnson's interpretations, as I consistently demonstrate, are not dependent upon any single note, but accumulate as a result of many comments. For that reason, I have compared Johnson's notes to those of previous editors. Shirley White Johnston, however, in "Samuel Johnson's Text of *King Lear:* 'Dull Duty Reassessed,'" *Yearbook of English Studies* 6 (1976): 80–91, has carefully compared Johnson's text with those of Theobald, Hanmer, Warburton, as well as a number of modern ones. She concludes, "Johnson's superiority over other eighteenth-century editors resulted not only from superior principles of editing and critical insight, but also from the closer attention he paid to textual details which might bear on the reader's understanding of the play" (p. 86).

19. For another reference to Shakespeare's sense of his audience, see *Merry Wives of Windsor* (2:523; 7:336). Johnson also comments on the importance of the servant's view of the master in *Timon of Athens* (6:231; 8:728).

20. Sherbo, in *Samuel Johnson* (p. 37), finds Heath's note similar to that of Johnson, but it seems to me that Heath emphasizes the spy in "God's spies" and Johnson focuses upon the perspective of God. However, be that as it may, one cannot fairly compare an interpretation that informs an entire edition with miscellaneous remarks.

21. See Larry S. Champion, *A Bibliography of "King Lear"* (New York: Garland, 1980).

22. Maynard Mack, "Actors and Redactors," in *Shakespeare: "King Lear," a Casebook*, ed. Frank Kermode (London: Macmillan, 1969), p. 78.

23. A. C. Bradley, *"King Lear,"* in *Shakespeare: "King Lear," a Casebook*, ed. Frank Kermode (London: Macmillan, 1969), p. 113.

24. Enid Welsford, "The Fool in *King Lear*," in *Shakespeare: "King Lear," a Casebook*, ed. Frank Kermode (London: Macmillan, 1969), pp. 145–49.

25. John Holloway, *"King Lear,"* in *Shakespeare: "King Lear," a Casebook*, ed. Frank Kermode (London: Macmillan, 1969), p. 224.

26. C. J. Sisson, "Justice in *King Lear*," in *Shakespeare: "King Lear," a Casebook*, ed. Frank Kermode (London: Macmillan, 1969), p. 241.

27. G. Wilson Knight, *"King Lear* and the Comedy of the Grotesque," in *Shakespeare: "King Lear," a Casebook*, ed. Frank Kermode (London: Macmillan, 1969), p. 136.

28. Robert B. Heilman, "The Unity of *King Lear*," in *Shakespeare: "King Lear," a Casebook*, ed. Frank Kermode (London: Macmillan, 1969), p. 178.

29. Jan Kott, *"King Lear,* or Endgame," in *Shakespeare: "King Lear," a Casebook*, ed. Frank Kermode (London: Macmillan, 1969), p. 291.

30. Stephen Booth, *"King Lear," "Macbeth," Indefinition, and Tragedy* (New Haven: Yale Univ. Press, 1983), p. 57.

31. Greenblatt, *Shakespearian Negotiations*, pp. 126–27. For a devastating deconstructive critique of Greenblatt, see Jonathan Goldberg, "Speculations: *Macbeth* and

Source," in *Shakespeare Reproduced,* ed. Jean E. Howard and Marian R. O'Connor (New York: Methuen, 1987), pp. 241–47.

32. Ralph Cohen, "Literary Theory as a Genre," *Centrum* 3 (1975): 45–64.

CHAPTER SIX
Imagination in *The Tempest*

1. For a discussion of the problem of the imagination in *Rasselas* as it pertains to the history of ideas, see my analysis in *Johnson, "Rasselas," and the Choice of Criticism,* pp. 96–98, in relation to Ernest Lee Tuveson, *The Imagination as a Means of Grace* (Berkeley: Univ. of California Press, 1960), p. 301. For the traditional view—that Johnson distrusted the imagination—see Raymond D. Havens, "Johnson's Distrust of the Imagination," *ELH* 10 (1943): 243–55; and for a more recent reinforcement of this position, see Jacob H. Adler, "Johnson's 'He That Imagines This,'" *Shakespeare Quarterly* 11 (1960): 225–28.

2. *The Works of John Dryden,* ed. Maximillian E. Novak (Los Angeles: Univ. of California Press, 1970), 13:2.

3. Rowe, *Works of Mr. William Shakespeare,* pp. xxiii–xxiv.

4. Gildon, *Works of Mr. William Shakespeare* 7:825.

5. John Holt, *Remarks on "The Tempest"* (London, 1749), p. 17.

6. *The Correspondence of Thomas Gray,* ed. Paget Toynbee and Leonard Wimbley (Oxford: Clarendon Press, 1971), 1:359.

7. Joseph Warton, *The Adventurer,* no. 93, 1753.

8. Samuel Taylor Coleridge, *Shakespeare Criticism,* ed. Thomas Middleton Raysor (London: Dent and Sons, 1960), 1:116.

9. Ibid., 2:131.

10. Ibid., 1:116.

11. Ibid., 1:118–19.

12. Parker, *Johnson's Shakespeare,* pp. 120–21, argues that Johnson did not highly regard *The Tempest,* for it is one of the four plays left without a stricture in the 1765 edition. It seems to me that Johnson's stricture of 1773 only summarizes what was already implicit in the notes. It must be kept in mind that Johnson's interpretations are built up by a process of accretion that involves his own notes and the skillful use of notes of others. Parker, in my view, is partially misled, because he seems to have used Sherbo's edition and thereby did not have access to others' notes left in Johnson's edition without comment.

13. Coleridge, *Shakespeare Criticism* 2:136.

14. Samuel Johnson, *A Journey to the Western Islands of Scotland,* ed. J. D. Fleeman (Oxford: Clarendon Press, 1983), pp. 89–91.

15. Coleridge, *Shakespeare Criticism* 2:137–38.

16. Frank Kermode, ed., *The Arden Edition of the Works of William Shakespeare: "The Tempest"* (Cambridge, Mass.: Harvard Univ. Press, 1958), p. 123. See also Stephen

Orgel, ed. *The Tempest* (Oxford: Oxford Univ. Press, 1982), p. 197. For other instances in the *Notes* where Johnson locates the importance of reason and passion in a love relationship, see *Merry Wives of Windsor* (2:472; 7:330); *Much Ado about Nothing* (3:241; 7:371); *All's Well That Ends Well* (3:360; 8:395); *Cymbeline* (7:284; 8:882); *Othello* (8:347; 8:1021).

17. Coleridge, *The Friend*, in *Collected Works of Samuel T. Coleridge*, ed. Barbara E. Rooke (London, 1969), 1:514–22.

18. James Engell, *The Creative Imagination: Enlightenment to Romanticism* (Cambridge, Mass.: Harvard Univ. Press, 1981), p. 57. Carol Lynn Hee, in "Fancy's Wing: The Imagination in Johnson's *Preface* to Shakespeare," *South Atlantic Quarterly* 81 (1982): 87–93, argues that Johnson's view in the *Preface* is ambivalent. My interest is in a section of the *Preface* as it bears upon the *Notes* to *The Tempest*: in this context, Johnson's view is balanced rather than ambivalent.

19. Engell, *Creative Imagination*, p. 338. For an alternative position based on the awareness that most discussions of the imagination are tacitly committed to Coleridge's method of approach, see Siskin, *Romantic Discourse*, pp. 45–47.

20. For an essay stressing the imaginary boundlessness, see Reuben A. Brower, "The Mirror of Analogy," in *The Fields of Light* (Oxford: Oxford Univ. Press, 1951); and, for an opposing view, see Frank Davidson, "*The Tempest*: An Interpretation," *Journal of English and Germanic Philology* 62 (1963). The most interesting recent work on *The Tempest* is that of Stephen Orgel. See the introduction to his edition of the drama (Oxford: Oxford Univ. Press, 1987), pp. 1–89, and "Prospero's Wife," *Representations* 8 (Fall 1984): 1–13.

CHAPTER SEVEN
Evaluation of Closure in *Hamlet*

1. In the notes to *Coriolanus*, Johnson defines "judgment" as "the faculty by which right is distinguished from wrong" (6:556; 8:809).

2. *Selected Prose of T. S. Eliot*, ed. Frank Kermode (London: Faber and Faber, 1975), p. 47. P. R. Grover uses Johnson, in "The Ghost of Dr. Johnson: L. C. Knights and D. A. Traversi on *Hamlet*," *Essays in Criticism* 17 (1967): 143–57, to show the didactic morality of two modern *Hamlet* critics. Grover seems to equate morality and didacticism, which I distinguished in chapter 1.

3. Harold Jenkins, ed., *The Tragedy of Hamlet*, by William Shakespeare (London: Methuen, 1982), p. 435.

4. See George Steevens in *SCH* 5:444–59. For a recent attempt to treat Johnson as a melancholiac like Hamlet, see James Lill, "Some Apocryphal Additions to Johnson's Notes on *Hamlet*," *South Atlantic Quarterly* 78 (1979): 33–41.

5. John Dover Wilson, ed., *The Tragedy of Hamlet*, by William Shakespeare (Cambridge: Cambridge Univ. Press, 1954), p. 152.

6. Jenkins, *Hamlet*, p. 437.

7. T. J. B. Spencer, ed., *The Tragedy of Hamlet*, by William Shakespeare (New York City: Penguin Books, 1980), p. 223.

8. George L. Kittredge and Irving Ribner, eds., *The Tragedy of Hamlet*, by William Shakespeare (New York: Franklin Watts, 1967), p. 177.

9. Dover Wilson, *Hamlet*, p. 168.

10. Spencer, *Hamlet*, p. 249.

11. Jenkins, *Hamlet*, p. 273.

12. Dover Wilson, *Hamlet*, p. 189.

13. Spencer, *Hamlet*, p. 265.

14. Kittredge and Ribner, *Hamlet*, p. 195.

15. Dover Wilson, *Hamlet*, p. 190.

16. Jenkins, *Hamlet*, pp. 484–85.

17. Ibid., pp. 487–88.

18. Ibid., p. 487.

19. Ibid., p. 488.

20. Dover Wilson, *Hamlet*, pp. 210–11.

21. Jenkins, *Hamlet*, p. 514.

22. Ibid., p. 529.

23. Ibid., p. 345.

24. Kittredge and Ribner, *Hamlet*, p. 209. For other references in the *Notes* to history as the situations of the dramas, see *The Merchant of Venice* (1:395; 7:218); *3 Henry VI* (5:197; 8:607); *Richard II* (4:83; 7:448).

25. The most pertinent definition of "variety" in Johnson's *Dictionary* is "change: succession . . . intermediation of one thing with another," which is illustrated by a phrase from *Paradise Lost:* "earth[s] yields." For Johnson, death, variety, and the plenitude of the earth clearly were intimately related.

26. Gildon, *Works of Mr. William Shakespeare* 7:417.

27. George Stubbes, *Some Remarks on "The Tragedy of Hamlet"* (London, 1736).

28. George Colman, *Prose on Several Occasions* (London, 1761), 2:113.

29. George Winchester Stone, Jr., "Garrick's Long-Lost Alteration of *Hamlet*," *PMLA* 49 (1934): 893. For a full discussion of Garrick's 1772 production, see Jeffrey L. L. Johnson, "Sweeping up Shakespeare's 'Rubbish': Garrick's Condensation of Acts 4 and 5 of *Hamlet*," *Eighteenth-Century Life* 8 (1983): 14–25, and my own essay, in the same volume, "The Comedy of the Graveyard Scene in *Hamlet*: Samuel Johnson Mediates between the Eighteenth and Twentieth Centuries," pp. 26–34.

30. Hill and Powell, 2:92. For other instances of notes on the mingling of comedy and tragedy, see the stricture of *Romeo and Juliet* (8:124; 8:957) and *Othello* (appendix; 8:1025).

31. Peter Winders, *Understanding "Hamlet:" A Study at an Advanced Level* (Exeter: Wheaton, 1975), p. 6.

32. Dover Wilson, *Hamlet*, p. 233; Spencer, *Hamlet*, p. 333; Kittredge and Ribner, *Hamlet*, p. 216; Jenkins, *Hamlet*, p. 548. For another version of this concept of death, see *Cymbeline* (7:357; 8:899).

33. Dover Wilson, *Hamlet*, p. 235.

34. Kittredge and Ribner, *Hamlet*, p. 216.

35. Spencer, *Hamlet*, p. 334.

36. Jenkins, *Hamlet*, p. 380.

37. Spencer, *Hamlet*, p. 331.

CHAPTER EIGHT

Aesthetic Empathy in *Macbeth*

1. Neal Oxenhandler, in "The Changing Concept of Literary Emotion," *New Literary History* 20 (Autumn 1988): 105–21, provides a good summary of the recent work in this field. Oxenhandler makes clear that the little fruitful, recent work comes from the hermeneuticists, because the structuralists and poststructuralists do not consider this problem worthy of their consideration.

2. See Scouten, *London Stage*, I, 3–99.

3. See Garrick, 3:6.

4. Ibid., 72. Johnson recognized that there was a tradition of harmless witchcraft—see *Midsummer Night's Dream* (1:106; 7:142). For other references to the evil of witches, see *Comedy of Errors* (3:111; 7:352); *The Winter's Tale* (2:276; 7:294); *Measure for Measure* (1:300; 7:186); *Othello* (8:467; 8:1046).

5. Cleanth Brooks, "'The Naked Babe' and the Cloak of Manliness," in *Shakespeare: "Macbeth," a Casebook*, ed. John Wain (London: Macmillan, 1968), p. 198. Herbert R. Coursen, in "Agreeing with Dr. Johnson," *Ariel* (Calgary) 10 (1979): 35–42, argues that *Macbeth* and *Antony and Cleopatra* are alike in a number of respects, particularly in that the protagonists know and fully face their fate long before it happens. It is, however, easier to understand this fatalism in a context of love than in one of crime.

6. Brooks, "Cloak of Manliness," p. 200. Because Johnson objects to the use of the terms "dun," "Knife," and "blanket" in *Rambler*, no. 168 (*Works* 5:127–29), he is thought to be insensitive to Shakespeare's imagery. Nothing could be farther from the truth. This *Rambler* essay uses these terms from *Macbeth* as examples of how vocabulary is historicized, words gaining and losing dignity in different ages.

7. Oscar James Campbell, "Shakespeare and the 'New' Critics," in *Twentieth-Century Interpretations of "Macbeth,"* ed. Terence Hawkes (Englewood Cliffs, N.J.: Prentice-Hall, 1973), p. 50.

8. Helen Gardner, "A Reply to Cleanth Brooks," reprinted in *Twentieth-Century Interpretations of "Macbeth,"* p. 80.

9. R. A. Foakes, "*Macbeth*," in *Focus on "Macbeth,"* ed. John R. Brown (London, 1982), p. 38. In the same volume, see Goldman, p. 219. David Lovett, "Shakespeare

as a Poet of Realism in the Eighteenth Century," *ELH* 2 (1935): 267–89, presented the position that Johnson developed the notion of realistic character, a view now generally assumed. (For his remarks on *Macbeth*, see p. 276.) This position is based upon a totalizing approach to Johnson's Shakespeare criticism which results in neglecting the interpretations of specific plays. Johnson develops the courage of Macbeth by stressing his ability to face his crimes. For other references to evil agents who act more like Lady Macbeth, see *King John* (3:477; 7:425); *Merchant of Venice* (1:402; 7:220); *Timon of Athens* (6:248; 8:736); *Cymbeline* (7:368; 8:902).

10. Robert Kimbrough, "Macbeth: The Prisoner of Gender," *Shakespeare Survey* 16 (1983): 175–90. Goldberg's "Speculations: *Macbeth* and Source" is a recent deconstructive analysis. But in focusing on authority and its excess, Goldberg leaves us in doubt what constitutes the tragic element of the drama. In this respect his essay, which involves, as I pointed out in chapter 5, a telling critique of Greenblatt's totalization assumption, shows the limitation of an analysis that avoids consideration of how *Macbeth* relates to the human predicament. For a view in essential agreement with Johnson on Macbeth's speech on the death of Lady Macbeth, see H. W. Donner, "'She Should Have Died Hereafter,'" *English Studies* 40 (1959): 385–89.

11. Here is one of the most telling examples of the limitations of the Yale edition of the *Notes*. This entire comment is omitted because it contains no remarks by Johnson.

12. Kenneth Muir, ed., *The Arden Edition of the Tragedy of "Macbeth,"* by William Shakespeare (London: Methuen, 1951), p. 16.

13. Thomas De Quincey, "On the Knocking at the Gate in *Macbeth*," in *The Collected Writings of Thomas De Quincey*, ed. David Masson (London, 1897), 10:393. Johnson's position on the unities has generated considerable debate. Thomas M. Raysor is one of the first to call Johnson's originality into question; see his essay, "The Downfall of the Three Unities," *MLN* 12 (1927): 1–9. He is here reinforcing David Nichol Smith, *Eighteenth-Century Essays on Shakespeare* (Oxford: Clarendon Press, 1903), pp. xxx–xxxi, and is himself reinforced by Sherbo and Stock. But it is important to note that even these scholars do not agree as to whether Johnson is more indebted to Farquhar or Lord Kames, the former denying delusion and the latter forwarding it. For specifics on the controversy, see R. K. Kaul, "The Unities Again: Dr. Johnson and Delusion," *Notes and Queries* (July 1962): 261–64; John Hardy, *Notes and Queries* (September 1962): 350–51; and Gunnor Sorelius, pp. 466–67, and April 1963, p. 156. When understood in relation to aesthetic empathy, Johnson's concept of delusion seems to me to fall between that of Farquhar and Kames, a position I advance in "The Witches in *Macbeth*: Samuel Johnson's Notion of Selective Empathy," *College English Association Critic* 47 (1984): 78–84. For a Bergsonian view of Johnson on the unity of time, see Wolfgang Bernard Fleischmann, "Shakespeare, Johnson, and the Dramatic Unities of Time and Place," *Studies in Philology* extra series 4 (1967): 128–34.

14. Julia Kristeva considers the fragmented self in *Desire in Language: A Semiotic Approach to Literature and Art* (Oxford: Basil Blackwell, 1980), pp. 125–47.

CONCLUSION
Toward a New Humanism

1. Macaulay's remarks are cited in D. Nichol Smith, *Eighteenth-Century Essays on Shakespeare*, p. xxxi.

2. Sherbo, *Samuel Johnson*, pp. 100–101.

3. Bertrand Bronson and Jean M. O'Meara, *Selections from Johnson on Shakespeare* (New Haven: Yale Univ. Press, 1986), p. xxxv.

4. Siskin, *Romantic Discourse*, p. 121.

5. Even as early as 1751, Johnson was fascinated by Shakespeare's ability to mingle comedy and tragedy. In *The Rambler*, no. 156, he cannot decide if this technique is to be followed by others or is the singular genius of Shakespeare: "These resistless vicissitudes of the heart, this alternate prevalence of merriment and solemnity, may sometimes be more properly ascribed to the vigour of the writer than the justness of the design: and instead of vindicating tragi-comedy by the success of Shakespear, we ought perhaps to pay new honours to that transcendent and unbounded genius that could preside over the passions in sport" (Walter J. Bate and Albrecht B. Strauss, eds., *The Yale Edition of the Works of Samuel Johnson* [New Haven: Yale Univ. Press, 1969], 5:69).

6. Johnson makes a point of commenting on the comic element in every tragedy; see *Timon of Athens* (6:192; 8:716); *Coriolanus* (6:627; 8:823); *Romeo and Juliet* (8:124; 8:957); *Othello* (appendix; 8:1025) for those not mentioned in the text. The only two not cited in this respect are *Titus Andronicus*, in which Johnson does not find "Shakespeare's touches very discernible" (6:364; 8:751), and *Julius Caesar*, which Johnson finds "cold and unaffecting" (7:102; 8:836). It seems to me that Johnson was particularly put off by the latter play because it is the only humorless tragedy attributed solely to Shakespeare.

INDEX

Action over character, 18, 117, 131–49
    passim, 153–70 passim
Adapting versus editing, 9, 37–50
    passim
Addison, Joseph, 91
Aesthetic empathy: in *Macbeth*, 6, 9,
    170–74; reader-response aspect, 12;
    and interpretation, 12, 173; in
    Johnson's *Preface*, 171; neglected
    premise of, 172, 195 (n. 14);
    exemplified by Johnson on
    Richard III, 172–73
All's Well That Ends Well, 184 (n. 17),
    191–92 (n. 16)
Alteration: Dryden's *Troilus and
    Cressida*, 38
Ambition, 155–56
Antony and Cleopatra, 164, 184 (n. 17),
    191–92 (n. 13)
As You Like It, 186 (n. 5)

Bibliography: the task of, 2; by satire
    related to ideology and theory, 11;
    with interpretation, 46; united by
    dramatic irony to ideology, 71–72
Blindness, 88, 160
Booth, Stephen, 108
Boswell, James: *Life of Johnson*, 35, 135,
    193 (n. 30)
Bradley, A. C., 105
Bright, Timothy, 137
Bronson, Bertrand, 175
Brooks, Cleanth, 4, 154

Caliban, 113–16, 121–24
Campbell, Oscar James, 154–55
Character: in historical context, 22;
    consistency of Shakespeare's, 115–16;
    over action, 117, 131–49, 153–70
Character criticism: Johnson refuses,
    18, 127; differs from his age, 113–17
Circle of love, 52–8
Closure, 6, 10; in *Hamlet*, 9; relation to
    judgment, 12; and modern criticism,
    130–31; death as subversion of, 148;
    and value, 149–51
Cohen, Ralph, 11, 181 (n. 1), 191
    (n. 32)
Coleridge, Samuel Taylor, 8, 9, 11;
    refers to Johnson on imagination,
    112; first to use organic structure for
    The Tempest, 117; versus Johnson,
    117–20; on Ariel, 120–23; disso-
    ciation of sensibility, 121; on ethics,
    121–22; relationship with Johnson,
    126–29; on dramatic delusion, 152
Collier, Jeremy, 16
Colman, George L., 94, 97, 144
Comedy, 13, 63, 146. *See also* Humor
Conscience of Macbeth: 164–65
Cooke, Thomas, 91–92
Copy text, concept of: 1
Coriolanus, 184 (n. 14), 185–86 (n. 5),
    188 (n. 13), 196 (n. 6)
Coursen, Herbert, 194 (n. 5)
Creative imagination, 11
Critical consensus, 6, 53–54, 55,
    139–40

Criticism: history of, 6; practical, 7; as
    a discipline, 7, 8, 9, 15, 33, 129, 178;
    formalist/structuralist aspect of, 12;
    and history of ideas, 127–29; ethical
    teleology of, 176. *See also* Theory
Cymbeline, 119, 188 (n. 13), 191–92
    (n. 16), 194–95 (n. 9)

Damrosch, Leopold, Jr., 5
Danby, John, 20
Danish court and Polonius, 134–37.
    See also *Hamlet*
D'Avenant, Sir William, 153
Deconstructive possibility in humor,
    178. *See also* Humor
Delusion and referentiality, 117–20
"Democratic hegemony," 10, 14
De Quincey, Thomas, 170–71, 195
    (n. 13)
Derrida, Jacques, 87
Didacticism: versus morality/ethics, 14,
    33; term used by Johnson, 15;
    Collier's, 16, 19, 28, 31, 69. *See also*
    Morality
"Dissociation of sensibility," 11,
    112, 121
Dollimore, Jonathan, 184 (n. 22)
Domestic politicized in *King Lear*,
    94–97
Double hermeneutic, 36, 50
Double perspective, 58, 63
Downer, H. W., 195 (n. 10)
Dramatic irony, 71–72, 88
Dryden, John, 1, 6, 8, 9; *Troilus and
    Cressida*, 37–50; *The Tempest; or, the
    Enchanted Island* (with
    D'Avenant), 113

Eastman, Arthur, 183 (n. 1)
Eddy, Donald D., 182 (n. 12)
Edinger, William, 5
Editorial decision, 10, 63. *See also*
    Interpretation
Edwards, Thomas, 93. *See also*
    Warburton, *King Lear*
Eliot, Thomas Stearns, 130

Emendation, 36, 44, 185 (n. 2)
Empathy, 171–72. *See also* Aesthetic
    empathy
Ethics, 10, 14, 33, 121–22, 151, 176. *See
    also* Morality, Theory
Evaluation, 2, 10, 130
Events versus characters, 113–17
Evil and the audience in *Macbeth*,
    165–66
Extraliterary critical goal, 10, 12, 152,
    157. *See also* Aesthetic empathy,
    Theory

Falstaff, 2, 9, 16, 17
—Johnson on: comic spirit of, 21–23;
    language, 22–26; awareness of
    appearance, 25; cowardice, 26;
    rejection of, 27; versus moderns, 27–
    34; punishments of, 29; imprisoning
    disturbs, 30; and moderns, 31. See
    also *Henry IV*, Humor
Falstaffian, or poststructural, stage, 179
Feminist criticism, 11, 84, 88. See also
    The Taming of the Shrew
Fineman, Joel, 87
Foakes, R. A., 155
Foote, Samuel, 92
Formalism, 12, 89–90, 109–11, 130–31
Friedman, Arthur, 4
Furness, H. H.: Victorian editor, 9;
    consensus versus stricture, 52; agrees
    with Warburton and Griffith, 53; on
    love, 57–58

Garber, Marjorie, 185 (n. 24)
Gardner, Dame Helen, 155
Garrick, David: *Catherine and Petruchio*,
    72–73, 76; resolution in relation to
    modern editors, 78; adaptation of
    King Lear, 93–94, 97; production
    of *Hamlet*, 144–48; production of
    Macbeth, 153–54
Gildon, Charles: on Falstaff, 17; on two
    parts of *Henry IV*, 19; on Hotspur,
    20–21; on death of Cordelia, 91; on
    Dryden-D'Avenant *Tempest*, 114; on

Ariel, 121; on humor in
graveyard, 143
"Glass" of satire, 71. *See also* Swift
Goldberg, Jonathan, 190 (n. 31)
Gray, Thomas, 115
Greenblatt, Stephen, 31–32, 108–9
Gunpowder Plot, 49

Hagstrum, Jean, 3–4
Hallam, Arthur Henry, 66
Hamlet, 6; modern editors on, 132–56
  passim; T. S. Eliot on, 130;
  metacritical perspective on, 140;
  Gildon on humor in, 143; Stubbes
  on, 143; Colman on, 144; Steevens
  and Garrick's proposal on, 144;
  schoolbook on, 149; Garrick's
  production of, 193 (n. 29)
—Johnson on: evaluation, 130; humor,
  130; accretive satire, 131; disunity,
  131–32; history in, 132–34, 142–43;
  versus moderns, 133; setting of, 134–
  37; Polonius, 135–36; madness, 137;
  role-playing, 137–38; mousetrap,
  138; critical accretion, 140; Jenkins
  and, 140; reason and passion, 143;
  humor in graveyard, 143–49; alterers
  of, 145; variorum technique, 145–46;
  spiritual viewpoint, 146; speaker,
  146; variety, 148; humor versus
  totalizing quest, 149–51; stricture,
  151; morality, 151; death of
  innocence, 189 (n. 17); comic
  element in tragedy, 196 (n. 6)
Hanmer, Thomas, 27, 153
Haring-Smith, Tori, 188 (n. 6)
Harrison, Charles T., 182 (n. 14)
Hartmann, Geoffrey, 188 (n. 3)
Hegemony of ideology, 33
Heilman, Robert, 56–57, 107–8
Henry IV, 14, 17, 18, 19–20, 21
—Johnson on: disapproval of the end,
  10; versus Upton, 17–18; refuses
  character criticism, 18–19; comic
  scene, 19; political message, 20–21;
  Hotspur, 21; moral issue, 21;

historical context, 22; Hal and
  Hotspur, 23; relation to *Henry V,* 24;
  on *2 Henry IV,* 26–27; versus
  moderns, 27–34; didactic
  interjection, 28; dissatisfaction at
  conclusion, 29
Henry V, 20, 183 (n. 11)
Henry VI, 185 (n. 5), 189 (n. 14), 193
  (n. 24)
Henry VIII, 185 (n. 5), 189 (n. 17)
Hermeneutics, 12, 129
History: of ideas, 6, 11, 112, 127–29; of
  criticism, 10, 12–13, 15, 51, 68–70;
  and politics, 42–46; in *Troilus and
  Cressida,* 43; versus psychology in
  Hamlet, 132–34; in *Hamlet's*
  references, 142–43; and witches, 166;
  humanity exists in, 166–67
Holistic empathy, 171–72
Holloway, John, 106–7
Holt, John, 115
Human: condition, 2; dilemma, 2, 10;
  predicament, 33, 151; situation, 177
Humanism, new, 3, 180 (n. 1)
Humanistic discipline, 128–29
Humanity: of *Macbeth,* 166–70
Humor: in *Hamlet,* 9; in tragedy, 12;
  undermines ideologies, 13, 174; of
  Falstaff, 22–29; of Olivia, 59; versus
  religion, 61; focal point in *The Taming
  of the Shrew,* 71–88; basis of critical
  goal, 130; on the graveyard, 143–49;
  defense of low humor, 145–47; black
  humor, 147–48; and variety of life,
  148; neglected by moderns, 149–51;
  exposes critical values, 150–57; and
  morality, 151; relates to earth, 152,
  177–78; enables literature to point
  beyond itself, 173–74. See also
  Henry IV
Humorlessness, 66–67
Humphreys, A. R., 27
Hurd, Richard, 74

Ideology: modification of, in *The Taming
  of the Shrew,* 6; related to criticism, 7,

Ideology (*continued*)
10, 14; beyond literature, 10; and
bibliography, 11, 71–72; and value,
12; undermined by humor, 13;
modified by ethics, 14; and morality,
32–34; and mimesis, 71; implicit
antifeminist, 72; basis of
disagreement, 87; and theory,
174, 177
Imagination, 112–13, 117–20
Imitation, 6
Intelligence, 140–43
Interpretation: evaluative, 2; loosely
defined, 10; and significant
conclusion, 10; art of, 12; and
judgment, 32, 37–42, 43; and
bibliography, 46–50; divorced from
editing, 63; related to textual issue,
85; of ends and beginnings, 129; and
empathy, 173; explicit, 176

Johnson, Samuel: creative imagination,
1; concept of wit, 3; *Lives of the Poets*,
3, 7, 36; commentary on his criticism, 3–5; morality, 4–5, 14–15, 88;
Plays of William Shakespeare, 5–9, 14,
15, 51, 175, 176, 178; *Vanity of
Human Wishes*, 6; ideology, 7;
Dictionary, 7, 33, 36, 39, 82, 125,
164; critical stance, 8, 10, 11; and
Coleridge, 11; history of ideas, 11;
judgment of closure, 12; humor in
tragedy, 12, 177–78; place in
Shakespeare scholarship, 12–13;
literary theory, 33; *Rambler*, 36. See
also *Preface, Notes to Shakespeare,* and
individual Shakespearean plays
Judgment, 12, 37–46
Julius Caesar, 196 (n. 6)

Kahn, Coppelia, 86–87
Kaul, R. K., 195 (n. 13)
Keast, William R., 9
Kimbrough, Robert, 155
King John, 194–95 (n. 9)

King Lear: moderns on fool, 99; tragic
concept of time in, 110
—Johnson on: return to original, 89–
90; opening scene, 93; Colman and,
94; domestic dilemma, 94–97; agrees
with Murphy and Edwards, 95; death
of Cordelia, 96–97, 102–4; on fool,
97–102; uses Warburton, 98;
supposed emendation, 99; versus his
predecessors, 100; madness, 100;
blinding of Gloucester, 101–2;
relation of subplot and main plot,
101–2; critics of his own day, 103–4;
poetic justice, 104; Hamlet's mirror,
105; Tate's version, 109; rash oaths,
189 (n. 12)
Kittredge, George Lyman, 99; edition
of *Hamlet* (Ribner, coeditor), 133–50
passim
Knight, G. Wilson, 107
Kott, Jan, 108
Krieger, Murray, 182 (n. 13)
Kristeva, Julia, 195 (n. 14)

Lacan, Jacques, 87
Lacey, John, 73
Laclau, Ernesto. *See* "Democratic
hegemony"
Lamb, Charles, 66–67, 69
Leech, Clifford, 20, 28, 31
Levin, Harold, 20
Levin, Richard, 186 (n. 2)
Lill, James, 192 (n. 4)
Literary criticism: and literary theory,
2; as a discipline, 2, 3, 7, 8, 9, 33,
129; related by morality to ideology,
2, 10; part of humanities, 12; and
comedy, 13; and history of ideas, 112;
and human situation, 177;
Falstaffian, 179
Literary theory, 2; in *Preface* and *Notes*,
3; history of, 6; and Lear, 6; second
step, 7; not totalizing, 8; with
practice, 8, 11; humorous closure, 9;

and mimeticism, 9; and aesthetic
empathy, 9; and bibliography, 11. See
also *Hamlet, King Lear, Macbeth*
Love, 57–58; of Miranda, 124. See also
The Tempest, Twelfth Night
Love's Labour's Lost, 185 (n. 5), 189
(n. 12)

Macbeth, 6, 9, 12; Brooks opposed by
Campbell and Gardner, 154–55;
recent critical polarity on, 155
—Johnson on: aesthetic empathy in,
152–53; humor, 152; active spectator,
153; sample of, 153; demonology,
153; solemn fiction, 153–56; witches,
155–60; estimable protagonist, 156–
60; and *Preface,* 157; Elizabethans,
157; variorum technique, 158; versus
Warburton and Muir, 158–59;
Macbeth facing horror, 159; Lady
Macbeth, 160–64; ethical faculty,
161; editorial revisions, 161–62, 169;
inner being, 161; atmosphere, 162;
virtue in evil, 163; Pope, 163, 167;
Warburton, 163–64, 168; conscience
recognizing hell, 164–65; allusion to
Antony, 164; witches' deception, 164;
audience bewitched, 165–66; the
unfathomable Macbeth, 166;
Macbeth's humanity, 167–68; tragic
dimension, 169; and modern
dichotomy, 169–70; an aspect of
Macbeth, 170–74; delusion, 171;
audience belief, 171; an alternative to
holistic empathy, 171–72; other evil
agents, 195 (n. 9)
McGann, Jerome J., 187 (n. 5)
Mack, Maynard, 104
McKenzie, D. F., 187–88 (n. 5)
Malvolio, problem of, 62–65
Measure for Measure, 185 (n. 5), 194
(n. 4)
The Merchant of Venice, 185 (n. 5), 193
(n. 24), 194–95 (n. 9)

The Merry Wives of Windsor, 184 (n. 14),
188 (n. 13), 190 (n. 19), 191–92
(n. 16)
Metacriticism, 6, 33, 140
Middendorf, John, 187 (n. 2)
Midsummer Night's Dream, 185 (n. 5),
189 (n. 12), 194 (n. 4)
Miller, J. Hillis, 7
Milton, John: *Comus,* 127; *Lycidas,* 35;
Paradise Lost, 97, 173
Mimetic: readings, 9; humor in the
graveyard, 143–49; question for
moderns, 104–11. See also *Hamlet,
King Lear*
Mimeticism: and modern theory, 11;
poses a question, 89–90; combined
with formalism/postformalism,
109–11. See also Theory, *King Lear*
Mimeticism, new, 12, 111
Mirror: of life, 75; of nature, 105; of
satire, 78–85
Modern critics/editors, 14–15, 19–20,
26–27, 31, 82, 99, 104–11, 128, 131–
51. See also *Hamlet, Henry IV, King
Lear, The Taming of the Shrew*
Modern Language Association (MLA),
7–8
Monaghan, T. J., 185 (n. 2)
Moral: issue in *Henry IV,* 21; outrage,
28; versus political/historical, 31;
versus ideological, 32; obligation of
metacriticism, 33; judgments, 50;
comedy, 63; and Malvolio, 64;
dimension in *The Tempest,* 124
Moralist: Johnson as most revered, 14;
separated from Pope, 71; focuses on
reform of sinner, 88
Morality: and didacticism, 2, 14;
modern neglect of, 3; on Johnson's,
4–5; versus politics, 14; relates
literary analysis to ideology, 14;
relates to human predicament,
33–34; and humor, 151
Morgann, Maurice, 16, 26
Morris, Brian (Arden editor of *The*

Morris, Brian (*continued*)
Taming of the Shrew), 19, 76, 78, 79,
    81, 83, 94–95
Morris, Corbyn, 17
Mouffe, Chantal. *See* "Democratic
    hegemony"
Much Ado About Nothing, 191–92 (n. 16)
Muir, Kenneth (Arden editor of
    Macbeth), 158–59
Murphy, Arthur, 93, 95

Nature: limits of, 120–23. See also *The
    Tempest*
Needham, John, 5
Notes to Shakespeare (Johnson): first
    book on, 3; as "naked criticism," 3;
    theoretical significance, 3–5; focal
    point, 6; in relation to *Preface*, 15,
    176; concept of emendation, 36;
    emendations not in text, 185 (n. 5);
    forbearance to predecessors, 186
    (n. 5); on Shakespeare's audience,
    190 (n. 19). See also *Preface*

Organic psyche, 170–74. See also
    Macbeth
Orgel, Stephen, 192 (n. 20)
Othello, 186 (n. 5), 189 (n. 17), 191–92
    (n. 16), 193 (n. 24), 196 (n. 6)
Oxenhandler, Neal, 194 (n. 1)

Parker, G. F., 5, 183 (n. 1), 191 (n. 12)
Passion: and reason, 120, 123–28, 143
Pepys, Samuel, 66
Play-within-a-play, 11. See also *The
    Taming of the Shrew*
Political versus moral, 31, 43, 50. *See
    also* Dryden, *Henry IV, Troilus and
    Cressida*
Politics: and history, 42–46. See also
    Troilus and Cressida
Polonius, 134–37
Pope, Alexander: Johnson rejects
    emendation of, 27; followed by
    Johnson, 53–54; as satirist, 71; first
    found Sly scenes, 72; explained by

Johnson, 79; Johnson prints same
    passage as, 84–85; Johnson disagrees
    with, 163; cited by Johnson, 167. See
    also *Henry IV, Macbeth, The Taming of
    the Shrew, Twelfth Night*
Postformalism, 10, 89–90, 109–11,
    130–31
Poststructuralism, 179
Practical criticism, 11
Practice. *See* Theory
Preface (to Johnson's edition of
    Shakespeare), 1–2, 4–5, 7; largely
    derivative, 3; theoretical significance
    of, 3; often printed on its own, 6;
    meaning of others' notes without
    comment, 20; mirror of life, 75; on
    combining comedy and tragedy, 148;
    on aesthetic empathy, 171; preference
    for comedies, 178. See also *Notes to
    Shakespeare*
Psychology versus history, 132–34

Rasselas (Johnson), 112, 191 (n. 1)
Raysor, Thomas, 195 (n. 13)
Reason. *See* Passion
Referentiality: and delusion, 117–20.
    See also *The Tempest*
Religious dimension, 124. See also *The
    Tempest*
Repression as obstacle, 160–64. See
    also *Macbeth*
Ribner, Irving. *See* Kittridge
Richard II, 9, 23, 184 (n. 15), 185 (n. 5),
    193 (n. 24)
Richard III, 20, 21, 172–73
Role-playing, 56–64. See also
    Twelfth Night
Romance, 127. See also *The Tempest*
Romeo and Juliet, 193 (n. 30), 196 (n. 6)
Rossiter, A. P., 20
Rowe, Nicholas, 29, 113–14, 169

Satire, 88
Satirical technique, 11
Seary, Peter, 183 (n. 1)

Shakespeare, William: editors previous to Johnson, 1, 9, 153. *See also* Hanmer, Pope, Rowe, Theobald, Warburton, and individual plays
Sherbo, Arthur, 5–6, 36, 175, 182 (n. 1)
Siebert, Donald, 182 (n. 13)
Sinfield, Alan, 184 (n. 32)
Siskin, Clifford, 177, 186 (n. 3)
Sisson, C. J., 106–7
Smith, David Nichol, 175
Smith, William, 92
Spencer, T. J. B.: edition of *Hamlet*, 133–56 passim
Steevens, George: first marginalized Sly scenes, 72–73, 187 (n. 4); probably began modern view of *Hamlet*, 133; removal of graveyard scene, 144
Stock, R. D., 5, 182 (n. 1)
Stone, George Winchester, Jr., 144
Stricture (Johnson's innovation), 35, 37–42, 50–52, 152–57
Stubbes, George, 143
Subversion, 88, 110
Swift, Jonathan, 35, 71

The Taming of the Shrew: Pope first found Sly scenes, 71; staging of, 72–73; bibliographic issue, 72; antifeminist ideology, 72; Garrick's version of, 73; Lacey's version, 73; history of printed text, 73–74; on Sly mirror, 74; two shrew traditions, 74–76
—Johnson on: separated from Pope, 71; sense of humor as focal point, 71–88; mirror of nature, 71; dramatic performance, 76; two plots, 76; moderns, 76–78, 82; satirical mirror, 76–85, 88, 188 (n. 13); variorum technique, 79; Pope, 79; difficulty for Warburton, 79–80, 83; versus Morris, 81, 85–88; uses Sly interlude, 83; feminine mirror, 84; passage from Pope, 84–85; Sly epilogue, 85
Tate, Nahum, 89–91, 109
Tatler, 75

Teleological: activity, 10; endeavor, 36, 70; nature, 50
The Tempest: Dryden and Rowe on Caliban's language, 113–16; character versus events, 113–17; Gray on verisimilitude, 115; Coleridge on organic structure, 117
—Johnson on: *Rasselas* and, 112; Coleridge, 112, 117–22, 126; his age of character criticism, 113–17; Warburton, 114–15, 121, 125; alternative to character criticism, 116; disapproval of *Cymbeline* and *The Winter's Tale*, 119; tolerates magic, 119; more serious than other romances, 119–20, 127; passion and reason, 120; dissociation of sensibility, 121; bounds of nature exceeded, 120–23; ingratitude, 122; subplot and main plot, 122; Miranda's love, 123–27; strategy of omission, 124; moral and religious dimension of love, 124; black magic, 125; most valued scene in romances, 126; conclusion on Caliban's language, 126–27; places in genre of *Comus*, 127; literature and other humanities, 128–29
Tennenhouse, Leonard, 182 (n. 24)
Theobald, Lewis: on Hal's soliloquy, 18; on *Richard III*, 20; on *Henry V*, 20; on Hotspur, 20–21; with Pope against Johnson, 27; used by Johnson, 42; follows Dryden, 45–46; followed by Johnson, 82; opposed to death of Cordelia, 91; on *Macbeth*, 157–58; serves Johnson's variorum technique, 158
Theory: and practice, 33, 71–72; and ideology, 174, 177, 186 (n. 3)
Tillyard, E. M. W., 19–20, 31
Time: flattened out by formalism and postformalism, 89–90; tragic concept of, in *King Lear*, 110
Timon of Athens, 184 (n. 14), 188 (n. 13), 190 (n. 19), 194–95 (n. 9)

Titus Andronicus, 196 (n. 6)
Tolliver, Harold, 20
Totalizing, concept of, 149–51
Tradition, *the*, 11; Johnson's voice
    muffled by consensus, 63–64
Tragedy: humor in, for Johnson, 12;
    concept subverts itself, 110
Troilus and Cressida
—Johnson on: alteration and edition,
    38; refusal to emend, 40; Dryden, 40,
    45–46; Warburton, 41, 44; use of
    Theobald, 42; hard on predecessors,
    43; judgment, 43; critical acumen,
    44; combines interpretation and
    bibliography, 46; variorum technique,
    47–48; history and politics, 49; and
    2 Henry IV, 50; Dryden as critical
    touchstone, 50; teleological nature
    of, 50
Twelfth Night: Furness's new variorum
    on, 51–70 passim; critical consensus,
    55; new variorum method, 61; humor
    and religion, 61; editing and
    interpreting, 65; Lamb on, 69
—Johnson on: history of criticism, 51;
    nature of variorum technique, 51;
    stricture, 52; Pope, 53–54;
    Warburton, 54, 57–58, 63; Viola, 55,
    58–62; role-playing, 56–58; lying
    versus fibbing, 56; difference
    neglected, 56–64; deception, 57;
    Furness, 60; humor versus religion,
    61; voice muffled by consensus, 63–
    64; problem of Malvolio, 62–67;
    moral in comedy, 63; his edition
    compared to new variorum, 63–64;
    double perspective, 66; natural
    perspective, 68; historical
    perspective, 68–69; didacticism, 69

Upton, John, 17, 93

Value: and closure, 149–51
Values: and ideology, 12; exposed by
    humor, 150–51; and ethical
    assumptions, 151

Variorum, new, 51–70 passim
Variorum technique: Johnson uses
    Theobald, 47–48; distinctive nature
    of, 51; predecessor's note takes on
    new meaning, 79; in graveyard, 145–
    46; Johnson uses Warburton and
    Theobald, 158
Victorian(s): Furness's edition of *Twelfth
    Night*, 51; lighten the vice of
    Malvolio, 64; versus Johnson on
    Malvolio, 65; and Johnson on the
    moral in comedy, 65

Warburton, William: final judgment of
    Falstaff, 17; on Hal's soliloquy, 18;
    on two parts of *Henry IV,* 19; on
    Hotspur, 20–21; accepts Pope's
    emendation, 27; Johnson rejects
    emendation, 40; Johnson a more
    careful bibliographer, 41; used by
    Johnson, 44, 98, 158, 163–64;
    Furness agrees with, 53, 54–60; and
    most eighteenth-century editors, 54;
    on humor of Olivia, 59; on moral of
    comedy, 63; Johnson clarified
    problem for, 79–80; refined by
    Johnson, 83–84; omits passage that
    Johnson and Pope print, 84–85; on
    opening scene of *King Lear,* 93;
    on the fool, 100; Johnson opposes on
    King Lear, 103; headnote to *The
    Tempest*, 114–15, 118; on consistency
    of character, 115–16; on Ariel, 121;
    Johnson's omission of a note of, 124;
    on black magic, 125; Johnson's
    strategy of omission of, 125; on
    soliloquy in *Hamlet,* 132; with
    moderns, 135–36; exemplary of
    eighteenth-century editors, 145–47;
    on witches as naughty, 157–58, 164;
    on psyche of Macbeth, 158–59; and
    Johnson on essential humanity of
    Macbeth, 168
Warton, Joseph, 93
Weimann, Robert, 71
Welsford, Enid, 99

Wentersdorf, Karl P., 187 (n. 4)
Whalley, Peter, 92–93
White, R. G., 55
Williams, William Proctor, 187 (n. 5)
Wilson, John Dover, 19–20; edition of
   Hamlet, 133–50 passim
Wimsatt, William Kurtz, Jr., 4
The Winter's Tale, 119, 186 (n. 5), 194
   (n. 4)
Witches: Elizabethan, 2; Macbeth seen

as under spell of, 156–60; evil not
   naughty for Johnson, 157–58;
   Johnson on deceptive nature of, 164;
   affect on audience, 165–66; enter
   Renaissance history, 166

Yale edition of *Notes to Shakespeare,* 20
Young, Karl, 183 (n. 1)

Zitner, S. P. 184 (n. 17)